Infinity for Marxists

Historical Materialism Book Series

The Historical Materialism Book Series is a major publishing initiative of the radical left. The capitalist crisis of the twenty-first century has been met by a resurgence of interest in critical Marxist theory. At the same time, the publishing institutions committed to Marxism have contracted markedly since the high point of the 1970s. The Historical Materialism Book Series is dedicated to addressing this situation by making available important works of Marxist theory. The aim of the series is to publish important theoretical contributions as the basis for vigorous intellectual debate and exchange on the left.

The peer-reviewed series publishes original monographs, translated texts, and reprints of classics across the bounds of academic disciplinary agendas and across the divisions of the left. The series is particularly concerned to encourage the internationalization of Marxist debate and aims to translate significant studies from beyond the English-speaking world.

For a full list of titles in the Historical Materialism Book Series available in paperback from Haymarket Books, visit: www.haymarketbooks.org/series_collections/1-historical-materialism.

Infinity for Marxists

Essays on Poetry and Capital

Christopher Nealon

Haymarket Books
Chicago, IL

First published in 2023 by Brill Academic Publishers, The Netherlands
© 2023 Koninklijke Brill NV, Leiden, The Netherlands

Published in paperback in 2024 by
Haymarket Books
P.O. Box 180165
Chicago, IL 60618
773-583-7884
www.haymarketbooks.org

ISBN: 979-8-88890-212-7

Distributed to the trade in the US through Consortium Book Sales and
Distribution (www.cbsd.com) and internationally through Ingram
Publisher Services International (www.ingramcontent.com).

This book was published with the generous support of Lannan
Foundation, Wallace Action Fund, and the Marguerite Casey Foundation.

Special discounts are available for bulk purchases by organizations and
institutions. Please call 773-583-7884 or email info@haymarketbooks.org
for more information.

Cover art and design by David Mabb. Cover art is a detail from *Construct
49, William Morris, Garden Tulip/Kazimir Malevich, Black Circle*, acrylic on
wallpaper (2006).

Printed in the United States.

Library of Congress Cataloging-in-Publication data is available.

If the infinite is unknowable, we are powerless. For our concept of the infinite is our concept of ourselves and our possibilities.

GILLIAN ROSE

∵

Contents

Acknowledgments

I am grateful to the editors of the journals and volumes in which these essays first appeared, and to anonymous reviewers who read them. They are as follows:

'Camp Messianism, Or The Hopes of Poetry in Late-Late Capitalism': *American Literature* (2004) 76 (3): 579–602

'The Poetic Case': *Critical Inquiry* (2007) 33 (4): 865–86

'Reading on The Left': *Representations* (2009) 108 (1): 22–50

'Affect, Performativity, and Actually Existing Poetry': *Textual Practice* (2011) 25 (2): 265–83

'Infinity for Marxists': *Mediations: Journal of the Marxist Literary Group* (online, 2015): 47–64

'The Prynne Reflex': *The Claudius App* (online, 2013).

'The Price of Value': in Rónán McDonald ed., *The Values of Literary Studies: Critical Institutions, Scholarly Agendas* (Cambridge: Cambridge UP, 2015): 91–104

'The Antihumanist Tone': in Alex Houen ed., *Affect and Literature* (Cambridge: Cambridge UP, 2020): 267–83.

'Modernism, Critical Theory, Rhetoric': in Stefanos Geroulanos, Peter Struck, and Sophia Rosenfeld, eds. *A Cultural History of Ideas* (Bloomsbury, 2021)

'Literary and Economic Value': *Oxford Research Encyclopedia of Literature* (online, 2017)

'Abstraction, Intuition, Poetry': ELH 88.2 (Summer 2021): 387–420.

I have benefitted over the years from the generosity of more interlocutors than I can recall, but I would especially like to thank my students and colleagues, present and former, at UC Berkeley and Johns Hopkins. Thanks to Sebastian Budgen, Steve Edwards, and Danny Hayward at Brill and the Historical Materialism Book Series, for enabling me to pull these essays together in a single volume, and to Alex Lewis for his expert copyediting of the final manuscript. Thanks, finally, to the many authors of HM volumes whose work has changed how I think and write about capitalism. I am honoured to be in your company.

Introduction

This book collects eleven essays I have written on poetry and capitalism in the last fifteen years. They cover material and ideas left unexplored in my 2011 study, *The Matter of Capital: Poetry and Crisis in The American Century*, but which form part of a notable shift in scholarship on North American poetry that has taken place in the last decade. Over these years a range of work has moved away from older literary periodizations, especially those formed by a modern-postmodern sequence, in favour of attempts to chart the history of poetry according to political and economic movements. More studies than ever have given serious attention to contemporary poetry. And there has been a shift away from the post-structuralist emphasis on textuality as the primary means to study the excitement or the specialness of poetic writing.

It was my aim in *The Matter of Capital* to suggest that the problems posed by capitalism formed a great unidentified subject-matter of English-language poetry from the interwar period to the turn of the twenty-first century. I argued that returning the study of poetry to 'subject-matter', rather than forgoing the study of form, allowed me to highlight the range of ways poets conceived of their historical situation, as well as their sense of what kind of thing poetry is. In particular, I argued that poets' historical self-consciousness was shaped by their sense of what kind of material life poems have. Trans-lingual, cross-period subject-matter – as in the medieval 'Matter of Britain' or the 'Matter of France' – became visible to me not only as a kind of topicality, but as an idea of a kind of distributed material existence that I found a range of poetry seeking to model. Much in the way the mid-twentieth-century internet was specifically designed to be dispersed, in order to minimise the damage of a nuclear assault, poets across the last century imagined poetry – especially when they imagined it threatened by the social atomization and economic commodification wrought by capital – as a low-lying, dispersed art-form whose continually unfinished character was its saving grace. I did not assume that this was actually true of poetry, of course, but left space open for new forms of readerly response to poems that enabled solicitude for the self-conception of the art to serve as part of aesthetic experience.

Preparing and writing that book opened possibilities for me, and made clear some problems, that I could not explore in the monograph itself. In particular I wanted to make more space for pushing back against the tendency in theoretical writing on poetry to ontologize the art form, which is to say the tendency to think philosophically about poetry at the expense of understanding it rhetorically. A related problem was that philosophically-oriented readings of the importance of poetry in the last quarter-century, even and especially when they aimed to give the art a present-tense urgency, tended to think historically only by way of broad-brush stories about 'modernity' that leaned on the actual history of capitalism while both existentializing it, and declining to study its particulars.

In *The Matter of Capital* it was important to my argument to focus on poetry that was not explicitly left-wing, socialist, or communist, since I wanted to show that even the least 'political' poetry was shaped by the imperatives and contradictions of life under capital. In these essays, by contrast, I have tended to focus on specifically anti-capitalist poetry. Across the course of the fifteen years in which I wrote them, I have also moved gradually to incorporate a more deeply grounded account of the history of capitalism into my arguments against modernity-theories. At first this meant thinking about poems in relation to the history of social movements, but ultimately it has come to mean returning to Marx's *Capital* to highlight the non-teleological, open-ended way Marx describes the horrible dynamics of accumulation.

The essays are as follows:

1   'Camp Messianism, Or The Hopes of Poetry in Late-Late
         Capitalism' (2004)

In this essay, I describe a rhetorical stance common to a range of poets on the political left who came of age in the 1990s, after the experiments and manifestos of the Language poets. I suggest that these poets are testing out an attitude toward capitalism that blends the melancholy historicism of the Frankfurt School with the archness of the queer practice of camp. I look at the variety of ways this blend of resources produces tropes of the future anterior, à la Benjamin and Adorno, but point out how these gestures are often given a lightness that departs from the dead-serious messianic claims of Benjamin in particular (that one day, for instance, the dispossessed will finally have recuperated even the distorted lives of the dead who lived before them). I suggest that the camp attitude both threatens to evacuate Frankfurt-style messianism – to see it as liable to devaluation through humor – but also creates a certain breathing room for it. I suggest that the complex tone generated out of this blend of attitudes is traceable back to a kind of *sub rosa*, vernacular reading of the history of social movements in the twentieth century, pitting the narrative of the political failure of the European working classes of the first half of the period against the later political successes of the LGBT movement in particular.

2   'The Poetic Case' (2007)

This essay describes a more ancient poetic *topos* than the turn-of-the-twenty-first-century trope of campily devalued messianic hope, but it is related. Beginning with the question of exemplarity – what is a single poem a 'case' of? – I suggest that there is a long history in theorising by poets of suggesting that the relationship between any given poem and the category 'poetry' is one of unrealisability – that is, an argument that suggests that no single poem could encapsulate all the characteristics of the category. The reasons for making this obvious-enough point, I suggest, have to do with how thinkers in the tradition of the 'defence of poetry' have responded to Plato's demotion of the claim that poets can instruct us on the workings of every human endeavour by suggesting that we live in a world of complex divisions of labor that poetry cannot overcome – at least until those divisions are themselves overcome. I suggest that poems, like defences of poetry, can offer versions of this *topos* – not only in serial poetry, where the promise of full realisation (of aesthetic pleasure, or of meaning) can always be deferred, but also in individual poems that, depending on their occasion, may wish to decrease the pressure on themselves to promise sure grounds for overcoming capitalism. I close my argument with attention to a poem by Jennifer Moxley that beautifully enacts a self-consciousness about how the relation between poems and 'Poetry' is one way to imagine poets' relation to political history.

3   'Reading on the Left' (2009)

This essay, which began as a talk at a conference meant to celebrate the 25th anniversary of the publication of Fredric Jameson's *The Political Unconscious*, offers a look at some exemplary instances of what has counted as 'symptomatic reading' in the Anglo-American conversation with French theory since the late 1980s. As I did in 'Camp Messianism', I begin by identifying the early twentieth-century heritage of left theory that took as its starting point the failure of the European and American working classes to overthrow capitalism. The idea of 'symptomatic reading' that grew out of this moment signified a reading that presumes to be smarter than its textual object (cf. Rita Felski), or that presumptuously superadds politics to texts that are not themselves 'political' (cf. Sharon Marcus and Stephen Best's 'Surface Reading', which was in fact the introduction to the journal issue in which this essay appeared). I suggest, though, that when we think about the earlier history of the 'symptomatic reading', such readings can't be reduced to one attitude or another, since their model is Althusser's interpretation of Marx's relationship to David Ricardo: Althusser reads this as a critical acceptance on Marx's part that the terrain of 'political economy' can't simply be erased in order to critique capitalism more accurately, but must be contended with by re-working its categories. This history both reminds us that the two poles of the debate that emerged in this period – symptomatic and reparative readings, suspicious and friendly – lead scholars to lose sight of the political context out of which the two poles developed in the first place. Moving from the debate about symptomatic reading to actual examples of it, I show that even for non-Marxist critics, the question of politics remains front and center. Looking at Toni Morrison's study of literary racism in *Playing In The Dark* (1992) and Lee Edelman's *Homographesis* (1994), I show how they both analogise interpretive politics to movement politics, imagining the antiracist critic facilitating a Civil-Rights-style healing and progress in Morrison's case, and the gay male reader committing to a survivalist war of position in the fashion of AIDS-activist militancy, in Edelman's. I suggest that, in 2009 at least, those movement-related styles of reading symptomatically were in the process of being supplanted by philosophical arguments that located militancy, not in an engagement with any one social movement, but in a kind of pre-social attitude of resistance that was 'ontological' in the sense of being prior to politics. Though this style of thinking emerged from outside literary criticism, I note that for theorists like Alain Badiou and Giorgio Agamben, militancy is linked to an idea of 'poetry' as itself austerely above, or prior to, enmeshment with the low-to-the-ground activity of political struggle. Wondering whether we had escaped the either-or bind of suspicious-versus-reparative reading at the cost of placing poems and the reading of poems too far above the fray, as a place of purity that secured but could not engage in materialist politics, I conclude with a reading of a poem by the Canadian poet Lisa Robertson whose own materialism places the here-and-now practice of rhetoric at its centre.

4   'Affect, Performativity, and Actually Existing Poetry' (2011)

This essay takes up the argument I began developing in 'Reading on The Left' – that actual poems give the lie to key theoretical claims made about them in the name of the category 'poetry'. I approach the matter from a different angle here, reflecting on the emergence of 'affect' and 'performativity' in the 90s and 00s as literary-theoretical keywords in the North American academy. On the American side, 'affect' and 'performativity' have come to be understood as examples of how 'language' supervenes in the attempts of a speaking or writing subject to control utterance – that is, the keywords are part of a larger allegory of the critique of the (Enlightenment, bourgeois) 'subject', where queer subjects are seen by critics as cannily mobilising an awareness of their non-self-identicality in the name of a subversive politics. But I am after something different. So the essay splits its effort between a revisionary look at the critical-theoretical origins of the terms in Europe, on the one hand, and their uptake in the early days of American queer theory, on the other. I turn first to De Man reading Kant and Derrida reading Hegel, demonstrating that their attention to mood and tone, over and against 'structure', lays the groundwork for the American version of affect and performativity. I show that the terms on which the post-structuralists imagined literary writing outmaneuvering structure were specifically anti-dialectical: the 'performativity' of sound-play in poetry, or chance operations, as in Mallarmé, are positioned against a dialectic imagined as lock-step and pre-determined. 'Affect', in this context, is primarily the critical affect of droll irony. I pivot, then, to work by Judith Butler and Leo Bersani, emphasising how the crisis of the AIDS epidemic produced a structure of feeling of militant solicitude for vulnerable bodies, and suggesting that there was lurking in the broadly anti-subjectivist and anti-humanist currents of queer theory a sensitivity to how the big-theory 'language' of post-structuralism could not succeed in being conceptually anterior to *rhetoric*, to embodied and circumstantial language. In closing, I look to the poems of mid-twentieth-century gay San Francisco poet Jack Spicer, who was trained as a linguist, and who used a highly self-conscious rhetoric of gaming and chance, in tandem with mischievous uses of grammatical and phonetic theory, to develop a rhetoric of militant tenderness for outsiders, hidden inside the idea of 'language'.

5   'Infinity for Marxists'

This short essay serves as a little *summa* of my brief against the ontologisation of poetry in the work of non-Marxist left theory (where 'ontology' means something like 'anteriority to predication'). Reading across the work of speculative realists, eco-critics, object-oriented ontologists, new materialists and historians of the book, I outline their various advocacies for the infinite – counterposed to the textual, the interpretive, the Enlightenment, and the dialectic, all of which are imagined in this discourse as cramped – as well as the arrogance of 'the human'. I note the syzygy, in this discourse, of anti-textualism and anti-dialecticality, anti-humanism and the critique of meaning *tout court*. But I also note that the supposedly un-interpretable 'assemblages' championed in this discourse not only go by a poetic name – the 'litany' – but that they are meant to provide exactly the sort of getting-out-of-oneself that the lyric poem has historically promised. I contrast this anti-critical championing of the ontology of the lyric, one last time, with an actual poem – in this case a poem from Dana Ward's volume *The Crisis of Infinite Worlds* (2013), which persuasively develops an idea of the infinite as a kind of mediation among people, experienced in poems as an embodied comportment carried out in language; that is, as rhetoric.

6   'The Prynne Reflex'

This essay marks a turn in the collection toward interrogating the modernity-narratives that shape not only our critical theories, but the thinking of poets themselves. It has a different shape than the other essays in the volume, since it involves a sustained reading of the work of one poet, the British writer J.H. Prynne. And it shifts from counterposing ontologised claims about 'poetry' with actual poems, to thinking about the implicit philosophical claims about poetry and history made *in* poems. I chose to write about Prynne because his work is a kind of limit-case for a particular left-wing modernism in which an abstraction away from scenic modes and direct address are imagined as part of a project of keeping the poetry un-commodifiable: the sheer difficulty of Prynne's work is seen by his advocates as proof of unimpeachable anti-capitalist militancy. Reading a selection of his work from the 1970s to the 2000s, I unpack the relationship between Prynne's critique of commodification, his gradual abandonment of direct address, and a fascinating soundplay in which the reversal of graphemes and phonemes is meant to signal the possibility of the de-commodification of human life. I describe the continuity of this project across Prynne's career, while suggesting, in conclusion, that it nonetheless pays a very high price for having pitted abstraction against commodification in this way, both in a political-economic sense (it linearises the capitalist accumulation it dreams of reversing) and in a rhetorical one (its imaginary relationship to the reader gradually becomes restricted to an endless education in 'damaged life'). I conclude by suggesting that what's missing in this dazzling poetic project is a sense of how capitalism produces not just commodities, but *value*.

7   'The Price of Value' (2015)

This piece further pursues some of the questions I opened up in 'The Prynne Reflex', regarding alternative ways to think about literary history and literary value together. I try two things here: first, I test out a poetic comparison across a longer historical distance than most field-based scholarship generally risks: in this case, between a canonical late antique poem (Boethius's *Consolation of Philosophy*, ca. 524) and a twentieth-century anti-capitalist poem with no guarantee of eventual canonical value (Jasper Bernes's *We Are Nothing And So Can You*, 2015). I suggest that to recognise formal similarities between the texts – their prosimetric alteration between lineation and paragraph, their phoneme- and grapheme-level fascination with chiasmus – might open paths for research into low-level but enduring poetic folkways that can't be captured by a literary history of period styles, or of successive modernities. Because the key formal similarities I identify also ramify to include both poets' sense of 'matter' – they are both using chiasmus to think about reversibilities between what we might call the material and the ideal – I suggest that we might also find a hinge between literary and economic senses of value buried in the comparison. Boethius's poem is a tale of sequestration, a prison poem, a death row poem, that imagines dematerialisation as freedom, as an escape from the prison of matter. Its Neoplatonic idealism is re-worked by Bernes as a way of thinking about capitalist accumulation and militant action alike as surpassing 'materialism': both require what we might call the 'ideal' – that which is latent, possible, inarticulate.

8   'The Anti-humanist Tone' (2020)

This essay is the first of two in the volume that explore the assumptions underpinning theoretical hostility to rhetoric. Drawing out similarities between early twentieth-century modernist work and later critical theory, I show that they share an antipathy to 'the human' shaped by a preference for a concept of abstraction as radical alterity to the human, that is, a concept of abstraction built on the sublime, as well as a deflationary sense of the relationship of the human either to an indifferent cosmos, as in the Nietzschean anti-humanisms of De Man and Benjamin, or of myth or the divine, as in the work of T.E. Hulme and T.S. Eliot. I show that even across a right-left political divide, these discourses share a notion of the aesthetic as a place of radical sovereignty – utterly superior to individual makers of aesthetic objects – that is linked to a concrete history of conservative class ideologies. I reply to this constellation of sovereignty politics, dispossession aesthetics, and absolutist versions of abstraction by noting a revival of work that imagines abstraction in less Nietzschean and more Hegelian terms, in which 'the abstract' is the whole, which does not obviate but animates each particular. And I suggest, in closing, that this totality frame is undergoing a revival in new Marxist theory that clears ground for mul-

tiple histories of anti-capitalism, one less focused on which class will prove
to be absolutely revolutionary, and more focused on the histories of social
reproduction that themselves emerge out of many varied relations to value-
production, not just wage relations. I close with a poem by Sandra Simonds
that uses the supposedly declensionary 'mythic method' (the high modernist
making-Ulysses of everyday folk in order to show how comic and pitiful regular
people are, from the perspective of superhuman divinity) to puzzle over social
reproduction instead, not least the social reproduction of literature through the
teaching of the humanities.

9   'Modernism, Critical Theory, and the Desire for Objecthood' (2020)

This essay further pursues one aspect of 'The Anthumanist Tone', that is, the
problems with the critical desire for sublime, radical alterity in aesthetic pro-
duction. It identifies a specifically anti-rhetorical aspect of that desire. This
piece demonstrates that the uptake of modernist aesthetic precepts in 'post-
modern' theory identified by Andreas Huyssen in *After The Great Divide* (1987)
also reworks the modernist championing of objectivity against personality and
ornament – that is, against rhetoric – into a periodising story, where the 'post-
modern' is a form of groundlessness that may be either lamented or celebrated,
but isn't, in any case, hard and obdurate – 'the post-modern', here, standing for
the ungroundedness of rhetorical assertion, free-floating exchange value, and
immaterial production, and 'the modern' standing for production, inhuman
objecthood, and pure use value. I push back against this story by showing, first,
how the moderns and the post-moderns alike misunderstand the character
of the inhuman objects they attend to, mostly because those objects are spe-
cifically capitalist machine-objects, less ontologically alien to the human than
socially *alienating*. Second, I show that the version of 'rhetoric' repudiated in
both modernist manifestos and post-modern theory is a narrow version indeed,
one that misses the social value of the situatedness of rhetoric by impugning
'ornament' and 'exchange' in the theoretical equivalent of (first right, then left)
populism. Turning in closing to a reading of similarities in the conceptions of
objecthood and rhetoric in the work of Hans Blumenberg and Fred Moten, I
suggest that attending to rhetoric as the practice of contending with the per-
plexity of situation – of sudden crises and ancient impasses faced by human
creativity – offers opportunities for better periodisation of the capitalist period,
one focused on struggle rather than on technology.

10   'Literary and Economic Value' (2017)

This essay, co-authored with Joshua Clover, works to expose the limits of post-war stories about the autonomy of the aesthetic that see it as imperiled or doomed – 'subsumed' is a recent usage – by the universal commodification of art. We do this by looking at the longer history of thinking about the relation between economic and aesthetic value, which we show has been shaped by a domain model that artificially separated aesthetic and economics, only to be dismayed, later, by their fusion. Following early work by scholars like Terry Eagleton, we highlight how Enlightenment-era attempts to separate out aesthetic value from its economic counterpart involved analogies between what were understood to be different cognitive faculties (reason and emotion, say), and relations among competing claims to political standing (between the bourgeoisie and the sovereign, most of all). By the twentieth centuries the analogies had become both more backgrounded and more baroque, leading, for instance, to the complex relay of analogical terms in Benjamin's theory of the constellation – where individual features of an artwork could be seen to be in potential rebellion against both its form and against ideologies of progress that dictated the form – or to the strange overlay of post-World War I geopolitics and fragmentary citation in T.S. Eliot's work, where part-whole relations, as in Benjamin, take on uncertain aesthetic value pending the eventual destiny of something like Christian culture. Liberal American conversations about literary and economic value after World War II worried over part-whole relations in terms of debates about works and canons, that is, the value of individual literary works in what seemed to be an ever-expanding multicultural canon. Post-war literary theories of economic and aesthetic value in a more Marxist vein turned to various narratives of the 'subsumption' of social life by economic values, either pessimistically imagining subsumption as a fatal error on the part of capitalism, since sociability is too unruly finally to organise according to economic principles (deriving from the Italian autonomist tradition, emphasising worker creativity), or as a terrible victory for capital, now free to morph into something qualitatively different and more sinister, like 'bio-power' (deriving, of course, from the Frankfurt School, before Foucault). But even these Marxist literary theories tended to ignore contemporary work in history and historical sociology that told capital's postwar history, not as a story about saturation or subsumption, but as one about ever-more consequential volatility leading to a crisis in capital's ways of producing profitable surplus value, and exchangeable use values. Seen from the vantage of this scholarship, it becomes clear that most discourses on the specific value of the aesthetic tend to lean too heavily on spatialised domain models of art and economics, and that they tend to insist on a separation of art and economics that rests on a false distinction between *politics* and economics. We conclude by urging a re-thinking the specificity of the aesthetic that does not think of it as a separate sphere, or as necessarily resistant to capital.

11   'Abstraction, Intuition, Poetry' (2021)

With this final essay I return to the baseline format of the volume – exploring a body of theoretical work with significance for how we read poetry, and then comparing its claims to the rhetoric of a contemporary poem. This time, however, I don't turn to the rhetorical liveness and situatedness of a poem to deflate the ontologising claims of anti-humanist or anti-Marxist theory. Instead, I begin with Marx and the Marxian tradition, laying out a path by which *Capital*, Volume I can help us think about the anti-solidaristic forces at work in contemporary capitalism, and then read a recent book of poetry that itself tests out the limits and possibilities of imagining oneself to be aligned with others, seen and unseen. The first part of the essay suggests that for today's struggles, which are coming to feel like a blend of 'identity' and anti-capitalist movements, we can benefit from returning to Chapter 25 of *Capital*, Volume I ('The General Law of Capitalist Accumulation'), specifically because it lays out how capital accumulation depends, not only on forcing populations into the wage relation, but also on keeping populations out of it, or expelling them from it. If the profitability of wage exploitation depends on unwaged, feminised reproductive labour, for instance, and on the imprisonment of no-longer-exploitable racialised populations, we begin to have grounds for linking feminist to antiracist struggles in fresh ways. And if we read Chapter 25 along with the subsequent chapters that focus on so-called primitive accumulation, we can begin to see a global dynamic between colonisers and colonised that prefigures and later mirrors this dynamic of tiered disposability and ever-shifting recipes of waged to unwaged exploitation. I frame this reading of *Capital* as a matter of isolating value as its key abstraction, and distinguish this from attempts to read *Capital* as primarily about 'property'. I take time to suggest, specifically, that this way of reading *Capital* in the Black Radical tradition, though it enables a critique of the limits of Marxism's ability to grasp the specificity of Black chattel slavery, also leaves open a door to thinking of Black enslavement and racialisation in terms of Marx's theory of value production. I close the essay by using this reading of Marx to focus on the dynamics of possession and dispossession in Stephanie Young's 2019 book *Pet Sounds*. In that volume,

Young uses the mode of autobiography and the form of the poetic sequence to track how seemingly fleeting or circumstantial encounters can deepen or ramify into the shape of a life, and which takes the occasions of these unexpectedly deep entailments of places and times, and of people with each other, to ask, shyly, what a solidarity might look like among people who don't 'deserve' to think of themselves as allied, because they are so different. I close by suggesting that, however counterintuitive it may seem to a generation of academic humanists who have been trained to critique 'the human', we urgently require a humanist study of the historical barriers to solidarity if we are to overcome them.

• •
•

Looking back at these essays teaches me about the long journey I have made from thinking about poetry in relation to capitalism, broadly, to thinking about it in relation to capitalist value-production, in particular. I hope that placing these essays alongside each other will allow their readers to see that movement more clearly than I could, at the time. And I hope that the place this volume leaves off will encourage fellow-travellers to pursue its open questions further. I will admit to wondering whether my own long learning curve en route to thinking about how value-production yokes us together and differentiates us is an ontogenetic recapitulation of philosophy's phylogenetic one: a century and a half of anti-Hegelianism, for instance, has arguably deferred the nourishing of habits of totality-thinking, and of honouring intuition, that I think we could all use as it becomes harder to deny that our many political and, well, existential struggles are part of a single problem.

Writing these essays, in other words, has led me to recognise the importance of a deeper awareness of the workings of the logic of accumulation at the level of the whole (if by 'logic' you'll allow me to mean a social dynamic that has achieved a long-term ability to overcome obstacles to reproducing itself, however violently). But the unfolding of that logic happens as history, of course, and I can see more clearly, now, that any further writing I do on capital and poetry – or on capital and people! – will need to draw on histories of both the geopolitics and the everyday experience of accumulation: not our familiar histories of 'modernity', but histories of the reproduction of property relations, for instance; or histories of anti-left and anti-communist violence. These are some of the histories that meet the granularity of literary writing halfway; bundled together with a capacity to think at the level of the whole, they might help us become more intuitively nimble when we try to name the many ways that value-production devalues most of us. What I mean is, if we could all develop a clearer picture, in the coming years, of the relationship between 'value' in its technical Marxist sense and its everyday humanist sense, I think we will have done about the best that intellectual work can be expected to do, when it forms part of a political struggle.

Washington, DC, September 2021

CHAPTER 1

Camp Messianism, or the Hopes of Poetry in Late-Late Capitalism

Recent innovative North American poetry is a good place for thinking about the status of a new aesthetics, since it's been busy writing one. I'm thinking of American and Canadian poets, most in their thirties and forties now, who are writing in light of the poetic and critical projects of Language poetry, though they are by no means simply following them out. These poets, referred to as 'post-Language' writers in the small-press world in which they've emerged, raise interesting questions about new habits of literary criticism, since their poems read both as theory and poetry. Although these poets have not yet produced a body of writing like the criticism and theory of the Language poets, their poetry reads like the yield, if not the foregrounding, of significant theoretical effort.

More specifically, many of the post-Language writers seem to have taken a kind of Frankfurt School turn in their poems, by which I mean not so much that they are crankily denouncing a culture industry – though they may – or critically miming 'authoritarian' types of language – though they do – but that they have become invested in a historical story about what Theodor Adorno called 'damaged life', or what Susan Stewart might call the 'fate' of the material world, its pasts and possible futures.[1] Unlike Adorno or Walter Benjamin, though, many of the post-Language poets have struck a kind of camp posture toward the 'damage' of late capitalism, in a way that borrows from but reinterprets both the messianism of Adorno and Benjamin and the subcultural (especially queer) trajectory of camp.

The best sketch I can offer of the Frankfurtian part of this historical story about a 'damaged' material life is to say that it's not just a story of the culture industry whose workings Adorno and Max Horkheimer detailed at midcentury, nor even of the 'late capitalism' Fredric Jameson first diagnosed in 1984; it's the story of something like really, *really* late capitalism; capitalism in a fully globalised and triumphal form, the destructive speed and flexibility of whose financial instruments alone make Nixon's lofting the dollar off the

---

1   See Adorno 1996; and Stewart 2001.

gold standard in 1971 look thoughtful and conservative.[2] Depending on how one understands the massive glut of capital unleashed on world markets since the collapse of the Soviet Union, capitalism has either taken on a new, omnipotently viral character (traveling across national boundaries, for instance, with the power to imperil entire economies for no other reason than to keep a tiny group of wealthy investors' portfolios mobile and artificially inflated); or it is in the last, seizing phases of a horrible addiction to its own mobility. In any case, the privatising, shock-treatment destruction of the post-Soviet economy in the early nineties, the collapse and bailout of the peso in 1995, the Asian currency crisis of 1997, and the bottoming out of the United States' supposedly post-historical new economy in 2000 – all these indicate a volatility to capital on an order of magnitude beyond even the ricochets of the early twentieth century.[3] If Adorno and Horkheimer made much of how the Enlightenment's dream of the equality of all people had become the nightmare of the interchangeability of all people, that interchangeability could now be said to have become entirely liquid, even quicksilver.

We might say that the camp aspect of post-Language writing, meanwhile, is the rueful astonishment that, against all odds, this liquidation is still not complete: post-Cold War global economic volatility has not resulted in wholesale disaster for the United States or Europe. Instead, late-late capitalism gives texture to our everyday lives more murmuringly: most of us are at least intermittently aware of being solicited day and night by a kind of manic mass culture that seeks, ever more aggressively, to stuff our attention to the gills. When Andrew Ross remarks, then, that camp 'is the re-creation of surplus value from forgotten forms of labor', he touches on a polemical affection for waste, which animates not just camp in its queer subcultural matrix but also in its migrations beyond subcultural boundaries – to mass culture (which tries to capture the dynamics of camp consumption in television, for instance, in programmes like Mystery Science Theater 3000, or in VH-1's 'Pop-up videos', or in fake-anachronistic sitcoms like 'That '70's Show') and to the literary culture of small-press poetry.[4] Mass-cultural camp invites us all to be clever; post-Language poetic camp, I hope to show, invites us to take up a polemical affection for what's obsolete, misguided, or trivial, and to risk the embarrassment of trying it out.

---

2   See Adorno and Horkheimer 2000; and Jameson 1991.
3   In the vast lay literature on the post-World War II financial system and its vulnerabilities, see Korten 1995; Guyatt 2001; Martin 2002; and Shutt 1998.
4   Ross 1999, p. 320.

So how do post-Language poets do this? How do they perform a relationship to the experience of a materiality that is both desubstantialised and supersaturating, subject to both lightning-swift consolidations and dispersals and to humiliating, vegetally slow decay? A first text for consideration:

> What gets *me* is
>> the robots are doing
>> *my* job, but I don't get
>> the *money*,
>>> some extrapolated node
>>> of expansion-contraction gets
>>> my money, which *I* need
>> for *time travel*.[5]

What gets *me* is how compactly this terrific little poem toys with, or speaks through, an affect that has transformed North American poetry in the last decade. At first, this poem by Kevin Davies seems to be just the swift dodge of a tedious sort of lecturing, political poetry. Yes, the speaker is complaining about the theft of his wages, but he does it science-fictionally, and by way of a dated science fiction, at that: there is no Matrix here, just 'robots' and '*time travel*'. But the campiness of the obsolete sci-fi conceit has something to play off against, namely, the description of the system that steals the speaker's wages, the 'extrapolated node / of expansion-contraction' – itself amusing in its succinctness but not quite the same as the clanking of the worker-robots. If the poem is a dodge, then, it's not quite dodging politics with humour: the truth of the poem lies elsewhere, in its rueful awareness of the obsolescence of its conceit. This awareness is not simply reflexive – not simply a modernist recognition of obsolescence – because the poem also performs the knowledge that even its obsolescence is obsolete. This performance – I think of it as a kind of stance – is designed to make the poem's last, emphatic phrase – '*time travel*' – escape, for a moment, its camp value and reveal an extravagant demand: that the speaker get his money *and* his history back, that he be freed to burrow back behind the process that made even the expropriating robots obsolete – or, perhaps, to lurch forward to a time when obsolescence will reveal itself to have been an unfinished piece of a story about the rescue of human vulnerability from the merciless abstraction of 'expansion' and 'contraction'.[6]

---

5   Davies 2000, untitled frontpiece.
6   In a very helpful essay called 'Globalit, Inc.; Or, the Cultural Logic of Global Literary Stud-

Read this way, Davies's poem is not far from the canonical modern artic-
ulation of a redemptive historiography – that is, from Benjamin's remarks in
'Theses on the Philosophy of History':

> A chronicler who recites events without distinguishing between major
> and minor ones acts in accordance with the following truth: nothing that
> has ever happened should be regarded as lost to history. To be sure, only a
> redeemed mankind receives the fullness of its past – which is to say, only
> for a redeemed mankind has its past become citable in all its moments.
> Each moment it has lived becomes a *citation à l'ordre du jour* – and that
> day is Judgment Day.[7]

This scenario echoes not only the short poem by Davies but also a whole vari-
ety of post-Language writing, like this poem in Lisa Robertson's *Debbie: An Epic*
(1997):

> maybe
> even
> this
> dress
> shall
> some
> day be
> a joy
> to
> repair[8]

And here, Davies again, from *Comp*'.s 'Karnal Bunt':

---

ies', Ian Baucom makes use of the figures of expansion and contraction to characterise the
current mode of capitalism (see Baucom 2001). He deploys these terms to invest the rhet-
oric of globalisation with a cautionary note: the 'expansion' of capital, he insists, means
also its 'contraction', that is, its concentration in fewer hands. Baucom offers this caution-
ary coinage in order to work against what he sees as a potentially romanticising tend-
ency to model literary studies on a new global situation that is, in fact, an uneven global
marketplace. I take Baucom's caution seriously; it is one reason I will rely here on the
Frankfurtian diction of a totality, whatever its problems, rather than on the word globalisa-
tion.

7 Benjamin 1969, p. 254.
8 Robertson 1997. *Debbie* has no page numbers.

> Every junked
> vehicle a
> proposition
> waiting for
> the right rustic
> welder
> after the war that
> never happened
> here.[9]

And Rod Smith, from *The Good House* (2001):

> Each reasonable house
> & each waking motion
> are votive, based on
> the wiley insurgence
> of awaiting worlds –[10]

Each of these poems (they are actually all stanzas or sections from longer poems) finds in its material at hand – a dress, 'junked' cars, the 'reasonable house' and 'waking motion' – a mute expectation of 'repair' or recuperation.

The character of this expectation is slightly different in each case. In the context of *Debbie*, it becomes clear that Robertson is implicitly imagining herself in the scene of repair; Davies understands the instances of his 'junked vehicle' logically, as 'propositions', but he complicates past logic the temporality of their being welded since their future is contingent on what 'never happened / here'; and Smith places not only his 'house' but also a human figure, with 'waking motion', in the way of expectation. The language in each poem is also differently political – only whisperingly so in Robertson (though, again, elsewhere she will show her cards), but frankly combative in Davies, with his hard-to-locate 'war', and slyly, ambiently resistant in Smith's 'wiley insurgence / of awaiting worlds'.

I realise that in offering a preliminary account of these poems my focus on modernist and mid-century points of comparison – camp modes of attachment and critique, and Frankfurtian tactics of re-reading history – raises the question, What about post-modernity? It is true, of course, that the two 'schools' of poetry to whom the post-Language poets are most indebted – the

---

9   Davies 2000, p. 61.
10   Smith 2001.

Language poetry of the 1980s and the New York school of the 1960s and 1970s – are both understood in American literary history as signally 'post-modern'. Are the post-Language poets post-modern?

This is a hard question. It is true that poets like Davies, Robertson, and Smith make use of the signal strategies of literary post-modernism as we've come to recognise it, especially its engagement with mass culture and a decoupling of signs from their referents. And it's true that these poets have also grown up with the peculiarly post-modern admixture of identity-based liberation movements and post-structural critiques of identity. But their poems seem to be written out of some set of conditions we are still struggling to name, conditions not quite matching the major accounts of the post-modern (hence, with my apologies, 'late-late capitalism'). At the very least, these younger poets are motivated by a different sense of historical situation – specifically, a different sense of the unfolding of a totalising political and economic system – than was felt by either the New York school or the Language poets.

Although vastly different, of course, both Language and New York writing developed in successive stages of the expansion of mass culture, and both drew energy from critiques of authenticity bound up in mass culture's unfolding. At mid-century, in poems like Frank O'Hara's 'Having a Coke with You' and John Ashbery's 'Daffy Duck in Hollywood', New York School poets made friends with popular and mass culture, deliberately braving the possibility of obsolescence or eventual inscrutability. Such risk-taking was meant to dislodge the idea of poetry from the formalist anti-modernisms of 'official verse culture', which presumed that poems were autonomous linguistic artifacts whose aim was to rise above their immediate surroundings and stake a claim to cultural permanence.[11]

Language school poets later developed a critique concerned not with the poet's cultural isolation as much as with the authenticity of lyric utterance – and, ultimately, of language itself – as a transparently truthful medium. Language poets, like the poets of the New York school, were interested in the relationship between mass culture and poetry, but rather than mining mass culture as a referential and affective resource, they tended to focus on its capacity to obscure social truths, especially the truth of the commodification of language. Deliberately fracturing syntax and troubling reference, Language poets developed a relationship between the poetic and the political not so much by striking the implicitly political posture of insouciance toward an official cul-

---

11   For a discussion of the character of 'official verse culture' (which is Charles Bernstein's phrase, coined long after the 1950s in reference to poetry of the 1980s), see Breslin 1983.

ture as by tearing away at its lies. If the relevant political backdrop for the New York school poets was the Cold War, for the Language poets, it was Vietnam.[12]

What kind of poetics the post-Language poets articulate, meanwhile, is a question understood so far primarily in terms of their relationship to Language writing rather than to the New York school, perhaps because the Language poets developed a large body of critical writing (and because they are the more immediate precursors). While I can't devote much space here to a comparison between Language and post-Language writing, I think it is important at least to mention some of the major arguments in the Language poets' critical writing in order to highlight what seems different now about the post-Language poets, especially in their understanding of linguistic materiality.

Language poets' contribution to the development of a post-modern poetics can be understood as an argument on behalf of three interrelated arguments about participatory readership, language and the commodity form, and the decentring of the post-modern political subject. These contributions have been widely discussed and analysed; in brief, I think it's fair to say that the notion of active readership lies at the centre of the Language poets' collective self-understanding.[13] Active readership points to a belief that difficult, unconventional texts, rather than being closed to readers, are actually more open than traditional literary texts because they don't smother or direct readers with too many genre cues, overdetermined tropes, clichés, or heavily rehearsed rhetorical movements – forms of what Language poets like Lyn Hejinian and Bruce Andrews refer to as 'closure'.[14] This 'rejection of closure', as Hejinian calls it, implies a scene of reader-writer collaboration meant to rescue language not only from cliché but also from commodification, from becoming a unidirectional, informatic, PowerPoint-y medium for social control. The argument for referentially disjunct, nonclosural texts as the appropriate scene for a collab-

---

12   For one consideration of the political background of Language poetry, especially in terms of its relation to the new social movements, see Kim 2001. Both Kim and Barrett Watten identify the emergence of Language poetry as a politicised avant-garde with the practice of criticism. For Kim, this means that the Language poets, in preserving a small-press 'outsider' status into the 1980s, actually ended up setting the stage for their (relative) canonization in university-based literary culture. For Watten, the 'turn to language' is articulated in a critical response to the failures of 'radical' poets like Denise Levertov to grasp the 'insufficiency of language to history' (Watten 2000, p. 182). For the Language poets of Watten's generation, this critique led to an exploration of the obduracy, even the opacity, of the relationship between politics and the linguistic sign.

13   The active-reader theory has received a good deal of attention from both post-Language poets and literary critics; see, for example, Gilbert 2002, and Altieri 1998.

14   For a key articulation of this theory, see Hejinian 2000, pp. 40–58.

orative decommodification of language has been made most forcefully by the
Language poet and critic Ron Silliman; this argument is linked, in the poetry
and critical writing of Bruce Andrews, to a theory of collaboration between
reader and writer that produces a mobile, protean, political subject along the
lines of the 'schizo' envisioned in Gilles Deleuze and Félix *Guattari's Anti-
Oedipus*.[15] As Andrews puts it:

> [Language poetics] doesn't call for a reading that rejects or negates the
> referential, or even the baldly representational forces of language,
> but one that resists letting those forces be confined and recuperated &
> territorialized. It would join in the adventure of keeping them active at
> the micro level, as singular & literal events – constantly varying, skidding,
> interpenetrating, mutually transforming, out in the open, on the surface
> ....
> Works are responses, and the praxis of the reader reconstructs this re-
> sponsiveness
> ....
> Here we're not looking for mastery, but passionate or even dizzying em-
> brace – of an *implicated* social body.[16]

These concerns with active readership, the decommodification of language,
and the production of a new, political subject, fully enfolded ('*implicated*') in a
mobile social body, are formally present in many Language poems. One canon-
ical example is Hejinian's *My Life*, which in its first edition contained thirty-
seven sections of thirty-seven sentences each, one section-sentence for each
year of Hejinian's life (the second edition, written eight years after the first,
adds eight sentences to the thirty-seven original sections, and eight new sec-
tions: guess why). These playfully arbitrary formal conceits allow Hejinian to
foreground the variety of means she deploys to establish connectivity among
her sentences:

> Back and backward, why, wide and wider. Such that art is inseparable from
> the search for reality. The continent is greater than the content. A river
> nets the peninsula
> ....

---

15   Silliman 1995 makes his case for understanding reader-writer collaboration as a decom-
      modification of language.
16   Andrews 2004.

> The Spanish make a little question frame. In the case, propped on a stand
> so as to beckon, was the hairy finger of St. Cecilia, covered with rings
>
> ....
>
> An extremely pleasant and often comic satisfaction comes from conjunc-
> tion, the fit, say, of comprehension in a reader's mind to content in a
> writer's work. But not bitter.[17]

Hejinian moves from one sentence to the next according to different principles
in different instances, and it is this connective variety that gives the poem life.
Sometimes the sentences move with a gesture toward logic. The second sen-
tence in this section, for instance, begins, 'such that'. Or the sentences might
represent two phrasings of the 'same' idea: 'The continent is greater than the
content' is followed by 'A river nets the peninsula', which allows Hejinian to
begin to isolate the difference particular figures make when called into the ser-
vice of the same concept – in this case, the concept of content surrounding,
rather than being encased by, form.

It is this last concept, really an argument, that seems typical of the attitude
toward linguistic materiality expressed in Language writing. While it is true
enough to say that Language writers are concerned with linguistic materiality
(since they are poets, it is nearly tautological to notice this), what's distinctive
is their relation to the aspectual character of this materiality. Language writ-
ing argues for understanding the medium of language as a kind of perpetually
mobile surround, which Hejinian typically calls 'context': placement, situation,
conjunction, animating constraint – the 'net' and the 'frame' – all serve to estab-
lish a scene that invites the reader to experience the toggle between material
and referential aspects of language as curious, as 'a little question frame' that
'nets' content but lets it go.[18] Poems like Hejinian's articulate linguistic material-
ity in terms much like those of a monist Deleuzian plenitude, where differences
are not metaphysical or categorical but '*implicated*'; they are folds. The relation-
ship between form and content in Language poetry takes on the character of a
materio-linguistic snapshot, where what is form one minute might be content
the next. It is a poetics of fluidity, and if we listen for it, I think we can hear in
it the echo of the post-1968 hope for a new, more fluid politics.

This set of beliefs and practices around the materiality of language is signi-
ficantly different from the testamentary, expectation-laden materiality in the
work of the post-Language poets who most interest me. The historical reas-

---

17   Hejinian 1987, pp. 84–5.
18   See Hejinian 2000.

ons for this difference are of course complex, and they are still being debated. Hejinian has recently suggested, controversially, that the new generation of poets has not been politicised as the Language poets were by the singular, defining experience of the war in Vietnam.[19] While this doesn't amount to the now-familiar Baby Boomer charge that Generation X is 'apathetic' or 'de-politicised' (which Silliman has suggested), it does raise the question of how different political moments breed different structures of political and poetic feeling. This is of course a complicated question; we might take a first attempt at answering it by way of the very largest abstractions to hand and try to understand the political affects of the two generations and the formal strategies that animate their work as expressing emphatically different moments in the unfolding of a late-capitalist totality:

> As for the current situation, ... [we can see] how the very mood and methodology of the analyses varied across the great internal polarity of voluntarism and fatalism (or determinism) according to the changes in the objective situation, and its great cyclical rhythms that alternate from situations of great promise and change ... to those of a locked social geology so massive that no visions of modification seem possible ...[20]

Fredric Jameson wrote this passage at the beginning of the 1990s, as part of an explanation of why he felt Adorno's work might, after what he felt were the post-structuralist highs of the 1970s and 1980s, be freshly relevant for political thinking. In 1990, at least, Jameson believed that Adorno, because of his willingness to work in isolation from an identifiable political movement, was a good model for the way critical thinking and political solitude might have to go together in a new post-modern dispensation that had done away with the types of cultural and historical memory that mass movements need. More than ten years later, Jameson seems to have been both right – there is undeniably a revival, in the English-language academy, of interest in Adorno – and wrong: late capitalism, perhaps in the emergent form of empire, is being written about as though it were all the more legible – and therefore more vulnerable to opposition – to a new generation of 'anti-globalisation' activists.[21]

---

19   For excerpts from Hejinian's and Silliman's remarks on this topic, and for responses to them by younger writers, see 'Forum: The Blank Generation?' Newsletter of the St. Mark's Poetry Project (February–March 2003), pp. 9–14.

20   Jameson 1990, p. 251.

21   For a recent example of this rhetoric of the emergent legibility of empire – American

The post-Language poets to whom I now want to turn, however, exhibit neither a post-revolutionary political apathy nor a specific set of anti-globalist affiliations. They are not 'movement' poets. But they do write with an acute knowledge of the susceptibility of their materials to historical change. What I would like to suggest in the rest of this essay is that the recent affective and strategic shift in American poetry can be described as a shift in attitudes toward the character of late capitalist totality. We might say that where the Language poets discovered a reserve of uncapitalised materiality in the lively, 'aspectual' character of language – so that the open-endedness of texts might outpace their superscription by languages of power – the post-Language poets, battered by another generation's-worth of the encroachments of capital, are not so ready to rely on those aspectual reserves. They can discern them in language, of course, and in material objects, but it's not their focus; instead, as I'll try to show, they expend their considerable talents on making articulate the ways in which, as they look around, they see *waiting*.

Perhaps the best place to begin is with a poem from Joshua Clover's manuscript *The Totality for Kids*. Since 1996, when he published his first book, *Madonna Anno Domini*, Clover has been trying to develop a new poetry of the city, with Paris as his model – a kind of post-Benjaminian, post-Situationist city, whose moods and contours are revealed by way of a perpetual and unstable movement between concretion and abstraction. Like Ashbery's poems, Clover's foreground the pathos of conceptualisation – how recursive it is, how helpless, even in its glories; but unlike Ashbery, Clover develops a quietly messianic sense that the city, and the aesthetic experience it fosters, awaits redemption. In this view, he follows Benjamin, for whom even ephemera – especially ephemera – could whisper to listening ears the story of how a mute material existence, completely overwritten by capital, might still one day become a tool for breaking it apart. As Clover puts it in the last poem in *The Totality for Kids*, 'What's American about American Poetry?':

> They basically grow it out of sand.
> This is a big help because it was getting pretty enigmatic.
> Welcome to the desert of the real,
> I am an ephemeral and not too discontented citizen.
> I do not think the revolution is finished.[22]

---

empire, here – see Roy 2003. Roy describes the Bush administration's international posture as 'tactless imprudence'.

22   Clover 2006, p. 63.

The Baudrillardian 'desert of the real', now more familiar to us from *The Matrix*, is – after all – a biblical desert of unredeemed wandering. Baudrillard's famous essay 'The Precession of Simulacra' opens with a simulacral 'quotation' from Ecclesiastes and begins as a meditation on the death of God. But Clover has none of Baudrillard's enraged despair with the Left. Although 'the revolution' that Clover counterposes to 'the desert of the real' is happening in a suspended grammar, detached from an object, that suspension may occur just because 'the revolution' has a temporality hard for him to see. Even the poem's fainting last line – 'I drift, mainly I drift' – recalls the situationist *dérive*, the deliberately unregulatable 'drift' that is meant to restore life to a too-regular city.

'Ceriserie', Clover's first poem in *The Totality for Kids*, meditates hungrily on where such life might hide:

> Music: the unless of a certain series.
> Mathematics: Everyone rolling dice and flinging Fibonacci, going to the
>   opera, counting everything.
> Fire: The number between four and five.
> Gold leaf: Wedding dress of the verb *to have*, it reminds you of of.[23]

There is a tiny messianic message, let me start by saying, even in the 'unless of a certain series': that music can withhold exact certainty from the 'certain series', or that there can be no truth unless there is music – not the rushed cacophony of everyone 'going to the opera, counting everything', but the music of 'fire', of what's *between* the numbers, unaccountable. 'Fire' is the poem's first foray into another materiality, the *serie-serie* of the 'Ceriserie', the series-series that both rests humbly in the interstices of the tossed dice of items in series and also promises to overthrow them by lighting up as pun and performance: 'Fire' is the tissue binding 'four' and 'five' – the tissue that, un-knotted and bright red, turns items into relationships, and numbers into words.

Not so 'Gold leaf', which a few lines before the ones I've quoted is associated with Enguerrand Quarton, the fifteenth-century painter who applied it so heavily. Unlike 'Fire', the 'Gold leaf' represents, like the 'robots' in Davies's poem, a sweet, bemusing anachronism, an artistic attempt revealed in retrospect as literal-minded; as a nice try; as trumped by subsequent history; as an object, that is, of camp affection. Clover puts it this way later in the poem: 'Enguerrand Quarton: In your dream gold leaf was the sun, salve on

---

23   Clover 2006, p. 3.

the visible world'. Quarton's 'salve', with which he suffused paintings like the *Coronation of the Virgin* (1454), is meant to supervene and redeem mere painterly reference, 'the kingdom of the visible'; to give 'the verb *to have*' a 'wedding dress'; to transform the genitive into the betrothed. But Quarton, endearingly, is a bit of a mess – 'swathed', earlier in the poem, 'in gold paint' and 'whispering come with me under the shadow of this gold leaf'. He cannot see, that is, the tightening noose of a modernity that will foreclose on any historical alchemy promising to make of possession a relation, a wedding, and that will turn 'Gold leaf', instead, into the chill 'red rock' of *The Waste Land*.

Robertson doesn't necessarily see this as a problem. In *Debbie*, she writes:

> I do not limit myself: I imitate
> many fancy things such as the dull red
> cloth of literature, its mumbled griefs.[24]

Although she shares with Clover a commitment to the recuperation of forms of material waste, Robertson has a different sense of what the candidates for recuperation might be, and by what means the recuperation might take place. Indeed, though she says she does not 'limit' herself, she is interested in ornament, and its uselessness, and she is everywhere an erotic poet, collaging from both modernity and classical tradition new configurations of old figures for pleasure. Her project, in books like *The Weather* and *Xeclogue* as well as in *Debbie*, has been to articulate something like a cyborg pastoral. Writing as one of 'Virgil's Bastard Daughters', she highlights at every turn the arbitrary and ideological nature of what she calls 'filiation', imagining in 'Argument' that history is simply a 'library', which might lend momentary legitimacy to a whole variety of recuperative claims: 'To narrate origin as lapidary, as irrevocable, is only to have chosen with a styled authority from the ranked aisles of thought'. Or elsewhere in the poem: 'filius/flunks'.

Though Robertson puckishly calls *Debbie* 'An Epic', it is really something like a prismatic pastoral, composed of 'episodes', 'parts', and unpaginated interludes, all gorgeously and adventuresomely typeset in varying text sizes and shades of gray, so that not even the physical matter of the text eludes what Robertson calls 'decoration'. There is no plot, although there is an astonishing array of poses and also a wide variety of background characters. Though only Debbie speaks in the poem, it is filled with 'nurses', 'majorettes', 'scholars', and

---

24   Robertson 1997, l. 609–61.

'shepherdesses' who loll and stroll and set themselves in the thickly textual landscapes Robertson paints. In a signal passage from an early section called 'Party Scene', the speaker asks:

> Do you remember the day we wanted
> to describe everything? We saw a
> euphoria of trees. This was the middle
> ground. Some women lounged on the clipped
> grass, shadows and intelligence moving
> lightly over their skin, compelled by
> the trenchant discussion of sovereignty.
> Others, in the background, rolled their pale
> Trousers to wade in the intimate sea:
> Their crisp gasps matched the waves. Freed scholars
> Strolled slowly in pairs along gravel
> Paths, reading from books the rhetoric
> Of perfidy. Succinct flowers thrust gauche
> Grammars into the air. In the upper
> Left corner improbable clouds grouped
> And regrouped the syntax of polit
> Esse: The feminist sky split open.[25]

Few poets these days brave this kind of utopian description. Robertson manages it, I think, because of how she foregrounds the 'improbable' – not just the 'improbable clouds', moving as if in conversation, and not just the 'gauche' grammaticality of flowers, as if their principles of growth were at last a language, but also the willful match between the crispnesses of waves and the gasps of the waders who step into them. It is, in short, a willful utopia, which overwrites the 'party scene' with an aspect of fulfillment that, it is hinted, cannot be found there. The 'euphoria of trees' in the 'middle ground', which gets listed first, seems indeed to ground the fanciful projections that follow and preserve, even in the pastoral, a narrative of the liberation required to get there – the 'sovereignty' won for women and 'freed scholars' by 'perfidy', by foregoing claims to legitimacy in favour of claims to ungrounded 'intelligence', which moves lightly, like weather, and opens up history: 'The feminist sky split open'.

It is perhaps a failure of my own imagination to want to probe such utopian passages for traces of conflict. But Robertson, too, seems to feel that the

---

25   Robertson 1997, l. 25–41.

argument from 'decoration' – that it is simply, gloriously, extra; that it is a supplement, and requires no ethical or political justification, no proper 'origin' – can't by itself address the problem of the entanglement of decoration in an unredeemed world. In a section of Debbie called 'As If the World's a Punctured Chit', she writes:

> The bridge and the river are
> not landscape – nor is this forest with its
> archival plenitude and entanglement.
> The clerical earth just exudes itself.
> – and the carved ruckus of milky bark
> spells a long diary of placation
> repeating ad infinitum We want
> to love. We want to love.
> Or the heart's cheap
> Dipthong snaps. Black ink trickles through my arms
> And it has written landscapes. The trees still
> pose embittered questions. Do
> bright thrones yield civil shade? Some day I shall
> laugh at even this obedience, wake
> in the middling shade of the library
> wander freely, calling out a name I hope[26]

This is a world not only overcome by a tyranny of exchange-value – made a 'chit' – but used, 'punctured', done with. It is still a richly textual scene – the forests' knotted plenty is 'archival', and the trees are transcriptions of a 'clerical earth' that is still, even deflated, writing itself – but the archive doesn't yield 'euphoria' here so much as a lonely, sad demand: 'We want to love', repeated in each mute material thrust of life up from earth, and bleeding out of every love-tattoo cut into 'milky bark'. Even 'the heart' breaks down into *he-art*, just what the thundering 'feminist sky' should have rinsed clear. The lines after the 'heart's cheap / Dipthong' seem crucial. Here and elsewhere in *Debbie*, Robertson equates ink with blood, writing with the body, and the poem with the landscape; but the embodied, erotic writing she vaunts is written, we can see, not only as a monologue: 'The trees still / pose embittered questions'. What they want to know, it turns out, is something about what the women in the earlier pastoral were discussing, that is, something about sovereignty: 'Do /

---

26   Robertson 1997, l. 316–31.

bright thrones yield civil shade?' It's a way of asking, you might say, whether mercy is a quality of Enlightenment: unanswerable question. And it obliges Robertson to turn, once more, to a dialectical 'some day' that will not only shed but also recuperate the pain of mute embittered questioning: 'some day I shall / laugh at even this obedience'. It is more persuasive, in its way, than the full-blown pastoral of 'Party Scene', since it foregrounds not the fancy of pure correspondences (between gasps and waves, clouds and syntax) but a not-quite posthistorical humanity where mediation, where language, has survived: one 'wakes' from the nightmare of history into the tree-like 'shade' of a library, no less, where there is world and time now for a future-anterior repair, and for the enjoyment of yearning: 'calling out a name'.

Rod Smith approaches the problem of a damaged materiality not so much by setting the scene for the pronunciation of a name as by meditating on the allegorical character of objects. And he finds, in his astonishing book *The Good House*, a moving inadequacy in their materiality:

> The good house feels bad about
> The territory
>   – the house seems
> to be a verb though it dislikes
> the term 'housing' – the house
> seems to be a bad dog & a
> live wire – the house is bored
> until people come over – the house
> is anxious to please guests –
> it is stupid & so thinks cordon
> means love – it is wise & so
> chooses –[27]

This 'house' is, yes, anthropomorphised, and allegorised, given attributes and placed in relationships, but part of the achievement of *The Good House* is that the 'house' is never left lying in a single rhetorical register or allowed to become only allegory, only anthropomorphic figure. It moves instead among modes of abstraction and concretion so ceaselessly that, reading the book, we are finally obliged to understand it as a kind of perpetually collapsing second-order allegory that performs and figures the vicissitudes of materiality – its dissatisfaction with itself as *material* – before our eyes, and for our ears.

---

27   Smith 2001.

This sounds essentially de Manian, I know – and Smith's writing is extraordinary in obliging readers to confront the movement between the figural and the performative that de Man argued was the very character of the materiality of language.[28] But for Smith, the character of materiality, even at its most mute, its most formal, is historical – that is, it acts out and compasses its inadequacy as material. As Smith puts it: 'There are 8 houses in the heart, / there should be 9'. Even the figural, these lines suggest, is not free from what it ought to be but isn't. There is no reason the '8 houses in the heart' shouldn't – or couldn't, for a more satisfied poet – complete the strophe; but the figure of the '8 houses in the heart' cannot be unhitched, for Smith, from what should be there. It is a historical and material condition of 'the house' to fail to be self-sufficient:

> the good house – it is heavy
> the good house – it exercises
> hope in the inhuman, is transformed
> by it –
>   becomes blatant in its strength
>   & is destroyed, the good
>   house must be rebuilt
>   carefully. The good house
>   is in conflict
> ordinary houses complete
> the smart bombs and are
> buoyant – victorious,
> brainwaves of shunt commotion,
> bestial then or not house[29]

---

28   See, for instance, de Man 1996b. There is a subtle and exceptionally elegant notion of the historicity of the materiality of writing in de Man, of course, a notion of history as the 'occurrence' of the transfer, in writing, between its 'cognitive' and 'performative' aspects – a notion of history as 'the emergence of a language of power out of a language of cognition' (de Man 1996b, p. 133). I cannot, here, compare the cognitivisms of, say, Adorno and de Man – another and more daunting project – but I can say, à propos of the two ways of understanding historicity and cognition, that where de Man rejects the idea of a dialectic in the materiality of language, Adorno sees the dialectic as the very form of that materiality – and sees the materiality of thought, furthermore, not as 'occurrence' (Adorno 1983, p. 408), but as what he calls 'the need in thinking', which is motivated not by the inadequacy of language to materiality but by its inadequacy to history – by the fact that our material productivity has not yet made of earth a paradise (Adorno 1970, p. 33).

29   Smith 2001.

The 'inhuman' and the 'bestial', here, are meant as a critique of 'blatant strength' as the 'buoyant' self-congratulation that forgets, in the midst of linguistic play, the *ought* at the heart of materiality – that it could be otherwise, that it could be, as Adorno might say, more humane: 'there should be 9'.

For Davies, meanwhile, the material world is overwhelming, and not in a nice way. As he puts it in 'Karnal Bunt':

> There's nothing superficial about the way all that stuff burrows into any available crack in the sidewalk, growing back, covering, by logical extension if not in fact, *everything*.[30]

'All that stuff', in Davies's poems, is the frightening array of material that has become commodified in late capitalism – not just the recognizably thing-like widgets on sale at the hardware store but also the 'node[s] / of expansion-contraction' whose materiality lies as much in their enmeshing network of objects as in the objects themselves. In the lines above, that network congeals momentarily, as it does in the untitled robot poem, around italicised speech, around the '*everything*' that is meant at once as the moment of collating divergent objects in the 'expansion-contraction' but also as the moment where the attempt to collate fails, and falls back on emphasis.

Elsewhere in 'Karnal Bunt', those italics are replaced with the comedy of pretending to have a lived attachment to incommensurably abstract, and complexly nested, nominalisations:

> I love to be an international unit in the measure of the loading of the fissures in the communal membrane into silos on a prairie in a basement by a government of souls in trouble at a party for a long time[31]

This nesting of abstract objects, and the pointed political irony of pretending that we can 'love' them, are part of an argument in Davies about the character of materiality in late capitalism. Like Smith, Davies sees the stuff of the world as wrong in its very quiddity. Where Marx, in the famous lines from 'Theses on Feuerbach', italicises the word 'change' – 'The philosophers have only *interpreted* the world, in various ways; the point, however, is to *change* it' – Davies writes, in one of the first poems in *Comp.*: 'The point, however, is to change it'.[32] As with Smith, materiality for Davies is not something worked on by his-

---

30   Davies 2000, p. 61.
31   Davies 2000, p. 54.
32   Davies 2000, p. 19.

torical conditions but actually produced by them: to change the world will have to be to change it, the stuff of the world, no aspect of which is simply 'pure' material, unhistorical; or, as Davies puts it a few lines later in the same poem: 'Class violence at the level of the seedling'. Polemical, yes; but not, in *Comp.*, ungrounded. The book's central poem, 'Karnal Bunt', names a fungal disease affecting wheat – wheat that the United States, affected by Karnal bunt in the late 1990s, managed to convince its trade partners not to scrutinise too closely.

What I like so much about Davies's poems is the unembarrassed glee with which he asks to be read polemically; indeed, at least one version of his argument about the saturation of the world with appalling materialisations of ever-tighter webs of capitalist relation is that we should not, at this point, even be arguing about whether or not such a web exists. And, again, the polemic is italic: '*You* know, the fact that we're ruled by the money that owns the people who have the money that rules itself –.' ...[33]

I hope I've managed to show that the 'votive' or propositional modes of expectation to which these poems gravitate implicitly distinguish them from the 'dark art' of the modernism we know best, in the academy, and from the blankness and euphoria Jameson suggests belong to the art of the post-modern. It is impossible to say, reading poems like these, whether we have therefore gone backward or forward – whether, for instance, these poems return us to the type of expectation Siegfried Kracauer attributed, in the Weimar period, to 'those who wait' while history horribly, unpredictably, seems to rouse itself into the form of a capital 'H'.[34] Certainly the comparison is tempting, though our conditions are different. What most chastens me on the edge of historical comparison, however, is the presence in these poems of types of materiality so gossamer, so nearly abstract – so nearly non-existent – that they feel as if they could come to us only from the fragile singularity of the history of the present. And the types of expectation by which Clover and Robertson, Smith and Davies animate such material feel similarly fragile, partly because they seem to reside neither in the form nor the content of the poems but somehow in their stance, in what Adorno would have called their 'comportment'. 'Great works wait', he writes, and their waiting is one way to think about the relation of their form to their content, of their politics to their aesthetics: it is unfulfilled.[35] This is especially true of a poetry that recognises that even its awareness of the obsol-

33   Davies 2000, p. 53.
34   Kracauer 1995, p. 137.
35   Adorno 1970, p. 40.

escence of its materials, as a literary strategy, is obsolete. It is in this sense that the poems I've been reading in this essay feel more like models than just instances – models of an aesthetics, at once enacted and theorised, groping for the future in the suffering of its materials.

I'd like to say a bit, in closing, about what I imagine are some of the questions left hanging by my discussion of these poems. First, I have foregrounded my own enthusiasm for them rather than subjecting them to critique; and second, I have focused, in reading them, on something like their content rather than their form. I have highlighted their preoccupations more than their techniques. What are the dangers for contemporary reading practice of a sympathetic, content-focused aesthetics? What might be its promise?

I think the most obvious risks run by the critical practice I've been testing here are a failure of critical distance and a literal-mindedness about content – so that a descriptive, advocating criticism is endangered by the possibility of becoming nothing more than an accompaniment to its object: packaging. Fair enough. Sympathy, and advocacy on the basis of content, runs counter to some of the most powerful and positive developments in late twentieth-century lit-erary studies – such as theory's claim to have extricated itself from pseudo-neutral assessments of value, or the attempts in feminism, queer theory, and U.S. ethnic and post-colonial studies to reveal pseudo-innocent content as a component of historical form.

These projects make up the centre of my own training, and I hold them dear. But I think we're at an impasse in literary studies, on the way to which we have sacrificed the critical potential of appreciation and advocacy in favour of what has become a rote 'problematisation' of texts, and a sadly narrow practice of appreciation that is only able to find subversiveness to admire. But what if the texts we admire, even the politically engaged ones, turn out to be not subvers-ive? What if their political efficacy has been evacuated or is pending? Ascribing performative success to these objects – to pick one of our favorite strategies of the last decade – and equating that capacity for performance with agency doesn't seem to do justice to the theoretical power of the idea of performativ-ity, which I take to lie not in our applauding the aesthetic object's performance but in our being unable to pin down when the performance is finished. Crucial to the sympathetic reading practice I want to advocate is an understanding that critical acts are not discrete. To dismiss appreciative or content-driven readings of texts on the grounds that they are insufficiently politicised, insufficiently counter-hegemonic, is to mistake the work of countering hegemony (if that's what we're doing) as individual work. When I read a text that interests me, espe-cially for its political-affective comportment, my impulse, my *critical* impulse, is: pass it on. Highlight it as best you can, read against the grain, or with it where you can, and make sure others take a look. This is as true for texts that I find repulsive as for those I admire: I don't imagine myself, as a critic, judging *by myself*.

This sense of critical reading as a self-insufficient act has historiographical implications for the dynamic of form and content. In particular, I think it is a living link both to camp and Left-messianic traditions of interpretation, for if both traditions insist that waste and trivia are potentially recuperable, they also imply that we might not be the final judges of what, in the object, was form, and what content. For instance, in reading some post-Language poems here, I have forgone looking at their (very interesting) line breaks and habits of syntax – not because these don't strike me as important but because those features of the poems are not what is most vividly emergent in them when they are grouped together. On the other hand, though I have been trying to foreground what I've called the preoccupations of these poems, those preoccupations don't quite amount to content either. I have been trying to articulate a stance or relation to a cultural problem that the poems are grappling with, which is the problem of how to have a live relationship to a material world whose temporal-spatial character is unreadable: an obsolescence on top of an obsolescence. The polemical affections of these poems for a 'good house', or a 'feminist sky', or for the lavish misguided-ness of an Enguerrand Quarton, are, yes, a kind of content; but they are also a relation to content – in other words, a kind of form.

It is the polemical character of this poetic stance that interests me most right now, since it is something we might imitate in our emerging critical practices. And what seems freshly polemical about some of my favorite post-Language writing – what I think we might treat as a model – is its sense that polemic is the element of the negative in affection, or in judgment. A critical or artistic attachment is polemical, dangerous even, not because of which protagonist it has chosen but because it models what it's like not to know the whole story of its object. The dream of a redeemed matter, that is, doesn't entail a positive vision of what that redemption will look like so much as a resistance to the idea that it will look like any one thing we know.

This seems to me the provoking thing about post-Language poetry's polemical affection, or its camp messianism: it is a new and interesting way of writing from within the presumption of totality. This is a large part of why I like these poems so much. And if we were to pick up on these cues and risk writing to our peers about what we admire or revile (without neutralising our opinions in advance by assuring our colleagues that yes, we too wish for the overthrow of hegemonic systems), I don't think we'd be giving ourselves over to a depoliticised humanism, or to mere impressionistic whimsy, so much as fostering a refreshed, and refreshing, negativity. Kevin Davies:

These cheesy little hypertexts
are going to get better.
I don't know
how *much* better, but *we'll see.*[36]

---

36   Davies 2000, p. 67.

CHAPTER 2

The Poetic Case

What might a poem be said to be exemplary of, today? How is its exemplarity shaped by discourse on poetry, on the aesthetic, on history? As far back as the *Republic*, debates about the value and the function of poetry have been tied to questions about the exemplarity of poetry as a kind of creativity, or representation, or labour so that, down to this day, much aesthetic and political theory still depends on a notion of poetry to explain what escapes (and urges on) conceptualisation in language and in social life.[1] But since the theory-revolutions of the 1970s and 1980s the poem's significance for historical thinking has dropped out of sight; especially in the Marxism of Fredric Jameson and his readers, narrative, rather than poetry, came to symbolise the historically and socially significant scene of human action.

The narrative that has become dominant since Jameson is a tragic one; the aim of this essay is to begin to disentangle Left aesthetics from that mode. Though I will be following through on arguments of Jameson's, I will also be reading against the grain of the terms he has bequeathed us. I will not only be arguing for a shift in our attention to different literary genres but also making a case for tuning in to different emotional structures than those to which the academic Left, at least, has become habituated. My argument will move from a consideration of how the tragic operates in Jameson's sense of history, to a range of poetic and aesthetic theory that posits forms of value other than those articulated in a tragic mode, and finally to a contemporary poem whose historical pathos derives from a fascinating palimpsest of anti-tragic arguments. What I have to propose is humbler than a political unconscious writ large, but I think its pas de deux of hope and disappointment may be something like what we need to read the history of the present.

---

1 Poetry and poetics have an important role to play, for instance, in the political thinking of Philippe Lacoue-Labarthe, Jacques Rancière, Alain Badiou, and Giorgio Agamben. See Lacoue-Labarthe 1999; Rancière 2004; Badiou 2005; and Agamben 1993 and 1999. I don't want to presume to amalgamate the work of all these very different thinkers, but it is interesting to note that they all interpret the relation between poetry and politics by establishing its specificity, sometimes (as in Badiou) even its singularity or (as in Lacoue-Labarthe) its absolute character.

1

In the long first chapter of *The Political Unconscious*, Jameson writes that, 'no matter how weakly ... all literature must be read as a symbolic meditation on the destiny of community'.[2] This is a less well-known pronouncement than the one that opens the book – 'Always historicize!' – but it is, Jameson suggests, a characterisation of the political unconscious itself – 'meditation' isolated in no one subject or any single period on a 'destiny' that Jameson argues must be understood historically as 'the experience of Necessity'. Interpreting this History requires assembling 'inert' historical data into a story of 'why what happened ... had to happen the way it did'; Jameson refers to this reassembly of data into History as 'the 'emotion' of great historiographic form'.[3]

In Jameson's interpretive system, a literary text must be read against 'pro-gressively wider horizons': first as an isolated 'symbolic act' that exists in chro-nological, punctual time; next as an 'ideologeme' that expresses features of ongoing class struggles; and then as an instance of an 'ideology of form', which orients the first two types of reading to an understanding of symbolic activity as giving form to simultaneous, co-existent 'traces or anticipations of modes of production'.[4] Against the backdrop of this widest horizon, the liberation of texts from mere inert chronology and into the pathos of Necessity gives 'the 'emotion' of great historiographic form' a particular shading; it is 'represented in the form of the inexorable logic involved in the determinate failure of all the revolutions that have taken place in human history'.[5]

These formulations have moved and inspired me since I first encountered them in the early 1990s. But I have always been struck by how the prospect of adhering to Jameson's interpretive system feels at once too difficult and too easy: too difficult because to take seriously the suturing of any given text into the simultaneity-rich history Jameson describes would be to delay that suturing, perhaps infinitely, while gathering data; and too easy because, once Jameson has described the widest backdrop against which texts may be read – the coexistence of traces of all modes of production and the determinate defeat of every revolution to date – it is very hard not to succumb to the temptation to skip to the end, as it were, and assign each text a place in universal history right off the bat.

---

2   Jameson 1981, p. 70.
3   Jameson 1981, p. 101.
4   Jameson 1981, p. 76.
5   Jameson 1981, p. 102.

I have also been unable to answer the question of whether, in Jameson's system, the deepest 'emotion' literary texts can yield is tragic. My uncertainty is linked to a confusion about phrasing the role of historical Necessity as 'the determinate failure of all the revolutions that have taken place in human history' rather than, say, the determinate coordination of all writing to the same system of abstraction that organises the life of the commodity. Why is 'failure' the normative standpoint for reading the political unconscious in or out of literature?

Not only do I feel a sheepish desire to redact or compress the Jamesonian narrative, but I'm not sure whether some of the emotions that most interest me in reading literary writing can count, in his terms, as truly 'historiographical'. So this essay will attempt to chart another way of reading, which takes seriously Jameson's insistence on a political unconscious – which tries to detect the trace 'meditations' on 'the destiny of community' at work in literary writing – but which arrives at a different understanding of the 'emotion' it puts in play.

For Jameson, mere chronology becomes a 'socially symbolic act' by being reconstructed into a tragic narrative of a very particular kind: the narrative of the failure of revolutions, which he conceives as the supersession of one set of historical conditions ('revolutionary') by another ('inert'). What this means, for Jameson's reading practice, is that the inert chronologies he wants to reconstruct into 'socially symbolic', affectively forceful interpretations are reconstructed as inert – as a story of becoming-inert, becoming-failure, that mere chronology, itself inert, has disguised. We move, in this style of reading, from a historical inertness to a tragic story of becoming-inert. This is not a circular interpretive practice, necessarily; it is a way of reading that turns interpretation to the task of reminding ourselves, you might say, how dead we have become.[6]

---

6 Narrative is not, of course, Jameson's only means of approaching the question of what can or cannot be made present to consciousness in the production of a text; in 'Postmodernism, or, The Cultural Logic of Late Capitalism', Jameson calls for an aesthetics of 'cognitive mapping' that would catch up to, and outmanoeuvre, the disorientation produced by postmodernism's technological sublime – famously rendered in that essay through the narrative of a shopper being unable to navigate the spectacular spaces of the Bonaventure Hotel in Los Angeles. The simultaneity of one's sense of placement in space, were it made possible again in post-modern spaces, would indeed share something with what I've taken as part of lyric experience, something of its instantaneity (see Jameson 1984). But the optative pedagogy embedded in 'cognitive mapping' – which, in the volume that later came to incorporate his essay, Jameson acknowledges was 'in reality nothing but a code word for "class consciousness"', is still hitched to a division between materiality and vitality whose source lies, not in Sartre's useful depiction of totality as an ongoing process of totalisation, but in his understanding of that process as a cycle that always returns human projects to the 'practico-inert', the used-up, the worked over (Jameson 1991, p. 418). Without dismissing the possibilities of

Even so, this reading style, grounded in a narrative of tragedy and supersession, forecloses the possibility of reading for the local affirmations, emphatic shifts in tone, and ecstatic simultaneity that have shaped the history of the lyric, as well as the history of poetry as an early name for what we would now call aesthetic experience. Three features of that history shape my essay. First, I traverse episodes in a gradual movement from a classical context in which poetry was a privileged name for all artistic creation to an aesthetic theory that depends on, but departs from, the tradition of seeing poetry as the metonym for all the arts. Second, I am moving across language that shifts from thinking of poetry as the name for a kind of thing made by poets – either literal writers of poems or artists generally – to thinking about aesthetic experience as marking a kind of human capacity, whether or not it produces traditionally aesthetic objects. And, third, I will be attending to the ways in which Western discourse on poetry is built so as to position any given poem as bearing value partly by way of its partial realisation of the capacities of poetry. When I turn to an individual poem at the end of this essay, then, I will be trying to read it, not as an instance of inertness made live by reconstruction, but as a partly realised instance of a discourse on poetry that avoids the deadness-liveness binary of Jameson's tragic model in favour of raising questions about poetic value – what poetry is good for and whether what it's good for can ever be realised.

This last point forms the crux of my essay. I believe that we are able to read poems through the lens of their partial realisation of the possibilities of the category *poetry* because the history of the Western discourse on poetry is itself built around recurring topoi of unrealisability. As I will detail below, these unrealisability topoi range from meditations on whether poem-making is a kind of labour to claims that poetry illuminates the unimportance or even pointlessness of all human labour.[7] The questions posed in such topoi are so basic that they are capable of making the category *poetry* straddle what we would now think of as two very different languages of value: an ancient language of use-value and a modern one of surplus-value. Questions about

---

an aesthetics of cognitive mapping, then, I want to clear space for other understandings of the political unconscious not premised on this undialectical division between the dead and the living. For the practico-inert, see Sartre 2004.

7 My term *unrealisability topoi* modifies a phrase of Ernst Robert Curtius's, 'inexpressibility topoi', which he used to name the poetic strategy of claiming, in medieval Latin poems praising royalty, that the overlord to whom the poem is addressed is too glorious or powerful to be compassed by any single poet or poem. See Curtius 1973, pp. 159–62.

whether a poem really is a made thing oblige us to think about something like the use-value of poems, what they are for, what they can do, and whether for-ness, telos, is really the right language for thinking about poems. Questions about the pointlessness of human labour, meanwhile, shine a light on what goes on in laboring activity, whether it can be said to be for something, a higher purpose, or whether it is simply toil or exploitation. A central argument of my essay is that, in the history of defending poetry, the topoi of unrealisability give poetry's defenders a way to suggest that the significance of poetry is not captured by the language of making or purpose but that it is a type of activity that puts pressure on the social meanings of both. And as the meaning of the social develops ever-greater complexity, relentlessness, and intensity, this demurral from instrumentalisation opens up a space of bewilderment about the present that is potentially critical, even as it risks valorising uselessness as such.

In what follows, then, I will visit some key moments in the 'defence of poetry' – a genre that returns, again and again, to questions of partial or impossible realisation. In particular, I will focus on the way implicit and expli-cit defences of poetry feed into a Left aesthetic tradition that keeps open the question of whether and how poetry – or, later, aesthetic experience – troubles our understanding of value as realisable in the first place. And I will argue that pursuing this trouble is exactly the way to begin reading a history of poetry that produces a historiographic emotion not quite captured by the story of the tragic and the inert.

2

To build an archive of rhetoric around poetry that centres on the question of the possible failure to realise its social value is to imagine that rhetoric as part of a long reply to Plato; so I think it makes sense to begin with a scene from the *Republic* in which this issue is addressed directly. In book 10 Socrates's discus-sion of poetry is almost entirely role based; he is irritated by a popular, unphilo-sophical attribution to poets of polymathy – the idea that poets, because they write about the whole world, must have expert knowledge of all trades, all skills, all professions. Plato counters this claim to universal poetic subject-hood by arguing, through Socrates, that poets are neither makers nor users of anything. Luring Glaucon through a thicket of leading questions, Socrates draws a distinction between the false universality of the poet and the func-tional dyad of maker and user – here, figured as the player and the maker of a pipe:

'A pipe-player, for example, tells a pipe-maker which of his pipes do what they're supposed to do when actually played, and goes on to instruct him in what kinds of pipes to make, and the pipe-maker does what he's told'.

'Of course'.

'so far as good and bad pipes are concerned, it's a knowledgeable person who gives the orders, while the other obeys the orders, and does the manufacturing. Right?'

'Yes'.

'Justified confidence, then, is what a pipe-maker has about goodness and badness ... while knowledge is the province of the person who makes use of the pipes'.

'Yes'.

'Which of these two categories does our representer belong to?' ...

'He doesn't fit either case'.[8]

Plato presents, against the claims of poetry, a political economy of pure realisation: a theory of production and consumption in which one transforms into the other with no overlap or residue. Everyone, that is, must have a single function, and there must be no gap between the production of a thing and its use, no deferral or ambiguity in realising the value of, say, a pipe. The pipe may not be played upon right away, but it must be immediately clear that being played upon is what it is for.

So this is what we might call the economic claim against poetry. Socrates's objection to poetry is not that it is a failed case, a secondary or copy, but that it is neither a case of production nor of consumption; it is a failed universality. My interest in this essay will be in responses to this accusation, especially when rhetoric around the utility or function of poetry proposes its unrealisability, when languages that defend the deferral or non-existence of poetry's utility defend it exactly for having no obvious end. Another way to describe what I mean by *unrealisability* is that it describes a condition of poetry as not most importantly a made thing or perhaps not a made thing at all. Certainly this is what Plato thinks; and one feature of the defence of poetry, as well as of the Left aesthetics that comes to draw on it, will be to accept Plato's characterisation and ask whether the not-made-ness of poetry is such a bad thing. This opens up other ways of thinking about the importance of poetry, not least as the scene of a perpetual making that never quite settles into the state of having-been-made. Unrealisability, then, might also be a name for the

---

8   Plato 1994, 353.

way in which any given poem can be read as much for its instancing poetry as for its separate status as individual poem.

In any case, these unrealisability topoi cluster around different kinds of questions from the Renaissance on – questions of sovereignty, of labour, of historical change and causality, of exploitation and value – but to read them from the long end of their deployment is to begin to be able to read a compressed history of the social relations, imagined and real, around the reading and writing of poetry. I think it makes sense to start looking at these unrealisability topoi in Renaissance replies to Plato because the Renaissance is the period when poetry begins to be understood once again as more than a school activity – not only as material for memorisation, or as a tool for learning the classical languages, but as a creative activity vulnerable exactly to Plato's charge of nonutility.

I will, then, conduct a brief and whirlwind tour of selected defences of poetry from the Renaissance on. This tour is meant to be neither comprehensive nor definitive; indeed it is deliberately eccentric and discontinuous. What will link my visits to these earlier defences of poetry is the topos of unrealisability and the joint it forms at the beginning of the modern era with certain ideas about labour, its value and its exploitation.

I begin with Philip Sidney's *Defence of Poesy*, which depicts the social competition between schoolmen and courtiers by way of a language of utility, of ends, and insists that poetry has an end, after all, even if it isn't immediately evident. Sidney, discussing oratory in his *Defence*, follows Aristotle by defining kinds of human activity in terms of their relation to 'virtuous action' and specifies that it is not an action's 'next end' – that is, its immediate utility – that matters for virtue so much as its 'further end', which is a little harder to pin down:

> even as the saddler's next end is to make a good saddle, but his further end to serve a nobler faculty, which is horsemanship, so the horseman's to soldiery, and the soldier not only to have the skill, but to perform the practice of a soldier. So that, the ending end of all earthly learning being virtuous action, those skills that most serve to bring forth that have a most just title to be princes over all the rest.[9]

Poetry's telos, then, is virtuous action, but not necessarily the poet's. Elsewhere in the *Defence of Poesy*, Sidney suggests that poets can fashion models or examples of governance superior to what – thus far, at least – has been found

9 Sidney 2002, pp. 219–20.

in nature and that these models can be of use to the queen. Indeed the canon-
ical rendering of the second nature of the made world in the *Defence of Poesy*
involves an implicit comparison of Elizabeth to the Cyrus of Xenophon's *Cyro-
paedia*:

> Which delivering forth [of ideal types] also is not wholly imaginative, as
> we are wont to say by them that build castles in the air; but so far substan-
> tially it worketh, not only to make a Cyrus, which had been but a particular
> excellency as nature might have done, but to bestow a Cyrus upon the
> world to make many Cyruses, if they will learn aright why and how that
> maker made him.[10]

Though Xenophon's Cyrus is a fictionalised perfection of the actual emperor,
Sidney suggests that the replication – and the replicability – of his ideality is a
form of service to the queen unique to the poet, useful to her in the perfection
of governance. Aristocratic court poets, then, become first among courtiers,
'princes over all the rest', by serving a higher authority, working for the sovereign
by miming sovereignty for her. As Robert Matz has shown, this canny rendition
of aristocracy-as-service allows Sidney to reply to detractors of poetry who see
it as having been reduced, since heroic times, to a decadent court pleasure.
Matz argues persuasively that Sidney's *Defence of Poesy* is as much a defence
of the idea of virtuous aristocracy as it is a defence of poetry, and he draws
our attention to the ways in which, in Sidney's hands, poetry's role of circulat-
ing models of virtue allows it to serve as a kind of rhetorical value adjuster. To
accusations that the aristocracy is simply feeding off the rest of the social body,
Sidney argues that this problem – which he tacitly acknowledges is real – can
be altered by the activity of poetry, which will serve as a corrective to aristo-
cratic excess and return the class system to its proper functioning.[11]

   This argument for poetry as the platform for class homeostasis survives past
the Renaissance, though it is called in to correct for different kinds of crises of
value. Beginning with Vico, and later among the romantics, we can see the par-
ticular not-quite production that is poetry brought to bear, not so much on the
question of decadence, but on the problem of the increasingly abstract char-
acter of social life. Vico's *The New Science*, for example, is an attempt at what
he called universal history – universal not only in its aim of comparing civiliz-
ations by abstracting them into stories of development, but also in its method,

---

10   Sidney 2002, pp. 216–217.
11   See Matz 2000, pp. 60–4.

which is to use philology to coordinate across cultures their different histories of kinship and state forms, habits of mind, and linguistic character.

Poetry has a central role to play in *The New Science*. Vico asserts that human language was originally full of vivid images – for gods and the powers of nature, especially – and that it became less 'poetic' with the development of modern government and science:

> the nature of our civilized minds is so detached from the senses, even in the vulgar, by abstractions corresponding to all the abstract terms our languages abound in, and so refined by the art of writing, and as it were spiritualized by the use of numbers, because even the vulgar know how to count and reckon, that it is naturally beyond our power to form the vast image of this mistress called 'sympathetic Nature'. Men shape the phrase with their lips but have nothing in their minds; for what they have in mind is falsehood, which is nothing; and their imagination no longer avails to form a vast false image.[12]

This will prove a very influential formulation; it is reworked two centuries later in the opening pages of *The Dialectic of Enlightenment*, where it buttresses Adorno and Horkheimer's argument that a ban on mimesis lies at the origin of the development of instrumental reason.[13] Vico's understanding of the cost of the development of abstraction is not dialectical, however; he believes in a combination of tragic and providential historical causality, in which cultures, even if they are destroyed by their own limitations, may be able to restart their development. Having positioned poetry at the origin of civilization, Vico sees it as a resource that later cultures can rediscover if they grasp a collective need for imagination as well as for abstract and empirical knowledge. Writing about this idea in Vico's philosophy, Isaiah Berlin says that for Vico the problem of rampant abstraction is that 'men have not realised their marvellous potentialities'.[14]

This positioning of poetic imagination as an unrealised potentiality will reverberate in the writing of the romantics. In the work of Schiller, Percy Shelley, and others, though, the theological mode subtending their historical claims about poetry will shift from the providential to the prophetic, not least because by the early nineteenth century poetry has begun to be classified as obsolete by a rising middle class that understands its interests in primarily material terms.

---

12   Vico 1984, p. 118.
13   See Horkheimer and Adorno 2002, pp. 1–34.
14   Berlin 2000, p. 60.

Shelley's 'The Defence of Poetry', for instance, is primarily a defence against Thomas Love Peacock's claim that, in an age that prizes facts, science, and technical utility, poets are committed to hopelessly outdated 'Cimmerian labours'.[15] Shelley's response to this claim is to insist that poetry can balance or compensate for excesses of what he calls the 'calculating principle':

> The cultivation of poetry is never more to be desired than at periods when from an excess of the selfish and calculating principle, the accumulation of the materials of external life exceed the quantity of the power of assimilating them to the internal laws of human nature.[16]

Like Sidney before him, Shelley wishes to defend poetry in terms of its capacity to repair an imbalance of value or accumulation in the social body; like Vico, he correlates periods of history and habits of mind. Under pressure to account for poetry's seeming supersession by the principle of utility, though, Shelley makes two additional moves.

First, he makes recourse to the language of prophecy; the poet, he says, 'beholds the future in the present'.[17] Second, he reworks the definition of utility so that it not only includes but is organised around poetry. This Shelleyan utility is linked to tragedy; poets, in his account, produce a kind of mixed pleasure and pain that is the highest pleasure, and 'the production and assurance of pleasure in this highest sense is true utility'.[18] The argument here is obscure, but made slightly less so by Shelley's use, in the passage describing pleasure and pain, of a verse from Ecclesiastes: 'It is better to go to the house of mourning, than to the house of mirth'.[19] Though the particular verse does not express it, Ecclesiastes is substantially concerned with the vanity of labour, its inability to realise human happiness; and it seems, if we put the pieces together, that Shelley's argument about tragic emotion as the highest utility is an argument for poetry's power to highlight the limits of human labour ability to answer larger questions of humanity's ends or uses.[20]

Shelley's ideas in 'The Defence of Poetry' are helpful in piecing together a genealogy of poetic discourse on value partly because they are broad. His ideas

---

15   Peacock 1923, p. 16.
16   Shelley 2003, p. 696.
17   Shelley 2003, p. 677.
18   Shelley 2003, p. 695.
19   Shelley 2003, p. 694.
20   Scholarship on Ecclesiastes returns frequently to this question, not least as it is raised by the insistent Ecclesiastian use of the Hebrew word *hebel* (*lbh*), which has been most frequently translated as 'vanity'. See, for instance, Miller 2002.

that poetry has the power to correct for excessive material accumulation and that technical labour cannot provide its own answers to the question of the ends of humanity allow us to see something like a perimeter of Left aesthetic theory that will remain stable down to the twentieth century.[21] Though his defence of poetry contains elements that remain useful for contemporary theory, however, it does not contain a theory of modernity per se; Shelley tends to rely, in phrases like 'periods of the decay of social life', on an implicitly cyclical historiography.[22] For a romantic aesthetics that tries to ground its claims for the value of poetry in an account of the rise of the modern, we have to look elsewhere; and it is in Schiller that we can find the most thoroughgoing and influential formulations.

In the sixth letter in his *On The Aesthetic Education of Man*, Schiller's argument centres on an account of the fragmentation of modern society that devolves from a comparison with ancient civilization:

> [The ancient mind] did indeed divide human nature into its several aspects, and project these in magnified form into the divinities of its glorious pantheon; but not by tearing it to pieces; rather by combining its aspects in different proportions, for in no single one of their deities was humanity in its entirety ever lacking. How different with us Moderns! With us too the image of the human species is projected in magnified form into separate individuals – but as fragments, not in different combinations, with the result that one has to go the rounds from one individual to another in order to be able to piece together a complete image of the species.[23]

For Schiller, having to 'go the rounds' of the social body just to piece together a whole human subject is disastrous. As he puts it elsewhere, 'Thus little by little the concrete life of the Individual is destroyed in order that the abstract idea of the Whole may drag out its sorry existence'.[24]

----

21 Robert Kaufman has worked assiduously to bring the contemporaneity of Shelleyan aesthetics into view for the twenty-first-century academy and, more broadly, to align the development of a romantic aesthetics of negativity with the aesthetic theories of Adorno and Benjamin and problems of Leftist politics today. His work at this juncture is immensely clarifying, and I feel a debt to it. For work most pertinent to the place of Shelley as precursor and reference point for a Left aesthetic theory, see Kaufman 1996 and 2001a. Also useful for a detailed account of the routes of transmission running from Shelley to Adorno and Benjamin is Kaufman 2001b.
22 Shelley 2003, p. 685.
23 Schiller 1967, pp. 31–3.
24 Schiller 1967, p. 37.

Schiller views this destruction of concrete existence as unavoidable: 'there was no other way in which the species as a whole could have progressed'.[25] By introducing the idea of historical necessity into the story of the fragment-ation of human capacity, Schiller obliges aesthetic theory – and the theory of poetry that forms part of it – to generate more complex concepts of part–whole relations. And in the sixth of the *Letters on the Aesthetic Education of Man* he produces a striking account of what we could call the causality of tend-encies, where individual causes contribute to an effect only apparent at the level of the system: 'one-sidedness in the exercise of his powers must ... lead the individual into error; but the species as a whole to truth'.[26] Schiller sees the implications of this causal mode in exceptionally stark terms, envision-ing philosophy, for instance, as a kind of terror: 'as long as philosophy has to make its prime business the provision of safeguards against error, truth will be bound to have its martyrs'.[27] Sidney had seen aristocratic virtue tied to a notion of sacrificial service; here, all humanity is subject to the possibility of sacrifice.

Schiller's martyrology of truth is resonant in Left aesthetics down to our day; Jameson depends on it when, reading Joseph Conrad's *Nostromo* at the end of *The Political Unconscious*, he urges us to see the novel's 'ultimate narrative mes-sage' as the 'disjunction between the movement of history and its enactment by individual subjects'.[28] For Jameson, to seek the 'ultimate message' of Conrad's novel is to understand the particular, the material, and the individual as per-forming a sacrificial function that allows latter-day readers to 'keep faith with' the possible realisation of a good totality we can never perceive except in the dialectical supersession of what has come before us; the characters in *Nostromo* serve 'merely to enable the coming into being after [themselves] of a new type of collectivity'.[29]

The indelibility of the language of sacrifice in Left aesthetics since Schiller does not mean, though, that it is the root formula for all subsequent rhetorics of deferred or unrealisable value. It is particularly well suited to theory that has been cut adrift from the energies of a live political movement; but in writers more closely aligned with present-tense class or movement politics, the com-plex form of historical causality Schiller helped make evident is lined up with other languages than those of tragic necessity and sacrificial supersession. The

25   Schiller 1967, pp. 39.
26   Schiller 1967, p. 41.
27   Schiller 1967, p. 43.
28   Jameson 1981, p. 278.
29   Jameson 1981, pp. 277, 279.

history of the defence of poetry and of the aesthetic makes persistent recourse to topoi of virtuality, potential, and prophecy before reaching, in Schiller, the scene of tragic sacrifice; but those optimistic languages don't seem able to meet the possibility of tragic social abstraction head-on. In the militant Georg Lukács, though – and, later, in the work of Gayatri Chakravorty Spivak – we can read the emergence of other topoi that reground the tradition of valorising making over the made, but in ways that are specifically geared to confront the abstract character of social life. I would like to think through two of these other topoi – of vigilance in Lukács and of tone in Spivak – before turning, finally, to a contemporary poem that traffics in them all.

3

Lukács, in *History and Class Consciousness*, identifies Schiller and Schiller's aesthetics as the ground for his own investigation of life under capitalism:

> By extending the aesthetic principle far beyond the confines of aesthetics, by seeing it as the key to the meaning of man's existence in society, Schiller brings us back to the basic issue of classical philosophy. On the one hand, he recognizes that social life has destroyed man as man. On the other hand, he points to the principle whereby *man having been socially destroyed, fragmented, and divided between different partial systems is to be made whole again in thought.*[30]

Lukács departs from Schiller by pointing out that man cannot be made whole again only in thought or by any single individual; but he hews to Schiller's emphasis on the aesthetic principle as a ground for the development of freedom. This is because, for Lukács, the aesthetic is still determined by a relationship between the given and the made, whereas a philosophy dominant since Kant has insisted that only what has been made by humans can be known.[31] But this emphasis on the made excludes the complex processes of making; by limiting philosophical reflection to the realm of the already produced, Lukács argues, the activity of thought becomes increasingly limited and less able to grasp anything that straddles the world of given matter and the 'intelligible' matter of the humanly made world. What's excluded in this narrowing of philo-

---

30   Lukács 1971, p. 139.
31   See, for instance, Kant 2000, p. 254.

sophical activity, Lukács suggests, is the entire realm of production, which is where social relationships under capitalism are formed.[32]

To describe these relationships, Lukács develops a language of reifying tendency and counterreifying vigilance. He describes the worker's coming-to-consciousness about the character of his exploitation this way: 'the worker ... perceives the split in his being preserved in the brutal form of what is in its whole tendency a slavery without limits'.[33] Because this exploitation is tendential and because it tends toward limitless exploitation, Lukács believes it must be met not with a single act of becoming-aware, but with a continual reassertion of immanent awareness of the workings of totalisation: reification 'can be overcome only by constant and constantly renewed efforts to disrupt the reified structure of existence by concretely relating to the concretely manifested contradictions of the total development, by becoming conscious of the immanent meanings of these contradictions for the total development'.[34] Not, in English at least, very pretty prose; but it helps clarify the particular function of vigilance in a reading practice that seeks to understand the exemplarity of its objects. For Lukács, aesthetic objects and experiences can be read as instances of a single totalising process, but one in which the character of the totalisation cannot be understood without reference to the constantly shifting ground of the particular. Another way to think about this vigilance would be to say that Lukács's insistence on the relations of making as more central to philosophy than the realm of the humanly made positions him alongside those thinkers who tried to separate the significance of poetry from manufacture – whether by emphasising its virtual force in Sidney, or by thinking of it as a reserve of human potential in Vico, or as the mark of a time other than the time of facture in Shelley, or (though I have not touched on it directly here) as linked to the capacity for play in Schiller.

The militancy of Lukács's project lends a fatedness to this way of interpreting aesthetic production, however; when he writes 'the fate of the worker becomes the fate of society as a whole', it is implicit that the aesthetic capacities of workers, always being tapped into by the processes of capitalist labour, are also tangled up in that fate.[35] This language of fate, however, limits the role of the aesthetic to an alternative potentiality that, under the right historical conditions, might serve as the ground for different forms of the realisation of human value. In political terms, this idea has tended to mean that only those whose

---

32   Lukács 1971, pp. 111–20.
33   Lukács 1971, p. 166.
34   Lukács 1971, p. 197.
35   Lukács 1971, p. 91.

labour is obviously an instance of capitalist exploitation – especially wage workers – can be imagined as the potential agents of revolutionary change. In aesthetic terms, the language of fate tends to burden poetic or artistic activity with an obligation to reflect, negatively, the operations of a capitalism we then believe we fully understand. Ironically, it took the long twentieth century of defeat and disappointment on the Left for its intellectuals to ask whether the split between the technical and the aesthetic under capitalism is best understood as a fated polarisation or sundering and to begin to think of the relationship between technologised labour and aesthetic experience in less binary terms.

In her 1985 essay 'scattered Speculations on the Question of Value', Spivak revisits the problem of the technical-aesthetic split, though it is not the binary she begins with. She asks, instead, whether and how First World intellectuals might imagine a political subject who is predicated neither in exclusively materialist nor idealist terms. To ask this question is to ask exactly how and to what extent subjects are determined by social forces. Are they simply made by them, or is there something else, some surplus in persons such that the forces that determine their formation do not do so entirely? One wants to avoid, Spivak suggests, thinking of people as simply the product of external forces but also thinking of people as somehow innately able to transcend those forces. Clearly, historical subjects are not purely determined by their histories; history keeps being changed by people. But if the idea of a transcendent will is too triumphalist an account of the realisation of a human subject that is both determined by and formative of history, what other narratives do we have? How can the subject of capitalism, for instance, be said to be more than the product of capitalist abstraction if he or she doesn't transcend it?

Spivak answers this question in literary terms. In an explicitly deconstructive reading of passages from volume 1 of *Capital*, Spivak moves away from the Lukácsian language of fate and towards an attention to what she calls, following Derrida, an 'apocalyptic tone' she hears in Marx's text.[36] But what is this tone,

---

36   Spivak 1988, p. 175. Spivak takes the phrase 'apocalyptic tone' from Derrida's 1980 essay, 'On a Newly Arisen Apocalyptic Tone in Philosophy', which reads a late work of Kant's, 'On a Newly Arisen Superior Tone in Philosophy'. Kant's essay is a polemic against the Christian neo-Platonists of his day, who mount an argument for the importance of emotion and intuition in philosophy. Kant's rejection of this argument is grounded, as was Plato's argument against the polymathy of poets, in the language of labour, which he links to the language of tone. He writes:

> In a word: all think themselves superior to the degree that they believe themselves exempt from work ... in this [mystical] philosophy one need not *work* but only listen

and what does it have to do with the unrealisability topoi or deferred realization that I have been tracing?

For Spivak, reading Marx, it is crucial to understand that the conception of the subject as the bearer of labour-power, of extractable value, is both historically contingent and, teleologically speaking, indeterminate. To conceive of subjects as 'superadequate' to their material engagements, as Spivak puts it – as bearing value not only in the labour they perform but in their capacity to labour – is possible only as the outcome of long struggles of dispossession; it is not a timeless idea.[37] Furthermore, Spivak argues, the historical struggle over exploitation is incomplete, and renewed at every moment in the circuit of capital, to which that historical capacity to exceed making lends a series of indeterminacies. As Spivak puts it, 'at each step in the dialectic something seems to lead off into the open-endedness of textuality: indifference, inadequation, rupture'.[38]

> to and enjoy the oracle within oneself in order to bring all the wisdom envisioned with philosophy into one's possession: and this announcement is indeed made in a tone indicating that the superior ones do not think of themselves in the same class as those who, in a scholarly manner, consider themselves obligated to progress slowly and carefully from the critique of their faculty of knowledge to dogmatic knowledge. (Kant 1993, p. 52)

We return here to the Platonic language of poetic class usurpation, though the centuries have honed and altered it. In Kant, the claim of poets to have made a thing without having actually worked to make it is twined together with the problem of mimesis, but not – as in Plato – at a metaphysical level. In this passage we can see that Kant imagines poets miming the aristocracy, adopting their 'tone', flaunting a labourlessness they haven't earned. Kant thinks this tone, should it spread too wide among pretenders to philosophy, will mean the end of the philosophical enterprise altogether, the abandonment of the hard work of conceptual reflection and determination. This is why Derrida turns the phrase 'superior tone' into 'apocalyptic tone': Derrida sees the twining together of the question of the end of philosophy with the more limited teleological question of the 'ends' of our activity, its aims, what it is meant to produce. For Derrida, working the double meaning of *ends* in French and English, the 'apocalyptic tone', the tone that announces the end, also announces the question of ends. In his essay, a phrase like 'the beginning of the end' can mean the beginning of the investigation of what we are for, or even the beginning of the discovery of what we might do, what we might make.

I read Derrida here, and Kant, in order to suggest that behind not only Spivak's analysis of value but all the texts I've set before you here there lies a problem, given the name *poetry*, that haunts our scenarios of the realisations of value with an abiding insubstantiality and that tethers even latter-day formulations of value to a social imaginary that, if it is much simpler than the economic relations it tries to explain, nonetheless keeps it honest; we don't know, yet, what is at stake in social production.

37   Spivak 1988, p. 161.
38   Spivak 1988, p. 160.

This 'inadequation', Spivak contends, prevents use-value from seamlessly becoming exchange-value becoming surplus-value, because keeping production running is not simply a means of the physical survival of workers – what Marx called 'socially necessary labor' – but of their emotional survival as well. Spivak calls the calculations sustaining such survival 'affectively necessary labor'. One implication of 'scattered Speculations on the Question of Value' is that the masters of capital (such as they are) must take despair into account as a component of the immiseration they skirt; it is to the affective body, at least as much as to the physical, that the rate of exploitation must be pitched.

I write *pitched* because Spivak suggests that the enmeshment of affect in the open-endedness of value is what produces the 'apocalyptic tone' she hears in Marx. That tone, then, is something like the sound of the rate of exploitation, differentially intensified across classes and sectors, and made most clearly audible in the 'super-exploitation' of women in the Third World.[39]

We have come a long way from the aristocratic-sacrificial poetics of Sidney, the humanist theologisation of poets in Vico, and the Ecclesiastian warning against the worship of technical labour in Shelley. But across the texts of these writers and throughout the development of aesthetic theory and its incorporation into Western Marxism there is also a staggered continuity of thinking about poetry – then the aesthetic and then the affective – as a ground or example of indirect, deferred, or impossible realisation of value. This tradition of unrealisability-writing has by no means always been critical (think of how deferred utility is realised in service to the sovereign in Sidney) but its resonances in Left aesthetic and critical theory make it possible to think about the defence of poetry, for instance, as part of the prehistory of dialectical thinking and, the other way around, to see dialectical criticality as bound up, even today, with a history of the aesthetic whose roots lie in defences of a broadly conceived concept of poetry.

But can the collocation I have offered help us read a poem? I think it can, and I would like to close by trying to show how. I'm not sure whether, by reading a poem at the end of this essay, I'm constructing a test case; if the precondition for its authenticity or experimental success would be to choose a poem as unlike the discourse I've traced as possible so as to measure the reach of that discourse, or bid for its universal validity, then I am not providing a test case. But the poem I have chosen, because it shares elements with the discourse I've been outlining, may help us think about the exemplarity of poems in

---

39   Spivak 1988, p. 167.

another way, by allowing us to see how much world can be touched on from within, or around, a given structuring language.

This poem, written by a young American poet who is well versed in the tradition of Euro-American Left aesthetic theory, is mimetic of parts of that tradition; but its mimetic relation to that discourse does not have to mean that the poem simply collapses into it. Instead it shifts the language of aesthetic value from an axis of realisation and failure-to-realise to a cluster of descriptions and performances of tone and comportment; indeed the poem quietly insists that tone and comportment are built out of resistance to the idea of realisation. And in doing so it serves as a reply, not only to the ancient insistence on usefulness, but to the modernist valorisation of tragedy and failure.

The poem is by Jennifer Moxley, from her 2002 volume *The Sense Record*. In its entirety:

ON THIS SIDE NOTHING

> The objects have gone quiet. Even old
> Mister Unicorn has run out of words,
> despite his painted red lips. Things inured
> to emptiness continue with their cold
> busyness. And thus the flurry of cash
> around the center silence still appears
> charitable tinsel, bright with the solace
> of distress, the joy of being in arrears
> so much more joyful than other joys. Songs
> unlike a virus have grown in this season
> of record rare, they sound an echo long
> in repose and leave conflicted reason
> to its bafflement. Things couldn't be worse,
> or could, we could resist, or complacent
> argue against resistance, neither course
> puts change at risk. Though we lay adjacent
> the cold garden wall and exquisitely sigh
> it will come, freed perhaps of our compelling
> but nevertheless compelled. It's well-nigh
> Christmas, snow covers the ground and is falling.
> the thirsty birds have re-opened our hands:
> though weary of ritual tending we deck
> the house yet again, reenact the ends
> of long antiquated customs, rectify

the aggressive apathy that binds us
to our friends. To what design? What lie lies
hidden in an ornament, in a truss
of tissue snug in a box? An old idea
forced into perverted service of the new
makes strange commerce of this cold affection
enfoiled in childish fables, a revenue
of hope out of the heart's aphasic diction.
And if it prove false, at least daily labor
will feel refreshed in the wake of leisure.
The bonvivant who repeats 'love thy neighbor'
does no harm, and Tennyson's sad measure
of years since we last saw our friend can bring
to mind a loss reduced from one December
to the next, a comfort and reminder
that we are at worst, on this side, nothing,
and risk nothing, to fight against and yet
not cut the feeling from our breast in queer
penance to a *blundering world*, to split
the will in two, to tell the truth, to fear
defeat, etc. The thought-ruined things
have done their work to keep our sentiment
in trust, though now we know we raised the scene
neither for ourselves nor for the love of it,
but out of some mislaid duty to form –
a table, a ribbon, a set of rules –
to adjust the love of a furious home,
but do not think we were born to be fools
nor bred to thoughtless and false happiness,
given our time's caution and your kind lash
it has never been easy for us to say yes.[40]

I think the first thing worth noticing about the poem is its particular super-
imposition of rhetorics; it is a Christmas poem, with Edwardian and Victorian
bearings, shot through with economic language: 'cash', 'charitable', 'arrears',
'rare', 'commerce', 'revenue', 'trust'. In puzzling over why, each year, her circle

---

40   Moxley 2002, pp. 9–10. An mp3 of Moxley reading this poem at the University of Maine in
      September 2003 is publicly accessible at www.writing.upenn.edu/pennsound/x/Moxley
      .html.

of familiars participates in the season's rituals – not least, it seems, the ritual-
ised rhetoric of loving one's fellows – the speaker worries over a question of
larger ends ('To what design?') and joins that worry to two others: the poten-
tial hypocrisy of idly favouring 'change' or 'resistance' and the possibly foolish
affective labour of 'rectify[ing] ... aggressive apathy', 'adjust[ing] ... love', or
'cut[ting] the feeling from our breast'. The poem also links the cyclical time
of the holiday to problems of memorial and to debt; she aligns her poem not
only with Tennyson's 'In Memoriam' but also with Edward Verrall Lucas's 1917
poem 'The Debt', from which Moxley takes the phrase 'blundering world'. That
poem identifies the aesthetic experience of all English people who survived
World War I as indebted to the sacrifice of the young soldiers who died in its
battles.[41]

The poem's title is a fragment of its emphatic answer to the problem of
whether merely managing feeling – wishing others well, disentangling aggres-
sion and apathy – can possibly serve as payment of the debt that the death or
injury of others incurs. The poet is agonisingly aware of the illusions in which
she traffics – that 'the flurry of cash' is actually 'charitable tinsel' or that 'resist-
ance' or arguments against it are of any consequence at all. Perhaps the bitterest
recognition in the poem is that beneath 'distress' is actually 'solace' – by which,
I think, the poet means the solace of finding that others have incurred injury on
her behalf, putting her joyfully, guiltily 'in arrears'. And by citing Lucas's poem,

---

41   Lucas's poem includes this passage about the aesthetic experience the living owe the dead
      soldiers, which he links, later in the poem, to collective guilt:
            So lone and cold they lie; but we,
            We still have life; we still may greet
            Our pleasant friends in home and street;
            We still have life, are able still
            To climb the turf of Bignor Hill,
            To see the placid sheep go by,
            To hear the sheep-dog's eager cry,
            To feel the sun, to taste the rain,
            To smell the Autumn's scents again
            Beneath the brown and gold and red
            Which old October's brush has spread,
            To hear the robin in the lane,
            To look upon the English sky.
            ....
            Those men who died for you and me,
            That England still might sheltered be
            And all our lives go on the same
            (Although to live is almost shame).
            (Lucas 1917, pp. 228–30)

so centred on the guilt of survivors, Moxley suggests that worry about others, or grief over losing them, may contain a germ of relief that they, not we, are the ones who paid the price of injury or death.

The violence and loss the poem hints at is figured through three overlapping moves: the reference to the loss of a friend, the link back to a poem of World War I, and the insistent foregrounding of economic language. This last move inflects the other two with a sense of system and circulation, which becomes clear in the poem's language of objects, through which all emotion is financed; material things have already 'gone quiet' by the poem's first line, silenced by the 'flurry of cash' around them, but they serve, despite being 'ruined' by thought, 'to keep our sentiment / in trust'. This service objects offer is mismatched, however, to the feelings of the season and to the subjects of those feelings:

> though now we know we raised the scene
> neither for ourselves nor for the love of it,
> but out of some mislaid duty to form –

Spivak might call this 'mislaid duty to form' a kind of inadequation; 'solace' and 'joy' are no match for the other, ambivalent feeling that invests itself in objects, carriers of the season's rhetorical force. This inadequacy, and the foolishness or even hypocrisy that it puts her in danger of, pushes Moxley to formulate two related positions: first, an ambivalent assertion of her harmlessness or worthlessness and, second, a defence of fellow feeling in the face of something like totalisation and paralysis.

At the poem's rhetorical centre, the occasion of grief is met with a Tennysonian 'sad measure' that allows the poet to feel her loss reduced from year to year; a strangely actuarial formula, it offers, for Moxley

> ... a comfort and reminder
> that we are at worst, on this side, nothing,
> and risk nothing, to fight against and yet
> not cut the feeling from our breast in queer
> penance to a *blundering world*, to split
> the will in two, to tell the truth, to fear
> defeat, etc.

Only by positing her worthlessness in the face of death – that she and her cohort are 'at worst, on this side, nothing' – is Moxley able to free herself from serving 'queer penance' to the 'blundering world' that, in Lucas's 'The Debt', blundered into war and tethered all sensory experience thereafter to the guilt of having survived it. Lucas's proposition, I should say, is less like an Adornian hesitancy about writing poetry after Auschwitz than it is a version of Sidney's language of aristocratic sacrifice as the guarantor of stable class relations; his soldiers die 'that England still might sheltered be / And all our lives go on the same'. Moxley, then, in rejecting Lucas's 'queer penance', is rejecting not the idea of guilt but the idea that it must crush all other feeling; loss and violence remind her 'to fight against' false solace, tinselled joy, but not at the price of 'cut[ting] the feeling from our breast', even though keeping it there may oblige 'the will' to 'split ... in two' and place the subject of feeling in the path of 'defeat'.

Moxley knows this counterformation, this defence of feeling despite its susceptibility to capture and falsification, places her on the knife-edge of the weakest forms of sentimentality. Her assertion of worthlessness is also, by way of reference to the 'bonvivant' who 'does no harm' in wishing others well, an assertion of her own harmlessness – an assertion that would seem to confound or back away from the poem's aggressive insistence that seeming innocence is no such thing. But the poem supplies a second, closing formulation that links this potentially irredeemable sentimentality to the conditions that produced it as an option: 'given our time's caution and your kind lash / it has never been easy for us to say yes'. This last defense of affirmation – and of poetry as an affirmative art – identifies the formalised and falsified emotion Moxley has been describing as the product of 'our time's caution' and the 'kind lash' of a heretofore invisible addressee. Both this 'caution' and that 'lash' are meant to encapsulate the structures of feeling of those who know they only bear the brunt of exploitation indirectly and who live, literally, at the expense of others. It is a guilty affirmation and a calibration of emotion registered in the 'rectifying' and 'adjusting' affective work the poem describes. What Moxley offers is a fellow feeling among all those who find, in the face of a hollow aesthetic (of 'songs'), the 'bafflement' of a 'reason' that cannot answer the question of what we are 'for'. And she insists on positing a 'we' regardless, against the 'you' that manages the rate of ruin with its 'kind lash'.

'On This Side Nothing' is not a poem of solidarity with the oppressed. It is an uneasy exploration of the reverb of oppression, as it registers in objects and sentiments consumed by the sheltered, and a defiant insistence that, despite its daily capture in the 'flurry of cash', emotion does not belong to it. I hope I've made it possible to sense, reading Moxley's poem, the different rhetorics of deferred or unrealisable value I have identified here. I hope it's possible to hear, in other words, Moxley making the poetic case, the case for poetry, once again, out of the checkered rhetoric of its defence. I cannot not hear, in this poem, Sidney's language of aristocratic sacrifice, displaced onto soldiers lodging in an earlier poem and another period; the Viconian presumption that poets (collectively evoked, I think, by the poem's closing 'us') have a historical claim to languages that precede abstraction; the tragic Shelleyan sense of the pointlessness of labour ('weary of ritual tending' or the poem's Ecclesiastian title); Schiller's dismay at the gap between the actions of the individual and the workings of the system ('freed perhaps of our compelling / but nevertheless compelled'); Lukács's vigilance around traversing this gap ('do not think we were born to be fools'); or, by way of Spivak, both affective labour and the rate of exploitation given tone ('rectify / aggressive apathy'; 'our time's caution and your kind lash').

Moxley's poem is a dossier, you might say, assembled on poetry's behalf; and as such it gains exemplarity as an instance of poetry, if we can give partial credit to the language of poetry's defence for shaping our sense of what poetry might be. Tangled into that exemplary case-making activity is a thickly layered text of propositions, no longer immediately evident as such, about poetry's place in the long development of value as a social abstraction; they form the poem's bridge between the feeling it affirms and the social violation it cannot escape. This feels like the poem's political unconscious – not a tragic emotion, built out of inert materials and reconstructed from the point of view of failure, but an assemblage, a case, fashioned out of historically divergent materials to create a tone – a tone that makes both affirmation and exploitation audible at once. I think learning how to listen for it is the central task of aesthetic theory today.

CHAPTER 3

Reading on the Left

My essay, like many of the others in this issue, began as a talk for the 2008 conference 'The Way We Read Now'. I was included on a panel called 'Hermeneutics Without Suspicion?' which raised the question of whether 'symptomatic' reading, especially in the wake of Fredric Jameson's work, was still a relevant or useful model for literary interpretation today (the conference's subtitle was, 'symptomatic Reading and Its Aftermath'). My paper attempted to disentangle the 'symptomatic' from the 'suspicious' by way of emphasising moments in Jameson's career where he advocates for certain texts rather than out-manoeuvres them; my larger aim was to link the hermeneutics of the symptom to a quest on the literary-academic left – sometimes 'suspicious', sometimes not – for models of revolutionary action, or militant comportment, that could replace the traditional Marxist championing of the industrial working class.

What I couldn't quite articulate at the time, though, were the reasons for a gap I saw between Jameson's style of 'symptomatic reading' and the variety of 'symptomatic' reading practices produced and consumed in the United States since the 1970s. The problem was not only that Jameson's practice of symptomatising texts did not necessarily seem 'suspicious' to me, or to involve an antagonistic relation to the texts he chose to read, but also that, despite his extraordinarily wide influence on literary study in the United States, there seemed to be almost no relation between his work and the other main strands of symptomatising reading that emerged in the period. At the time, I understood this gap in Jameson's own terms, as responses to failure – in particular, as readerly responses to the failure of the working class to become revolutionary in the twentieth century. In other words, I interpreted the kinds of symptomatic reading that emerged in the U.S. literary academy in the 1980s as part of a search for something other than a proletariat to valorise.

This seems accurate enough. Now, though, I'm inclined to reframe the matter a bit, and to suggest that the gap between Jameson's symptomatising readings and those of, say, deconstruction and multiculturalism has equally to do with the long history of anti-Marxism in the United States, which includes the strong discouragement of academics from Marxist analysis.[1] This history

---

1   There are many measures by which to gauge this history of American anti-Marxism. Employ-

of anti-Marxism has yet to be told as a coherent story with regard to post-war 'theory', and I couldn't begin to lay it out here. But even if we keep it in mind as a blunt, underdeveloped proposition, it becomes easier to make sense of Jameson's canonicity, since he is best known for a periodisation (modern-postmodern) and an axiom ('always historicize!') that do not immediately demand adoption by way of Marxist concepts. Jameson's great obsession, the problem of the non-revolutionary character of the twentieth century (or of the non-liberatory character of its revolutions), is easily set aside when he is read this way.

Ironically, then, it is possible to conduct a survey of American 'symptomatic' reading without much recourse to Jameson's work, since, as I'll try to show, what counts as a 'symptom' in those styles of reading has little to do with the notion of the symptom that emerges in the 1970s from within Marxism. Nonetheless, I think the styles of symptomatic reading that grew up in the United States in this period retain something that is now, in the new millennium, coming around to meet that Marxist formulation. So I will begin with the intra-Marxist Jameson, far though his work lies from the main line of non-Marxist symptomatic interpretation, as a way of beginning the story of left-wing literary-academic reading in the period from the 70s to today. After identifying three variations on symptomatic reading – a Marxist version, and then two multiculturalist versions, humanist and anti-humanist – I will try to suggest why symptomatic reading in a multiculturalist vein has been dislodged by forms of reading that lay emphasis on the history of the present. Then I will compare contemporary theories of what it means to historicise the present to Jameson's version, suggesting that they share a theory of causal necessity that is linked to theories of matter or materiality. And in closing I will point to ways in which a literary understanding of 'matter', very different from the philosophical sense that drives historicising theory, might help us work toward fresher ways to read now, and to read 'the now'.

---

ees of the State of California, for instance, must still sign, in 2009, a 'loyalty oath' that, while it no longer obliges the signer specifically to declare that she has never been a member of the Communist Party, is nonetheless shaped by the anti-Communism of the Cold War. This history also registers in the common gesture by which liberal intellectuals in the English-speaking world discount Marxist thought by depicting it as brainwashing, 'ideology', or hysteria – anything but intellection. A good example of this kind of work is Lilla 2001.

1   The Marxist Symptom

The foundational 'symptomatic reading' for twentieth-century Marxism is actually a friendly reading of a text, that is, Louis Althusser's reading of the text of *Capital*. If Althusser could be said to be 'suspicious' in *Reading 'Capital'*, it is because he is suspicious not of Marx's text, but of monocausal, economistic readings of it. Indeed, for Althusser, this is the critical force of the idea of a symptom: it is more complex than a mere reflection. I think a certain confusion begins here between two senses of 'symptomatic reading': first, symptomatic reading that allows us to see a text generating a concept of the symptom; and second, symptomatic reading that critiques a text for not being in control of itself. Althusser is reading Marx in the first sense. He is trying to get us to see that Marx's reading of the commodity in Volume I of *Capital* takes commodity relations to be, not mere reflections of a single process of exploitation, but rather the complex result of multiple processes that can't be understood without recourse to an account of the activities of exploitation. In particular, Althusser highlights the way that Marx begins *in media res*, not with the origins of capital but with its structuring activily, that is, commodity exchange. In this context, the critical advantage of the symptom over the reflection is that one can read texts as a Marxist without having to read them didactically. The need for this kind of reading emerges, in the 1960s and 1970s, as it becomes clear that the working classes of Europe and America may not be the engine of revolution or the subject of history after all, that they are too divided, too defeated, or too distracted to perform the role the revolutionaries of the nineteenth century first imagined for them. To read a text symptomatically in this context means to become more flexible in one's search for significant historical action in texts: literature can be read as more than a mostly empty repository of revolutionary acts; other acts besides revolutionary ones can be seen as historically significant, or aesthetically important, because of the ways they point to how human history is not only, or not yet, apprehensible as the pre-history of revolution.

This is where Jameson picks up on Althusser, especially in *The Political Unconscious*. Rather than choose a class to blame for the failure of the twentieth century to be the century of liberatory revolutions, Jameson incorporates revolutionary failure into his system of interpretation, and, in doing so, he makes it possible to think about the relationships among forms of historical causality, types of literary activity, and modes of critical reading without hitching those relationships either to the hope that one class will emerge as revolutionary, or to the accusation that it was the action or inaction of one class or another that prevented revolution from coming to pass. The question that haunts left criticism in the twentieth century – why wasn't this a liberatory age? – still shapes his work, but he refuses any single answer to it.

Jameson's particular twist on Althusserian reading is to make an analogy between structural causality in the social system and 'heterogeneity' or contradiction in literary works: rather than naming other classes, or social formations other than classes, to whose fortunes left intellectuals might pin their hopes, he makes an aesthetic turn that identifies in literary works the kind of fissures that reveal the failure, both of left-wing political hopes and of the projects of capital to quash them. He brings Althusser, that is, around to the language of literary modernism:

> It follows, then, that the interpretive mission of a properly structural causality will ... find its privileged content in rifts and discontinuities within the work, and ultimately in a conception of the former 'work of art' as a heterogeneous and (to use the most dramatic recent slogan) a schizophrenic text.[2]

That this aesthetic turn is still shaped by a notion of possible resistance by actual categories of people is made clear, in *The Political Unconscious*, by the contrast drawn between Althusser and Georg Lukács. For Lukács, the industrial working class was the engine of historical change, and the realist novel was the expression of its emergence, since, regardless of the political orientation of realist novel-writers themselves, the codes of realism demanded an expanded social palette. To move from Lukács to Althusser on aesthetic matters, as Jameson does, is therefore also to imply a post-Lukácsian understanding that heterogeneity in the work of art, even failure, is expressive of the pending problem of there being no obvious successor to the working classes as the engine of history. Jameson's literary modernism, then, his aesthetics of fissure and failure, is also always a political agnosticism about who might replace the working classes, and a flexibility about how it might be useful to read in the meantime.

This flexibility makes possible a kind of symptomatic reading that is also a friendly reading, along the lines of Althusser's reading of *Capital*. Indeed this is the Jameson I know best, the Jameson making what seem like untimely defences of writers like Jean-Paul Sartre and Theodor Adorno at moments – in 1971, in 1989 – when those thinkers seem discredited or superseded. In these moments, a 'symptomatic reading' involves figuring out how history and the text have come around to meet each other once again, how what once seemed

---

2   Jameson 1981, p. 56.

like weaknesses in an argument, or in a mode of presentation, can come to find new force, or even truth, in a later period. So when Jameson argues, in *Marxism and Form*, that Sartre's subjectivism, démodé in the Althusserian 70s, is actually exactly what the foment of the time calls for; or when, in his book on Adorno, he points out that Adorno's much-derided quietism, seemingly surpassed by the subversive energies in Michel Foucault, in Jacques Derrida, in Jacques Lacan, is in fact the ground for a kind of dialectical patience that the global rightward shift demands – in these moments, Jameson's symptomatic style of reading emerges not as a hermeneutics of suspicion but as a hermeneutics of *situation* – a kind of reading that proposes texts for our attention because they seem useful for historicising the present.[3]

What's important here is not so much that Jameson's readings of Adorno and Sartre are friendly rather than suspicious, but that he models a reading practice in which what nourishes a revolutionary comportment, or a proto-revolutionary one, will be different under different circumstances. This is another sense in which his reading style can be said to be symptomatic – his own readings are themselves self-consciously symptomatic, that is, complexly and unstably a product of their own time.

I say 'unstably' because in *The Political Unconscious* Jameson works up a highly unstable compound of Althusser and Sartre, old enemies, in order keep the objectivism of Althusser's 'structural causality' from becoming a scientism, even as the Sartrean language of the inert, to which I'll turn in a moment, threatens to topple that structuralism by positing a matter ontologically prior to human action. But Jameson thinks that it's worth the intellectual risk: as the global shift to the right gains momentum, he is aware that any persuasive account of the ongoing relevance of Marxism will have to be able to offer critics a reading practice that makes sense of defeat – something the Althusserian model tends to do only in the mode of blame, of blaming would-be revolutionaries for their lapses into ideology. So he turns to Sartre, to a language of Necessity that is meant to be logical but not universally valid, 'represented', as Jameson puts it, 'in the form of the inexorable logic involved in the determinate failure of all the revolutions that have taken place in human history'.[4] In describing the work of the interpreter, Jameson locates this idea of Necessity in relation to the Sartrean categories of the inert and the practico-inert, which represent, respectively, the dead matter that precedes human labour and the unsettling autonomy of matter once it has been worked on. He writes:

---

3   See Jameson 1974 and 1990.
4   Jameson 1981, p. 102.

> Whatever the raw material on which historiographic form works ... the 'emotion' of great historiographic form can then always be seen as the radical restructuration of that inert material, in this instance the powerful reorganization of otherwise inert chronological material and 'linear' data in the form of Necessity: why what happened ... had to happen the way it did.[5]

Notice the linkage here between the idea of matter as 'inert' and the idea of causal necessity. In this Sartrean parable, events can be revealed to participate in causal necessity because matter precedes human action, ontologically and logically: it is there before us, and can therefore be said to have a determinative effect on human action. Since 1981, Jameson's linkage of causation to a notion of inert matter that awaits 'restructuration' has made a good claim to be just what historicising readers need in an unrevolutionary era: it seems to suit perfectly an era of defeats for the Left. But there is an intellectual and historiographical price to pay for this logicisation and ontologisation of 'matter', which is that it tends to muffle our ability to understand capital as experimental and uncertain – a feature of its workings that has become central to our understanding of capital in the current financial crisis. I'll return to this problem a bit later, since it resurfaces in a different, but equally ontologising, theory of matter in the era of globalisation. Meanwhile, though, there is a second, circumstantial limitation on the explanatory power of Jameson's method of historicisation – which is that in the 1980s and 1990s, many readers on the left were experiencing the era as anything but unrevolutionary.

2   The Multicultural Symptom

Though we tend to frame the 1980s in U.S. political history in terms of the rise of the right, it is also true that those years were the great period of academic multiculturalism in the humanities, the period in which the 'culture wars' were won, by and large, by teachers and scholars working to open up the canons of literature (especially American literature) to other voices – 'other voices' being both a feminist and an ethnic-studies catchphrase of the period. These struggles, which were not confined to the university, permanently altered the syllabi of children's literature and high school curricula and, in commercial publishing, opened the way to the more global understanding of literature in English that

---

5   Jameson 1981, p. 101.

we now take for granted. Toni Morrison's Nobel Prize in 1993 was the capstone of this period, serving not only as a recognition of her literary achievement but also as an endorsement of U.S.-style expansions of the literary canon. So a variety of readers would have had cause to experience the category of 'literature' in the 1980s as undergoing a 'revolutionary' period in the restricted sense that it saw the academic fulfillment of earlier, more properly political struggles.

In the political realm, meanwhile, the period did in fact witness the upsurge of a confrontational, direct-action movement in the form of AIDS activism, which created a generation of activists who became expert not only at organising mass demonstrations but also in speaking the languages of government health policy, science policy, and even of science itself. The AIDS Coalition to Unleash Power (ACT UP), which spearheaded this activism, had chapters in every major city in the United States, with 'affinity groups' devoted to a host of issues affecting people with AIDS; virtually all of the AIDS service organisations in American cities today owe their existence to this period of activism. The epidemic, which fueled particularly vicious forms of homophobia, and suffered alarming neglect by the Reagan and Bush I administrations, produced a militant consciousness in many gay men and lesbians of the time, who were led to rethink not only their relationship to government and its services but also to categories like family and community, which were tested and reworked in the crisis. The catchphrase of the movement, 'silence=Death', conveyed succinctly the sense that the epidemic was creating persons with nothing to lose from radicalisation; it formed a key part of the protest in the 1987 March on Washington for Lesbian and Gay Rights, which brought more than half a million people to the capital.[6]

Both the multicultural expansion of the canon and the militancy born of the AIDS epidemic affected literary reading in the 1980s and early 1990s, in ways that form a countercurrent to the Jamesonian story of revolutionary failure. In terms of how these developments fit into the broader story of left politics in the period, I think we can say that two things happened to left-leaning U.S. literary criticism at this point. One was an opening-out of the search for historical actors, either as the new revolutionaries, or as the sub-jects of modes of action that are liberatory without being punctually revolutionary. The other was a shift

---

6   The archive of AIDS activist work was itself built in a movement context, but there is of course a large body of academic work on it by now. The best history of the intersection of activism and medical policy remains Epstein 1998. For a collection of influential essays that were written on the ground during the first decade of the epidemic in the U.K. and the U.S., see Watney 1994.

from the search for a replacement for the working classes to a sustained critique of the acquisitional middle class. The first describes what I think of as broadly multicultural reading practices, which point to the historical agency of other actors than, say, the white middle-class man; the second set of practices, which took up the tools of psychoanalysis and deconstruction, critique the idea of the autonomy of the liberal political subject that the middle-class white man comes to represent. In the first case, to read critically is to excavate the historical violence, and the causal contingency, by which the liberal political subject achieved his autonomy – by the becoming-significant, for instance, of his race, or his sex – and to leverage knowledge of this violence and contingency to point out that subjects other than the white man can act significantly. In the second case, to read critically is to point out that the indicatively white male political subject, at least as he appears in literary texts, does not in fact enjoy autonomy: autonomy is seen as residing in the textual system, which not only trumps the subject through its systematicity but also carries traces of what that subject can't bear having made manifest, that is, evidence of his heteronomy. Together these two developments count for much of what we have come to think of as 'symptomatic reading' in the United States; against Marxist symptomatic reading, we might indeed call them the two major variations on 'American symptomatic reading', which amount to humanist and anti-humanist multiculturalisms.

In different ways, both of these kinds of reading put pressure on the category of 'the literary'. Toni Morrison's 1992 *Playing in the Dark*, for instance (which is subtitled *Whiteness and the Literary Imagination*), relies on Freudian ideas about unconscious habits of fetishisation, condensation, and displacement in order to develop an account of how white American writers figured blackness by paying attention to the actual depiction of black persons, as well as to the unconscious stress she believes white writers felt in attempting to prevent those depictions from becoming an overwhelming formal problem. In Morrison's analyses of white writers' texts, the pressure to address histories of racial violence threatens to deform those texts, indeed to press them past the bounds of the literary. Reading Willa Cather's late novel *Sapphira and the Slave Girl* (1940), in which an elderly, disabled, slave-owning white woman becomes obsessed with the possibility that her faithful husband is having sex with a young slave woman, Morrison homes in on the over-determined character of Sapphira's behavior, which finds no plausible explanation in the novel. As Morrison points out, this behaviour makes no characterological, narrative, or historical sense: Sapphira arranges for the slave girl to be raped, hoping thereby to destroy her husband's sense of pleasure in possessing the girl, Nancy; but we are given no grounds for judging whether Sapphira is paranoid, and in any case, Morrison notes, there was no concept of black women's chastity in the history of U.S. slave-holding, so that Sapphira's scheme to have Nancy 'despoiled' is incoherent.[7]

This is a 'symptomatic' reading, then, in that it judges the author to be not fully in control of the production of her text. More interesting, though, are the measures by which Morrison assesses this 'symptom'. She observes that Cather, almost as if to compensate for the incoherence of plot and character created by the casuistical situation of Sapphira's evil and Nancy's virtue, indulges in an epilogue to the story in which, many years after Nancy successfully escapes to the north, a stand-in for the young Cather returns with Nancy to present her to her mother, the former slave Till. In Morrison's eyes, this only makes matters worse, since the scene of mother-daughter reunion is thus focalized around the young author-to-be, for whom the agony of maternal separation, and the pathos of reunion, become mere staging for the emergent narrative skill of the white child. This is a serious list of literary flaws. What's startling, then, is Morrison's conclusion:

> The final fugitive in Cather's novel is the novel itself. The plot's own plotting to free the endangered slave girl ... is designed for other purposes. It functions as a means for the author to meditate on the moral equivalence of free white women and enslaved black women.[8]

In this phrasing, the flaws in Cather's novel make it not a failure, but a loss – the loss of a potential story in the history readers and writers will need if they are ever to come to terms with the heritage of slavery. Morrison's reading of *Sapphira and the Slave Girl* is symptomatic, and it is critical, but her aim in identifying the symptom is to create space in the American history of race for damaged literary texts. Her narrative is one of healing, though neither the author nor the text can benefit from it; the forgiving of author and text – for forgiveness is what's at stake – is rather part of a healing process in the history of American racism, which exceeds literary writing. Cather's novel may have become 'fugitive', barely a novel, but it (and its author) can now be read as part of an extra-literary history of damage and deformation. To read 'symptomatically', for Morrison, is to set aside 'literature' as the master-category of reading.

It takes more effort to track the position of the category of the literary in the deconstructive flank of American symptomatic reading, partly because it does not locate 'symptoms' in any one author or text. Where a multicultural reading

7   Morrison 1993, p. 25.
8   Morrison 1993, p. 27.

like Morrison's exceeds the bounds of 'the literary' by way of a humanism that elevates the writer into the position of exemplary personhood (writers, for Morrison, are worth studying on something like their own terms, as writers), deconstructive, anti-humanist symptomatic reading is interested in getting behind personhood to the question of what systems or structures shape it, make it possible. But what is at stake in the turn to systems or structures?

Lee Edelman's *Homographesis* of 1994 is a culminating example of the anti-humanist turn in American symptomatic reading – 'culminating' because it brings deconstruction back around to the question of the political stakes of reading for actual persons, even as it reserves the intellectual right to understand personhood in terms of textuality. The genius of Edelman's book is to tell a story in which a whole category of persons in the modern era – gay men – are made to stand in for something like writing and reading: their bodies are understood as especially legible, even as they present problems of legibility recognisable to the professional scholar of literature as problems of interpretive endlessness, of too much meaning. 'Homographesis', for Edelman, is meant to name both the social and cultural processes by which gay men become equated with writing, and the interpretive strategies by which professional gay textual scholars can expose those processes as 'reductive' and 'repressive'.[9]

For Edelman, the violence of homophobia, at least as it is directed at gay men, is linguistic, in an epistemological and metaphysical sense: homophobia works as a kind of demand in the medium of language that gay men correspond to the hostile fantasies about them. This demand for exact correspondence is not only levelled at gay men, however – Edelman makes clear that straight men's presumption of wholeness, and self-evident personhood, is bought at the price of masking an ambiguity and open-endedness of language that he thinks is its essential quality. To expose self-identity as containing difference, then, is both to loosen the bonds of homophobia on gay men and to show up the pretensions to uncomplicated masculinity of straight men: they are, gay and straight men alike, both more and less than what the culture has made them out to be.[10]

There is an irreducible humanism in this linguistic account of homophobia. In this light, Edelman's project is cultural, psychological, and historical; indeed it is multicultural. Queer theory, as he puts it, is

---

9   Edelman 1994, p. 23.
10   See Edelman 1994, p. 14.

the study of the historically variable rhetorics, the discursive strategies, and tropological formations in which sexuality is embedded and conceived; it suggests that the differing psychologies of figuration in different places and at different times bear crucially on the textual articulations and cultural constructions of sexuality; and it suggests that the sphere of gay criticism need not be restricted to the examination of texts that either thematize homosexual relations or dramatize the vicissitudes of homosexual/homosocial desire.[11]

This is a humanist, multiculturalist argument for the expansion of a canon, and for attention to historical and psychological variability. It also contains an anti-humanist counter-current, however: in the same paragraph in which Edelman makes his bid for the importance of studying human and historical variability, he writes: 'The project of homographesis would locate the critical force of homosexuality at the very point of discrimination between sameness and difference as cognitive landmarks governing the discursive field of social symbolic relations'.[12]

So the work of the anti-homophobic scholar is a kind of textual scholarship, isolating metaphors ('the very point of discrimination between sameness and difference') – but the goal, unlike that of traditional textual scholarship, is not to produce the cleanest, most authoritative text. Metaphors are now understood as 'cognitive', that is, in the language of the social sciences (Edelman does not call metaphors 'imaginative' or 'intellectual' or even 'mental' landmarks). Indeed the phrase, 'the discursive field of social symbolic relations', points directly back to Levi-Strauss's structuralist anthropology, which itself was built out of an analogy to Saussurean linguistics.

In terms of the category of 'the literary', then, this style of reading involves subsuming the specificity of literature under a metaphor of 'writing' as legibility, cognition, symbolisation, governance, philosophy, and philosophy's disciplinary anxiety. In a brief reading of Marcel Proust at the beginning of *Homographesis*, for instance, Edelman interprets a scene in which Proust's narrator recognises M. De Charlus's homosexuality retrospectively as a recognition of 'writing itself', though the narrator's figure for his belated recognition is specifically of seeing letters assemble themselves into an order – that is, a figure for a socially and educationally specific process of becoming literate.[13]

---

11   Edelman 1994, p. 20.
12   Ibid.
13   See Edelman 1994, pp. 18–20.

As with Morrison's humanist symptomatic reading, then, Edelman's anti-humanist reading subsumes 'literature' under another category – here, a cognitivised 'writing', to which homosexuality has also been subsumed. In Morrison's case, the identification of Cather's symptom is aimed at healing literature, so to speak, by giving it a clearer sense of its history, and thereby allowing literature to move on. It would seem, in Edelman's case, that gay men are being advised to participate in a perpetual discursive skirmish with heterosexual men and along the way to seize their spectacularised gay identities, which threaten male heterosexuality so as to make it anxious. This would be a way for gay men to 'enjoy their symptom', as Slavoj Žižek would put it; this is certainly the direction Edelman's work has taken since the early 1990s.[14]

The ideas of history behind these humanist and anti-humanist multiculturalisms are quite different – one imagines something like progress, the other an endless war of position – but I think they share the confidence of the social movements out of which they grew. One way to confirm this is to compare them with the Jamesonian narrative, which is so emphatically formed through notions of failure. The Marxist symptom and the multicultural symptom are not just temperamental 'opposites', however, one 'optimistic' and the other 'pessimistic'; they represent two poles in a contradictory historical development. American multiculturalist reading practices grew out of the successes, in the 1960s and 1970s, of the civil rights movement and the new social movements, like feminism and gay liberation, that modelled themselves on it – while Marxist models of historical necessity read the same period in terms of the decline of working-class militancy and social democracy.

Read from a different angle, the tension between Marxist and multiculturalist models of reading is linked to a contradiction built into the new social movements themselves. On the one hand, they seemed to sidestep the endless factionalism and cumulative defeatism of the European Marxist left: they were grassroots movements without party structures. On the other hand, they tended to forsake a critique of capital as old-style politics and ended up focusing on injury and its repair at the expense of the question of liberation: they became practical, institutional.

As these social movements grappled in the 1980s and 90s with contradictions external and internal (between identity and the critique of identity; between grassroots organising and institution building), they became less distinct from liberal civil society, and they gradually lost their grip on the imagination of left-leaning intellectuals. During the same years, however, the profile

---

14   See Žižek 2001; and Edelman 2004.

of global capital emerged with ever greater clarity, bouncing back from the oil shock of 1973 in a trans-Atlantic rightward turn that loosened up market regulations, facilitated the implementation of new, highly speculative forms of 'wealth', and launched migrations of labour across national boundaries on an unprecedented scale. These developments have produced a wholesale abandonment of post-structuralist thinking in the humanistic academy, which has been reduced to fire-sale prices as its advocacy for textuality as a model for culture (or becoming-literate as a model for political activity) seems less and less relevant in what looks like a new era of *number*. What has emerged instead is a constellation of critical thought that reframes the contradictions of the age of new social movements in terms of a new situation and aggressively reasserts *subjectivity* as the ground of politics. The model of reading that has developed alongside this new critical thought is less 'symptomatic' than exemplary, as in: who is the exemplary subject in the era of global capital? I would like to outline the features of this latest style of reading in what follows, focusing on how it tries to understand politics through a grasp of the special character of the contemporary, of something like a 'situation' that calls for heroic action.

3   After the Symptom: Situational Reading

I don't mean to say that this style of reading is not 'symptomatic' in the broad sense of being diagnostic: indeed diagnosis of the contemporary is exactly what motivates it. But it does not read the contemporary scene for indications of a masked or occluded reality; whatever 'symptoms' it sees are eminently present. But the urge of this style of reading toward the exemplary makes it hard to describe by way of the 'symptom' in a literary sense, since the work I am thinking of – writing by Antonio Negri and Michael Hardt, by Giorgio Agamben, and by Alain Badiou – has largely forgone the operation of reading literary texts in order to reposition them in a wider frame. Instead, this style of reading begins with the assumption that the wider frame, or situation, is the starting point and then turns to literary texts for relatively transparent support for one kind of action or another in that situation. Gone is the attempt at elevating 'writing' to a commanding position among the incommensurable disciplines; gone too is the valorisation of failure on its own terms. In their place we find a return to reading writers for the kind of personhood they depict or exemplify. So there is a continuity between this kind of reading, which has a strong humanist component, and the humanist multiculturalism of, say, Morrison. But these writers are less interested than Morrison in recuperating ambivalently progressive writing, and more interested in assembling a canon of something like heroes or saints.

The work of Hardt and Negri, Agamben, and Badiou overlap in many ways. Hardt and Negri follow Agamben in developing a concept of the 'biopolitical'; Agamben and Badiou have both written books on Saint Paul; Badiou and Hardt and Negri have been at work outlining new forms of militancy to meet the present. There is also significant disagreement among these writers – Badiou in particular is dismissive of both Agamben's work on Paul, and of Hardt and Negri's alliance of their concept of 'the multitude' with the anti-globalization movement. What they all have in common, though, is an urgent message that a new era has arrived, and a sense that reading, such as it is, must emerge from the urgencies of the contemporary situation.

What the situation is, exactly, differs among these thinkers, and I will sketch their respective senses of it further on. First, though, it's worth noting a certain irony, which is that the prominence of Agamben, Badiou, and Hardt and Negri on the American literary-academic left can be understood as registering the decline of American exemplarity for European intellectuals. From the mid-1960s to the early 1990s, grassroots politics in the United States held a special place in left-wing European thought: from Herbert Marcuse's interest in (and adoption by) 60s youth movements and Guy Debord's situationist reading of the 1965 Watts uprising in Los Angeles, on through to Derrida's remark in the mid-1980s that 'deconstruction *is* America', the United States was a metonym for the possibilities and the contradictions of the period that Jameson, himself making a global exemplar of American art and architecture, helped popularise as 'post-modern'.[15] But Badiou's work is emphatically centred on the politics of France; Agamben's makes central the experience of the mass murder of European Jews; and Hardt and Negri's co-authored work emphasises the theoretical importance of migrant populations around the globe. Whether we understand this turn away from the United States as the result of failures in its multiculturalist and grassroots politics, or of developments outside the United States, it is true that all the most widely circulating theoretical languages for the present are post-American in some sense – and I think this is a significant part of their appeal for Americans, either because they are eager to break from the solipsism engendered by U.S. exceptionalism, or because they are exhausted by hunting for possibilities of resistance from deep within the centre of the imperium.

For Badiou, calling for a return to the exemplarity of a militant stance he sees in Saint Paul, the political scene is particularly French, and defined by factional struggles on the post-war left. In the preface to the English-language edition of

---

15   See Marcuse 1969, Debord 2008; and Derrida 1986.

his 2005 *Metapolitics* he outlines these struggles, fondly recalling the Maoism of the 70s, when 'everyday life was entirely politicized' and 'daily activism was the done thing'.[16] This activism was positioned against both the official politics of the French Communist Party and the decay of the spirit of the student uprisings of May 1968, neither of which was as spontaneous as the Resistance of the 1940s (Badiou's main contemporary model of militancy). For Badiou, everything hinges on an exasperated critique of liberal parliamentarianism, which, politically, tends toward identification of the state with the common good and, philosophically, tends toward the endless expostulation of opinion instead of the pursuit of truth. As he puts it, opinion is 'forever disjoined from all truth. We know what this idea amounts to: sophistry ... sophistry dedicated to the promotion of an entirely particular politics. In other words: parliamentary politics'.[17] This distinction between philosophy and sophistry, or truth and opinion, dates to Plato, and in attempting to establish it as the criterion for an authentic politics, Badiou dismisses the politics of multiculturalism in favour of a small canon of writers, philosophers, and political figures who embodied, in his mind, an ontological resistance to what 'is'. Mao heads up the list, as does Paul; also present are his own father and a cluster of limit-modernists like Paul Celan, Stéphane Mallarmé, and Samuel Beckett – a canon of literary extremity also dear to the post-structuralists whom he despises.[18] What unites these literary figures for Badiou is their placement in situations where the Leninist question of 'what is to be done' had an obvious answer, an answer requiring no thought or reflection: resistance happens ineluctably – or, as he puts it, 'by *logic*'.[19] Inasmuch as these literary figures are to be 'read' at all, they serve as examples of militancy.

I think Badiou's work has touched a chord among leftist academics in Bush-era America because his exasperation with liberal humanism finds a mirror in the capitulation of the Democratic Party to Bush's 'war on terror', and the militancy he calls for can be imagined as an antidote to that liberal giving-away of political ground. Obscured in the U.S. context has been Badiou's bizarre interpretation of his modern *locus classicus*, the French Resistance, which he leverages, not only against the Marxist concept of class as an engine of historical change, but also against sociability, opinion, thought itself. It is beside the point, he writes in the preface to *Metapolitics*, 'to assign the study of the Resistance to sociological or institutional representations. No group, no

16   Badiou 2005, p. xxxiv.
17   Badiou 2005, p. 14.
18   Badiou 2005, p. xxxii.
19   Badiou 2005, p. 4.

class, no social configuration or mental objective was behind the Resistance'.[20] Even his sympathetic translator is left to wonder how a politics like this, so insistent on the idea of any reflection at all as liberal nattering, can imagine change.[21]

One answer, it turns out, is poetically. Badiou is appealingly schematic when he describes the historical relations between philosophy and poetry, which he understands to have developed along three lines: a Parmenidean postulation of the oneness of all knowledge, a Platonic exile of poetry from legitimate thought, and an Aristotelian impulse to categorise it. One key to Badiou's appeal to literary scholars in particular, I think, is the simple but bravura gesture he makes, in *Infinite Thought*, of introducing a fourth option – which, if you believe there have only ever been three, is breathtaking in its freshness. This fourth relation, which is actually as old as Romanticism, assigns the role of 'presence', or unmasterable intensity, to poetry and rewrites philosophy's role as occasional visitor to its realm, where it learns commitment.

The literary canon that facilitates such a relation must remain narrow, as you might imagine. Only the most intense of poems can plausibly be taken as establishing this kind of relation to philosophical thought: what could Frank O'Hara teach Plato of commitment? And even in the case of Celan, certainly unsurpassed in linguistic and experiential intensity, Badiou's reading assimilates his poems into the category of 'poetry' in general, where 'poetry' figures ontological excess. He writes:

> When Celan tells us:
>   Wurfscheibe, mit
>   Vorgesichten besternt,
>   wirf dich
>   auf dir hinaus.
> Which can be translated as:
>   Cast-disc, with
>   Forseeings bestarred,
>   cast yourself
>   out your outside.
> ... [this means that] one must be *poetically* ready for the outside-of-self. For the nomination of an event – in the sense in which I speak of it, that is, an undecidable supplementation which must be named to occur for a

---

20   Badiou 2005, p. 5.
21   See Badiou 2005, pp. xxii–xxiii.

being-faithful, thus for a truth – *this* nomination is *always* poetic. To name a supplement, a chance, an incalculable, one must draw from the void of sense, in default of established significations, to the peril of language. One must therefore poeticize, and the poetic name of the event is what throws us outside of ourselves, through the flaming ring of predictions.[22]

Badiou's assimilation of *ecstasis* to militancy and his assimilation of poems to 'the poetic name of the event' severely contracts the imaginable canon of 'poetry' even as it elevates the role of 'the poetic' to co-chairmanship with philosophy in the sciences of the human. This tiny canon comes at a cost: only by being more militant, more rigorous than Plato himself, it seems, can poetry share space with philosophy. Badiou's thematic reading of the content of Celan's poem as getting the reader ready for *ecstasis*, however, reveals the poem's secondary status, since upon arrival of the logically necessary event, the militant subject will have no need of poetry, indeed of language, in order to act.

In Giorgio Agamben's work, the contemporary situation is defined, much as it is for Badiou, as a moment when issues internal to philosophy emerge as the truth of human history. For Badiou that truth is revealed in moments where 'logic' supervenes all other considerations to produce blind, heroic action; for Agamben, that truth is revealed in a coincidence between what he thinks of as a conceptual tangle between 'biological' and collective life (*zoe* and *bios*, in Aristotle), and its manifestation as the overriding political problem of the age. Once again the story of history is assimilated to the story of 'Western metaphysics', although with Agamben it is not the exile of writing from the authenticity of the voice that defines philosophy and therefore provides the key to understanding history, but rather the undecidability built into the question of whether our humanness is creaturely or political.[23] The historical event that exposes this undecidability as the new truth of history is for Agamben, as it was for Hannah Arendt, the mass murder of the European Jews, as well as the subsequent refugee crises of the twentieth century. The refugee and the concentration camp prisoner are for Agamben exemplary figures of the human because they force the question of what we are to become, what aspects of 'biopolitical' life we are to emphasise if we are to survive as a species. Only the dispossessed, he argues, can make a humane future, because they are unhitched from the ancient viciousness of territoriality. He makes this explicit in a 1994 essay called

---

22   Badiou 2005, p. 75.

23   See Agamben 1998.

'We Refugees', which takes its title (and no little of its argument) from a 1943 essay of Hannah Arendt's. Describing a cosmopolitan Europe in which nobody would claim citizenship in any state, he writes,

> This space would not coincide with any homogeneous national territory, nor with their *topographical* sum, but would act on these territories, making holes in them and dividing them *topologically* like in a Leiden jar or in a Moebius strip, where exterior and interior are indeterminate. In this new space, the European cities, entering into a relationship of reciprocal extraterritoriality, would rediscover their ancient vocation as cities of the world. Today, in a sort of no-man's-land between Lebanon and Israel, there are four hundred and twenty-five Palestinians who were expelled by the state of Israel. According to Hannah Arendt's suggestion, these men constitute 'the *avant-garde* of their people'. But this does not necessarily or only mean that they might form the original nucleus of a future national state, which would probably resolve the Palestinian problem just as inadequately as Israel has resolved the Jewish question. Rather, the no-man's-land where they have found refuge has retroacted on the territory of the state of Israel, making holes in it. It is only in a land where the spaces of states will have been perforated and topologically deformed, and the citizen will have learned to acknowledge the refugee that he himself is, that man's political survival today is imaginable.[24]

For Agamben as for Badiou, the figure of the Möbius strip is useful for how it is not the dialectic – which, for Badiou, reduces history to mere circularity.[25] In this passage, the Möbius strip captures what Agamben understands to be the undialectical directness of forms of state power that act on 'life itself'. This emphasis on alternatives to the dialectic is key to his thinking. In his work on Saint Paul, Agamben argues that what Paul exposes is an unsynthesisable remnant in human experience, something that the operations of reason cannot overcome or sublate. This remnant can be understood as that which is uncaptured in our collective experience of time, and which therefore perpetually keeps open the possibility of something entirely other, some different experience of time, appearing to us. In his Paul book, the problem of dialectical thinking is that when it is confronted with this unsublatable gap in human experience, it tries to paper it over – or worse, force it shut. Agamben's example

24   Agamben 1995, p. 119.
25   For a helpful exposition of the figure of the Möbius strip in Badiou's thinking, and its relation to his interpretation of the Hegelian dialectic, see Barker 2002, pp. 40–1.

of this problem is the late dogmatism of Lukács, who faced the gap between
theory and political practice, the working classes and the Communist Party, by
choosing the party line on its supremacy over the proletariat.[26] In his deploy-
ment of these examples and figures, then, Agamben imagines that the undia-
lectizable dispossession of the refugee goes deeper than the exploitation of
the working classes, and eludes what he takes to be the dogmatic militancy
of a Lukács. In the distance between the figure of the dogmatic Lukács and the
sleek topology of the Möbius strip lies the source of Agamben's appeal in the
English-language literary academy: the cosmopolitan replaces the militant and
a sense of ontological crisis (what is inside? what is outside?) replaces a theory
of revolution.

This anti-dialectical stance expresses itself in a formalist reading practice
that, like Badiou's, turns to poetry for exemplary instances of an alternative
understanding or experience of time. In his book on Paul, Agamben interprets
a well-known sestina by the twelfth-century Occitan poet Arnaut Daniel called
'The firm will that enters my heart'. He describes the play of rhyme in the form
of the sestina as 'a soteriological device' that obliges the reader to experience
a kind of recurrence that disrupts 'linear homogeneous time', because the six
end-words identical to each stanza appear not only in a different order in each
of a sestina's first six stanzas but also one last time, reshuffled and compressed
into a final three-line stanza. This property of the form leads him to argue that

> the sestina – and, in this sense, every poem – is a soteriological device
> which, through the sophisticated *mēchanē* of the announcement and
> retrieval of rhyming end-words (which correspond to typological rela-
> tions between past and present), transforms chronological relations of
> time into messianic time.[27]

Unlike Badiou, whose universalisation of 'poetry' from Celan's poems depends
implicitly on an understanding of the urgency of the moment in which Celan
wrote – that is, during and after the mass murder of the European Jews – Agam-
ben does not suggest that there is anything about Daniel in particular, or the
itinerant status of the troubadour, or the special place of Occitan-Provençal in
Ezra Pound's influential construction of the history of the modern lyric, that
leads him to choose this example: indeed he makes no remark on its historical
particularities at all. He is not even especially interested in the content of the

---

26   Agamben 2005, pp. 32–3.
27   Agamben 2005, p. 82.

poem, though arguably, like the other historical details he forgoes inspecting, it might have made the tie between the poem and the letters of Paul (since, after all, the figure of the 'strong will that enters my heart' is easily read in religious as well as romantic terms). Instead, Agamben assimilates Daniel's poem into 'the poetic' as such, collapsing Daniel's sestina into its form, 'the sestina', and the form into 'every poem'. Where for Badiou 'the poetic' earns its place by defining a realm inhabited by a small band of poetic militants, in Agamben's case 'the poetic' wins particularity as an instance of language that comes to an end, and which therefore raises philosophical and religious questions about what endings are, as well as what salvation from them might look like (the 'soteriological device'). Just as Agamben understands the age undialectically, as a case *in extremis* of mass dispossession that opens onto the possibility that those in possession (of goods, of land) might one day let possession go, so does Agamben's soteriological 'poem' stage escapes from linear time by becoming a small exemplary case of its disorder: topology become typology.

The intense pressure Agamben and Badiou put on the category of 'poetry' to be a lever for understanding the urgency of the present makes one wish not only for the liberation of actual poems from such frameworks but also for a more nuanced understanding of the contemporary 'situation'. Michael Hardt and Antonio Negri, among the theorists of the present who have enjoyed wide popularity in the U.S. literary academy, certainly provide this. This is partly because, alone among the theorists of the contemporary who have achieved the widest readership, they tell a comparative story, a story that links Europe and the United States to the global south. And because they take the idea of 'the global' seriously, they are much more wide-ranging in their examples of political activism and militancy than either Badiou or Agamben.

They are also more dialectical. The story they tell about the current state of capitalism is of capital responding to the creativity of workers by retooling itself to meet a situation that workers alter. It is a story they tell and retell from different angles, but the central version of it involves linking traditional labour struggles with youth struggle, linking struggles over the means of production with a reworking of what counts as production in the first place. It begins as a story about labor unions and young people in the global north in the 1960s and 1970s and the pressure they put on capitalism:

> The social struggles [of this period] not only raised the costs of reproduction and the social wage (hence decreasing the rate of profit), but also and more important forced a change in the quality and nature of labor itself. Particularly in the dominant capitalist countries, where the margin of freedom afforded to and won by workers was greatest, the refusal of

the disciplinary regime of the social factory was accompanied by a ree-valuation of the social value of the entire set of productive activities. The disciplinary regime clearly no longer succeeded in containing the needs and desires of young people. The prospect of getting a job that guaran-tees regular and stable work for eight hours a day, fifty weeks a year, for an entire working life, the prospect of entering the normalized regime of the social factory, which had been a dream for many of their parents, now appeared as a kind of death. The mass refusal of the disciplinary regime, which took a variety of forms, was not only a negative expression but also a moment of creation, what Nietzsche calls a transvaluation of values.[28]

This emphasis on the creativity of refusal by young people in the postwar global north has two significant meanings for Hardt and Negri, both of which they italicise. First, they take this refusal as evidence that '[this] *"merely cultural"* experimentation had very profound political and economic effects' – by which they mean a range of developments, from the creation of a 'youth market' to the expansion of a service sector designed to meet new desires.[29] Capital, that is, was obliged to respond to what Hardt and Negri think of as 'new subjectivit-ies'. Second, they take the example of youth counterculture as a signal instance of 'change from below' – or, as they put it, 'Capital did not need to invent a new paradigm (even if it were capable of doing so) because *the truly creative moment had already taken place*'.[30]

But Hardt and Negri's scenario of youthful creativity as the engine that drives changes in capital begs two questions. One, is this kind of creativity available to more directly exploited populations? And two, what does it mean to call 'cre-ative' a refusal that is met so emphatically with a subsumption? That is, why emphasise the creativity of youth culture when it so quickly became a mere market?

In answering these questions, Hardt and Negri tread lightly on the causal links between the rise of new forms of labour in the global north (which they call, in rotating fashion, 'post-Fordist' labor, 'affective labor', and 'immaterial labor'). In this they lag behind thinkers like Gayatri Spivak, who in 1985 had already pointed out that new information systems, which sped up the flow of data in the north and made possible a futurist vision of the home office and the telecommute, were causing an intensification of exploitation in the global south, essentially a work speedup in response to sped-up demand in the

---

28   Hardt and Negri 2000, pp. 273–4.
29   Hardt and Negri 2000, p. 274.
30   Hardt and Negri 2000, p. 276.

north.[31] Like Spivak, however, Hardt and Negri draw attention to the becoming-parallel of exploitative processes in north and south, so that the growth of the service sector in the north, which obliges workers to give over their creativity to seeming nice, or to solving minute problems of client whim, is part of the same process by which the dispossessed of the south are forced into creatively defending their livelihoods and their resources. For Hardt and Negri, 'creativity' in the south looks different, both because the global poor of the south are often the guardians of traditional knowledge that benefits everyone and because they are on the front lines of struggles that implicate everyone. Hardt and Negri's examples stress battles to preserve biodiversity, which they call a form of 'wealth' especially concentrated in the global south.[32]

As for the question of why we should construe as 'creativity' the kinds of refusals of life under capital that seem simply to breed more sophisticated responses from capital's machinery, Hardt and Negri have a slightly unstable answer that splits the difference, you could say, between the social and the ontological. They clearly believe that the priority of inventiveness from below, however constantly it is met with counter-invention by capital, gives those 'below' the edge in seizing their situation and changing it. This seems a perpetual condition of social relations since the rise of capital. But they also seem to believe that this era is special because of the way capital has been obliged to take hold of affect, of creativity, in ever more 'immaterial' ways, raising the possibility that the intensification of capital into the realm of the 'biopolitical' will trigger a massive rejection of its demands, since capital may be approaching too close, as it did in the era of child labour, to a kind of absolute exploitation.

The persuasiveness of these arguments has been at issue since the publication of *Empire* in 2000, perhaps no more acutely than in Gopal Balakrishnan's early and pointed observation that the difference between the multitude and the empire is not so much that the multitude is inventive and empire reactive, but that the empire has more guns.[33] I am going to demur, however, from the question of whether Hardt and Negri have an effective political programme to propose (they don't claim to).

I'd like to spend a moment, instead, to suggest what might be the appeal of work like *Empire* and *Multitude* for readers in the literary academy. I think it lies in Hardt and Negri's argument that, as capital is obliged to colonise more and more 'immaterial' aspects of the labour process, commodifying affect, bodily comportment, information, and knowledge, this colonisation deforms older

31   See Spivak 1988, pp. 154–78.
32   See Hardt and Negri 2004, pp. 131–2.
33   See Balakrishnan 2000.

class categories and makes it harder to describe the world in terms of an industrial proletariat and a capitalist class. In *Multitude*, they call this 'the socialization of all the figures of labor', meaning that older categories – peasant, proletariat, service worker – are alike caught up in new imperatives of capital so that 'the struggles of each sector tend to become the struggle of all'.[34] Though they caution that this 'socialisation' does not mean that all struggles are alike, or that all exploitation is equally intense, their stance clearly makes room for the affect-workers of the northern literary academy to imagine themselves in alliance with the exploited of the global south.

Hardt and Negri's concept of the becoming-social of labour finds expression in the composition of their two books as well. One thing to notice about *Empire* and *Multitude* is that they incorporate a far wider canon of texts than do Agamben or Badiou: they include quotes from ancient and modern literary sources, from popular songs, from political thinkers and economists. Interestingly, though, Hardt and Negri make almost no space for poetry in their work, perhaps because the modern lyric, the most extractable form, lays greater emphasis on individual subjectivity than on the kinds of collective experience they are interested in tracking.

This move in the direction of culling prose sources across fields and genres also leads Hardt and Negri away from the close reading of literary texts. Instead, they strew mention of them throughout *Empire* and *Multitude* in the forms of anecdote, epigraph, sidebar, and what they call 'excurses'. The overall effect of this incorporation of literary material into the two volumes is that each citation carries a lighter burden of exemplarity, and takes on the ready-to-hand character of the aphorism. In pursuing this activity of literary assemblage, Hardt and Negri prove themselves humanists in a textual sense: among other things, *Empire* and *Multitude* are left-wing commonplace books, stuffed full of aphorism, products of the kind of rhetorical invention that reassembles texts to suit an occasion: indeed at the end of *Multitude*, they make specific recourse to the idea of *kairos*, or occasion, in order to highlight that they do not a have a political programme, that programme making is the job of activists, but that they are calling for a kind of *reading* that helps prepare for, and clarify, activism.[35] This inventive textual practice, and its relation to a sense of situation, is perhaps best encapsulated in the very first of their hundreds of citations, a song lyric by Ani DiFranco that appears on the front page of *Empire*: 'Every tool is a weapon if you hold it right'. So the concept of creativity and inventiveness

---

34   Hardt and Negri 2004, p. 125.
35   See Hardt and Negri 2004, p. 357.

that is Hardt and Negri's key to rethinking capital, and the source of the most controversy in their work, has a literary and rhetorical corollary in how they put their books together: they tell a story of inventiveness by way of sustained textual invention.[36]

4   Criticism, 'Theory', and Matter

I conclude my survey of contemporary 'reading on the left' with Hardt and Negri not only because their work, among the major critical theories of the day, offers the most thorough account of the present, but also because it completes a certain critical arc that begins with Jameson. As with Jameson's work, Hardt and Negri's is rooted in an understanding of capital that hinges on the question of the priority of matter and labour. Their emphasis on the primacy of labouring creativity, which has a fifty-year history in Italian *operaismo* ('workerism'), and which has philosophical roots in Spinoza's monism, is a precise counter-position to the Sartrean materialism of Jameson, which gives 'inert' matter priority over human praxis. So we could say that these two accounts of literature's relation to history and politics since the 70s, because they are so firmly rooted in philosophical accounts of matter and labour that worry the question of which comes first, leave us in a kind of manic-depressive readerly situation, where we are invited to read according to whether post-proletarian social movements – multicultural, anti-globalising – are failures awaiting redemption, or upsurges of irrepressible creativity. Either way the post-1968 history of reading on the left, viewed in this light, becomes a history of rushing – first with high hopes, then in disappointment – from one potential exemplarity to the next.

I would like to propose that we literary critics consider another option, which, put most briefly, is the option of thinking of ourselves *as* literary critics, instead of as 'theorists', or activists. Activists we may become – wonderful to think! – but the kinds of things we might learn, in developing literary-critical knowledge, seem to me to have a different relation to politics and history than

---

36 In this practice of assemblage and invention, Hardt and Negri's work parallels two developments in contemporary literary studies: a shift in the scale of reading, driven both by technologies of digital reproduction and data storage, which make it possible to develop new forms of pattern-recognition across many more texts than could be carefully read by a single scholar, and by a new comparativism, which insists on tracking the often-surprising circulation of texts across linguistic and geographical divides. Franco Moretti's recent work on the novel, and Wai-Chee Dimock's research into the 'deep time' of circulation, are defining examples of these new developments. See Dimock 2006, and Moretti 2007.

what was on offer in the age of 'theory', which tried to mediate between criticism and activism by imagining the relation between the two as necessary, or as definitional (not least in a compressed code that went: writing-is-reading / reading-is-literacy / literacy-is-empowerment / empowerment-is-activist). In fact, as I hope I've managed to suggest, 'theory' tended to assimilate literary texts, not to politics, but to philosophical questions about necessity, or about universality and particularity. So let me turn for a moment to a defence of literary criticism that slightly predates the left-wing reading I've outlined here.

In 1957, at the height of the Cold War, Northrop Frye argued in the 'Tentative Conclusion' to *Anatomy of Criticism* that 'no discussion of beauty can confine itself to the formal relations of the isolated work of art; it must consider, too, the participation of the work of art in the vision of the goal of social effort, the idea of complete and classless civilization'.[37] Lest he be mistaken for a Communist, Frye makes clear that his understanding of 'class' is Arnoldian, not Marxist; 'classlessness' in this account amounts to urbanity, to good taste. But alongside the rear-guard action in Frye's formulation there exists a progressive truth, which is this idea of the participation of 'the work of art' in imagining society as other than itself. This is what Jameson means when he writes, retooling Frye in *The Political Unconscious*, that 'no matter how weakly ... all literature must be read as a symbolic meditation on the destiny of community'.[38] Note that this is not a definition of literature; it identifies in literature something Jameson thinks we must attend to. For Frye and Jameson alike, criticism *tracks* literature; they have a mimetic relation, and negative, 'symptomatic', or even antagonist readings by critics of literary texts do not change this relation – they merely strike different notes on its scale.

What this suggests to me is that the more deeply we allow ourselves to understand literary texts as being written out of histories of struggle, of liberation, of toil, the less pressure we will feel to read them 'theoretically', to super-add an activist orientation to them, since they will all the more clearly be documents of a history of human struggles to be free – not least free, for readers of nineteenth- and twentieth-century writing, of the consequences of capitalist exploitation. One thing that emerges, when we allow ourselves to imagine a mimetic relation between literature and criticism along the axis of 'the destiny of community', is the possibility that reading literary texts for marks of how they imagine themselves as literary, as part of the history of literature, is not only self-referential, but referential of literature's shifting position in the history of 'social effort'.

---

37   Frye 1957, p. 348.
38   Jameson 1981, p. 70.

I think allowing for the simultaneously social and intraliterary orientation of our objects of study at the outset places the search for scholarly objectivity on firmer footing: objectivity is to be found not in the ability of literary scholars to read texts from frameworks that bear no trace of the objects they study, but in the historical story that emerges when we read texts for how they participate in the history of what, at different times and places, 'the literary' has meant.

There are many avenues along which we might construct histories of the literary imaginary of literary texts. Because the frame of my essay has been the post-1960s history of 'reading on the left', though, I'd like to highlight one possibility in particular. I have tried to suggest that the strong situational forms of reading that bookend the last third of the twentieth century depend on theories of matter bound up in what comes first – matter 'itself', or human action upon it? I have also tried to suggest that this logical and ontological problem is not well suited to confront the problems of materiality with which literary history presents us – that the philosophical phrasing of what matter is does not match very well the history of literary objects imagining themselves to be one kind of 'matter' or another. I have also argued that the political comportment we are invited to adopt by Jamesonian and Negrian materialisms (or Sartrean and Spinozan materialisms) has tended to fork, meta-historically, in the late twentieth century: we should read for optimism or pessimism, or (put modally) for tragedy or comedy.

So I feel enabled by work like Jameson's, and Hardt and Negri's, to understand literary history as part of a broad history of social and political struggle, and eager to expand our understanding of 'political struggle' so as to include under its rubric struggles to survive, to love, to live in safety and in joy that may not at first have seemed 'political' *per se*. And I am convinced that to read literature as part of a human struggle to be free necessarily includes reading literature for its engagement with 'matter' – with its production, its appearance, its working and reworking. But I think we need an account of literary materialisms closer to the ground of literary history than what is on offer by the strongest left-wing theoretical materialisms, which quickly become full-on philosophies of history before they have really absorbed the particulars of literary history (which, after all, may seem a mere by-way or rest stop in the rush to theorise History, capital *H*). I don't mean that the 'literary' is a single thing, or an unconstructed thing, or that it is not riven by internal contradictions; but I think there is a record, in the writing we have come to call 'literary', of how that writing conceives of its literariness, and I think that record could inform a history of 'matter' that makes more sense for literature. My own investigation into this question in the archive of twentieth-century poetry in English suggests, for one thing, that the history of poetic materialism is less heroic, less clearly tragic or comic, than the theoretical accounts would suggest, and more scatter-shot, more ad hoc, and more protective of 'poetry' than prescriptive of political action. It is also more linked than we might think to the educational traditions by which written poetry has been made part of the body of 'literature' in the West – more linked, that is, to the long history of poetry as a tool and occasion for the teaching of rhetoric and grammar, where 'matter' has its own meanings.

5   A Poem

I'd like to conclude with a brief reading of a contemporary poem. Poetry is underrepresented in the post-1968 English-language literary criticism of the Left, even as it has emerged, at least in North America, as an extremely fine-grained and inventive medium for understanding the present – not least the present in which capital has achieved the spectacular form Guy Debord described for it in 1967, where the awesomeness of capital's productive power mediates all social relations.[39] So while I don't mean for the poems that follow to bear excessive exemplary weight, I do think there's an interesting story to be told about twentieth-century poetry and twentieth-century capital. And one chapter of this story has to do with how English-language poets since the 1980s have deployed figures of literacy and reading, not as 'post-modern' or self-referential tropes, but as indices to the history of poetry and to how its assembly of textual 'matter' competes with the massive organisation of matter under capital. This is true when Michael Palmer writes, at the beginning of his astonishing 1988 poem 'sun',

> Write this. We have burned all their villages
> Write this. We have burned all the villages and the people in them
> Write this. We have adopted their customs and their manner of dress[40]

Or when Lyn Hejinian, in her 1994 volume *The Cold of Poetry*, writes,

> 'Depress the world'
> with true literary realism – that is, words
>   as they are[41]

---

39   See Debord 2006.
40   Palmer 2001, p. 233.
41   Hejinian 1994, p. 163.

Or when Harryette Mullen writes, in the *abécédaire* (called 'Jingle Jangle') she includes in her 2002 collection, *Sleeping with the Dictionary*,

> Backtrack backpack Bahama Mama balls to the wall bam-a-lam band-
> stand
> Battle in Seattle beat the meat bee's knees behani ghani best-dressed.[42]

All these poems, which are in conversation with the influential avant-garde movement called 'Language Poetry', riff on figures and concepts of the acquis-ition of literacy in order to investigate what kind of 'matter' poetry might be – and, often explicitly, to set that matter against other 'matters' that seem to operate on a much larger scale (Vietnam, in Palmer's poem; or 'the world' in Hejinian; or the 'Jingle Jangle' of spectacular noise that includes 'The Battle in Seattle', in Mullen).

The poem I'd like to look at, which participates in this recent poetic history, is from Lisa Robertson's 2001 book *The Weather*. Robertson grew up poetically in the very active scene around the writer-organised Kootenay School of Writing in Vancouver, though she now lives in the United States. *The Weather* grew out of research into what Robertson calls 'the rhetorical structure of English met-eorological description'. Written during a fellowship at Cambridge University, it cites and reworks language from BBC shipping forecasts, Sprat's *History of the Royal Society*, Wordsworth's *Prelude*, and William Cobbett's *Rural Rides*, among many other sources. It is prefaced with a passage from the *Arcades Project*: 'Architecture, fashion – yes, even the weather – are, in the interior of the col-lective, what the sensoria of organs, the feeling of sickness or health, are in the individual'. The book is organised in sections named for the days of the week, punctuated by shorter parts called 'Residence at C'. Here is one of those parts:

> Give me hackneyed words because
> they are good. Brocade me the whole body
> of terrestrial air. Say spongy ground
> with its soft weeds. Say self because it can.
> Say arts of happiness. Say you have died.
> Say sequin because the word just
> appeared. Say weather take this adult
> from its box. Memorize being sequined
> to something, water. Everything you forget

---

42   Mullen 2002, p. 34.

inserts love into the silent money.
Memorize huge things of girders greased. Say
the water parting about the particular
animal. Say what happens to the face
as it gala tints my simple cut
vicious this afternoon the beautiful
light on the cash is human to guzzle
with – go away wild feelings, there you go
as the robin as the songsparrow go
the system shines with uninterrupted
light. It's petal caked. Leaves shoot up. Each
leaf's a runnel. Far into the night a
sweetness. Marvelous. Spectacular. Brilliant.
Clouded towards the south. It translates
Lucretius. Say cup of your heart rush
sluice is yellow sluice Kate Moss is Rousseau
have my arms. Say impasto of
atmosphere for her fur. Halo open
her face. Misplace the death. All the truth
under the tree has two pinky oozy
names. Say trying to possess or not. Say
if you thought love was ironical. If
pleasure emancipates, why aren't you some-
where. Sincerity.[43]

The poem begins in praise of deep mundanity, of the 'hackneyed words' about the weather that we use to pass the time, placeholder language that keeps us in each other's company though it may not carry lots of information. But the weather is a topic, in the old sense of a topic in rhetoric, and the rest of the poem plays with the idea of poetry as a school art, medium for rhetoric but also for grammar and for elocution. It is written largely in imperatives: Say this, say that. Memorise. 'It translates / Lucretius' – the most didactic poet on the least exotic subject, the nature of things. The poem is engaged in something like a humanist project of stylistic pedagogy, arranging utterances in anthology form. It is itself, I think we can say, hermeneutical: the reader of the poem is not the only one doing the work of interpretation.

---

43   Robertson 2001, pp. 14–15.

The poet is also engaged in a memory practice, in the form of an anatomy of pleasures she is worried she'll forget. It's an anatomy not only of 'the whole body / of terrestrial air' but also of the 'self', the 'adult', the 'particular animal' – its face, its haircut, its feelings, its heart, its arms. Memorising these, the poem suggests, is a stay against the problem of money; but money is fused with the medium of perception, light:

> Everything you forget
> inserts love into the silent money.
>
> the beautiful
> light on the cash is human to guzzle
> with
> ...
> the system shines with uninterrupted
> light.

Robertson seems to be saying that any lapse of our attention to what we love hurries love off to capital; she is noticing that it is perfectly human to want to soak up the light, but that whatever it falls on, it is always falling on cash, so that one cannot perceive without ingesting it; and she is saying that there is no pause in the light, so that to seek pleasure is to become sutured – 'sequined', in the poem's language – to an unending process that sounds a lot like the spectacle.

Robertson's speaker is a feminist, and she wants to believe in a politics of the body and its pleasures, but the twining together of beauty to money has left her dismayed:

> If
> pleasure emancipates, why aren't you some-
> where. Sincerity.

So what, as they say, is to be done? The poem does not answer this question, but the one it does pursue may be more appropriate to literary criticism: what's going on? I think poetry is especially useful as a record of how print textuality, passed down to us out of a humanist configuration of rhetoric, grammar, and criticism, is constantly being refigured and retooled into new forms of textual matter so as to meet what capital makes into material. Some poetry seeks to keep up with it, to outmanoeuvre it; some poetry seeks to stave it off; some poetry seeks homoeopathic contact with it, so as to make itself immune to it.

These relations are all experimental, and they are liable to failure; indeed, in a Sartrean mode we should expect them to fail. But their failure is not the most interesting thing, or even the most literary-historically important thing about them. Even if revolution remains the limit-horizon against which we measure literary dreaming, its wishes for arcadia or its visions of suffering, that does not mean that the critic has only the measure from text to revolution to name. We don't know what revolution will look like, what it will seize hold of, because the history of the capture of material life by capital, and of resistance to it, is still being written. And in any case, cultivating revolutionary consciousness may not be a job we need to do; the comment boxes underneath the articles on the subprime mortgage fiasco show clearly enough that in a crisis, everyone is capable of systemic thinking. But we may be the best trained in the custodial job of maintaining and arranging texts according to the anatomies they suggest, and the questions they pose: do feelings move as fast as money? Does language? Assembling the textual body that tracks these questions, even if they shift like clouds, can help us rethink the meanings of literary and rhetorical materiality; and I think we can learn from this assembly a little bit about the workings of another 'matter' – matter in the sense of the deeds of a mighty protagonist, as Arthur's were known by the name The Matter of Britain, or Charlemagne's The Matter of France. I think if we can learn to read the weather we will better understand The Matter of Capital.

CHAPTER 4

Affect, Performativity, and Actually Existing Poetry

This essay thinks about how the conjunction of the keywords 'affect' and 'performativity' in U.S. literary studies encodes a theoretical story about literature and politics, especially poetry and politics, that has drifted from the actual poetry written in the States since the mid-twentieth century. In the first part of the essay I try to piece apart this theoretical story, and in the second I turn to the work of the poet Jack Spicer, who is enjoying a significant revival in the U.S. at the moment, as a way of beginning to tell stories about poetry and politics other than the affective-performative one that became so dominant in the era of the American consumption of French theory.

First, though, I should note that in the American literary academy, the field first called to mind by the words 'affect' and 'performativity' is the field of queer theory – which begins with deep debts to French post-structuralism but quickly puts French theory's presuppositions and insights to quite different use. Judith Butler's work in the early 1990s on the performative and citational character of sexuality made it possible for scholars of sexuality to imagine strong accounts of sexual identity that were not etiological – an immense benefit after more than a century of pathologising, origin-obsessed descriptions of sexual identity in the medical and social sciences. In a similar way, the work of Eve Kosofsky Sedgwick on the dynamics of shame – especially as she began to make use of models of affect like those of Silvan Tompkins – allowed scholars in the humanities to imagine that affect could be studied, not only for its origins, but for its variety. Sedgwick's work was especially emphatic in its detourning of the question 'why are there gay people in the world?' – which she rightly took to imply an obsession with figuring out how to engineer their presence out of it.[1]

In the 1990s, then, queer theory formed a riposte or counter-movement to the becoming-scientific of American psychoanalysis, whose mutation into professional psychology and psychiatry at mid-century was closely tied to the military's need to assess the fitness of soldiers for the work of war. Queer theorists, as if in response, turned to literary writing, especially fictional narrative, to overturn the categorical and pathologising styles of knowing that the military-industrial boom had helped facilitate. Fiction in particular provided

---

1   See, of course, Butler 1990. Sedgwick's work on Tompkins is redacted in Sedgewick 1995, and her remark about the will to erasure lurking in the desire to know the 'cause' of homosexuality can be found in Sedgewick 1993.

these scholars a rich terrain by which to study the ways in which the seeming autonomy of character was in fact enmeshed in other features of storytelling – was inseparable, in fact, from plot, discursive aspect, and point-of-view. And in a Foucauldian turn, in these accounts enmeshment was cousin to freedom, since, unlike bourgeois notions of the autonomy of character, queer-theroetical accounts focused on affect and linguistic performance saw character as *relational*.[2]

So the conjunction of 'affect' and 'performativity' in U.S. literary studies has strong liberatory overtones. But the rise of those two keywords is linked back to the emergence of a post-structuralism with different aims and somewhat different coordinates, which for my purposes here include a preference for poetic over fictional examples and an anti-scientism aimed, not at the professionalised therapeutic arts, but at the scientific pretensions of Marxism.

This pre-history also has roots in the Second World War. In post-war France, the diverse writers of the *Tel Quel* group began to carve out a notion of literature as 'writing' that emphasised, instead of the genius of any particular author, or the canon-worthiness of any particular text, the self-reflexive, theoretical practice shared by writers of poetry, fiction, journalism, and philosophy. This reformulation of literature into 'writing' drew on both the semiotics of Barthes and the Russian Formalism of the 1920s, which was being translated into French in the late 1960s and early 1970s. Through its many twists and turns (apolitical beginnings, an alliance with the Communist Party of France, its dalliance with Maoism) the *Tel Quel* group argued for a medium-specificity of 'language' that was innately political, and in need of no external ideological support for its politics. This put them at odds with Sartre, whose engaged existentialism presumed that authors, not writing, were the vector of politics. This politicisation of 'language', then, was also a critique of existentialist Marxism.[3]

By the time of the rise of literary post-structuralism in France and the U.S., this earlier debate had congealed into a kind of fossil-layer under the ground, invisible to surface observation but rich in useful fuel. To get a clear sense of the relationship between politics and literature in this work therefore requires a bit of lingering: its polemics are often embedded in what seem like purely local gestures. But I would like to linger briefly with some examples of it because, at least in the U.S., its sidelong propositions about the political character of literature became reflex assumptions before they were ever made explicit.

---

2   Again, Sedgwick's work is crucial here. See essays collected in Sedgewick 1997.
3   For good English-language work on the post-war milieu of French intellectual life, and the germinating conditions of post-structuralism, see Marx-Scouras 1996, Holsinger 2005, and Cusset 2008.

The late work of Paul de Man, especially the work collected in the volume *Aesthetic Ideology*, gives a good sense of how 'affect' and 'performativity' were used in his writing. In the well-known essay 'Phenomenality and Materiality in Kant', de Man locates a 'deep, perhaps fatal break' in Kant's *Critique of Judgement* (1790), which is caused by Kant's inability to understand that words for beauty are not simply part of a catalogue – they cannot be typologised or made into a system without cost to their nuance.[4] To put it another way, de Man is impatient with Kant's reduction of language to 'a system of tropes', not least after Kant has been obliged to acknowledge, in attempting to develop an account of the sublime, that there is a dynamic and not merely descriptive relation between language and the world in the moment of sublimity. As de Man phrases it, 'From the pseudocognition of tropes, language has to expand to the activity of performance'.[5] What 'performance' means here is a kind of preconscious mimesis or echo-system in which words and phrases call each other up like a rebus, in a drive more powerful than even the driest of philosophy can regulate. De Man calls it 'the play of the letter and the syllable' – and he says it forces even Kant to modulate from a faculty model of psychology to one 'mediated by affects, moods, and feelings'.[6] This appearance of linguistic play in the activity of writing, when the writer cannot help but, say, include in his text multiple words with '-ll' in them – this appearance is what de Man means by the performative, and he views it as a kind of mundane violence (it leads us to break down words into their component parts) that philosophers ignore at cost to analytic clarity.

One way to read the idea of the performative in de Man, then, is as a mark of the differences in analytic rigour between disciplines. In another late essay, 'Kant's Materialism', de Man writes that 'Kant is never as bland as when he discusses the emotions', suggesting that what his writing misses is the 'interpretive sensitivity, the affective cogito that one can capture in Montaigne, in Malebranche, or in the Romantics'.[7] It's not just that Kant's philosophy is weak on the emotions because of a weakness in his understanding of language; it's that the performative powers of language, which de Man suggests Kant understands full well, simply cannot be incorporated into any philosophy in a Kantian vein.

When de Man refers to 'Kant's materialism', then, he is being ironic: the formal system into which Kant attempts to incorporate affect, mood, linguistic

---

4   de Man 1996a, p. 79.
5   Ibid.
6   de Man 1996a, pp. 89, 80.
7   de Man 1996a, p. 123.

performance – this system has already de-materialised matter after the manner of a comfy beachside encounter with a storm far from shore: 'Poets, in Kant, do not embark on the high seas'.[8] He has still more stringent ironies reserved for the misguided 'materialists' of the contemporary literary academy: 'Theoreticians of literature who fear that they may have deserted or betrayed the world by being too formalistic are worrying about the wrong thing: in the spirit of Kant's third *Critique*, they were not nearly formalistic enough'.[9]

Lest the Marxist materialist miss the irony, de Man makes sure to dismiss the critical force of their other key concept. In another late essay on Kant, de Man rejects the notion that the movement by which philosophical contemplation is disrupted by linguistic performance can be understood by way of the dialectic:

> At that moment things *happen*, there is *occurrence*, there is *event*. History is therefore not a temporal notion, it has nothing to do with temporality, but it is the emergence of a language of power out of a language of cognition. An emergence which is, however, not itself either a dialectical movement or any kind of continuum ...[10]

This anti-dialectical loyalty to the pre-contextual 'event', so closely linked in de Man to properly professional literary reading, is cousin to another key anti-Hegelian moment in French post-structuralism, which is to be found in the work of Jacques Derrida. Briefly, then, I'd like to turn to a crucial theoretical story of Derrida's.

Over the course of his long career, Derrida revised his thinking about literature, philosophy and politics countless times, but his early work is very clear in establishing a set of founding relays among those domains. So I'd like to take a look at his influential 1966 essay, 'From Restricted to General Economy: A Hegelianism without Reserve'. The piece leans on Alexandre Kojève's Marxian interpretation of Hegel in order to produce an allegory of Hegelian negativity as industrial labour; then, enabled by this analogy or allegory, it turns to Bataille and a Kierkegaardian absurdism to argue that the negative must be understood in terms other than those to which philosophy submits it; the negative, for Derrida, is constantly being brought into philosophical service – exploited, he suggests – as the other of meaning, providing the prompt to philosophical concept-honing. But it cannot be assimilated to such uses.

---

8   de Man 1996a, p. 127.
9   de Man 1996a, p. 128.
10   de Man 1996a, p. 133.

Derrida's essay makes two key moves that, taken together, proved extremely persuasive on American shores. One is to transpose the question of the exploitation of labour into a philosophical register, by reading it as the capture and exploitation of negativity by philosophy, where it is forced into the work of systematic thinking. The other is to suggest that the true character of the negative is expressed in chance and in play, and that this true character of the negative is best understood in literary terms – or, more specifically, modernist poetic terms, best exemplified by Mallarmé's *Un coup de dés jamais n'abolira le hasard*. Derrida gestures at Mallarmé's poem this way:

> The poetic or ecstatic is that *in every discourse* which can open itself up to the absolute loss of its sense, to the (non-)base of the sacred, of nonmeaning, of un-knowledge or play, to the swoon from which it is reawakened by a throw of the dice.[11]

This move is significant because, having transposed the question of labour into a philosophical question of negativity, and having implicity posited the modernist poetics of Mallarmé as a privileged site for the expression of the negativity that philosophy seeks to capture, Derrida aligns the poetic specificity of the modernist lyric with the uncapturable life-force of the rebellious worker. He contrasts the 'master' of Hegel's master-slave dialectic with a Bataillean 'sovereign' who laughs at philosophy's mere 'amortisation' of the negative, who laughs at death: 'laughter alone exceeds dialectics and the dialectician'.[12] Noting that 'philosophy is work *itself*' for Bataille', he adds that Hegelian *Aufhebung* is 'laughable' because it is merely a '*busying*' of discourse' that starts panting as it 'reappropriates all negativity for itself'.[13] Philosophy, here, is a huffing bourgeois.

Now the bourgeoisie, as a mercantile or a professional class, are not entirely, or not necessarily, the same as the industrial capitalist class that actually *would* compel labour; so we should note another slight shift or transposition in the Marxian critique here. Similarly, note that it is not capital, but the dialectic, that is the enemy – so that the militant worker, when the moment of rebellion finally becomes possible, rebels not against capital, but against philosophy. Indeed, at the moment when Derrida's allegory depicts rebellion, 'the negative' – figured, Derrida says, in the Hegelian slave, who Derrida says Kojève suggests is the worker – at the moment of rebellion, the worker looks more existential than

---

11   Derrida 1980, p. 261.
12   Derrida 1980, p. 256.
13   Derrida 1980, pp. 252, 257.

militant.[14] Indeed he looks more like a Resistance fighter in World War II than a proletarian. Here is Derrida's gloss on the negative in Bataille:

> [it] can no longer be called negative precisely because it has no reserved underside, because it can no longer permit itself to be converted into positivity, it can no longer *collaborate* with the continuous linking-up of meaning, concept, time, and truth in discourse; because it literally can no longer *labor* and let itself be interrogated as 'the work of the negative'.[15]

Note the italicised word 'collaborate' in this passage, which to my ear is a giveaway signal that the allegory of the negative-as-worker has now received an overlay of wartime militancy.

What all these deft allegorical, anthropomorphic, and transposing gestures accomplish, for Derrida, is the insight that German dialectical philosophy is no match for French literary modernism:

> In interpreting negativity as labor, in betting for discourse, meaning, history, etc., Hegel has bet against play, against chance. He has blinded himself ... to the fact that play *includes* the work of meaning or the meaning of work.[16]

In 1966, this overlay of the figure of the militant Resistance fighter on top of the figure of the worker, who is cannier than the philosopher-bourgeois about the work-cancelling play that modern poetry highlights, is a kind of backward glance. But it is also an echo of a contemporary development in French politics. Here is a key passage from the 1966 Situationist pamphlet *On The Poverty of Student Life*:

> For the proletariat revolt is a festival or it is nothing: in revolution the road of excess leads to the palace of wisdom. A palace which knows only one rationality: the game. The rules are simple: to live instead of devising a lingering death, and to indulge untrammeled desire.[17]

The distribution of this pamphlet by the students of the University of Strasbourg helped trigger, two years later, the student alliance with workers in the

---

14   Derrida 1980, p. 276.
15   Derrida 1980, pp. 259–60.
16   Derrida 1980, p. 260.
17   See Ford 2005.

uprisings of May 1968; and it remains an exemplary text for non-Communist Party, Marxist anti-capitalism in France. I cannot trace the lines of commonality or influence between Derrida and the Situationists with much precision here; it is hard to say whether Derrida is leaning on rebellious student energies, or the students are picking up on something that Derrida is also aware of, a critique of Communist Party politics that is registered as a romantic (here, Blakean) critique of Hegel (the 'lingering death' of the dialectic as work, as opposed to 'untrammeled desire', which Derrida renders, in the title of his essay, as 'Hegelianism without reserve').

What has become clear with time, though, is that the leveraging of modernist poetry into an anti-dialectical argument with Hegel (and implicitly, doctrinaire, party-line Marxism) becomes *the* gesture into which the idea of 'poetry' is incorporated in the French theory that travelled to American shores in the 1970s and 1980s. This anti-dialecticism is emphatically present in Julia Kristeva's 1974 *Revolution in Poetic Language*, which pits the disruptive literary practice of Mallarmé and Lautréamont against a psychoanalytic subject falsely unified by the state and society. And it organises Jean-Luc Nancy's 1982 *The Inoperative Community*, which cites Bataille's remark in *Literature and Evil* (1957) that 'Literature cannot assume the task of directing collective necessity' in order to position a Levinasian-Heideggerian understanding of poetry as an 'interruption' against both those literary texts that seek after mere produced beauty, and that late Marxism that imagines state-managed 'productivity' as the only engine of history.[18] This is not to mention the work of Gilles Deleuze and Félix Guattari, or, more recently, Alain Badiou, who have all kept alive, from very different philosophical positions, the practice of pitting one literary modernism or another against a cartoon of Hegel made to stand in for something like either the rigidness or the insufficient militancy of the French Communist Party.

So when we speak, in the U.S. at least, about 'affect' and 'performativity', we are not only silently glossing the rise of an American queer theory in which both keywords signal the escape from an orthodoxy – either Freud's, or that of a scientised psychoanalysis. We are also glossing a French intellectual and political history in which literary studies, under cover of structuralism, lays claim to the autonomy and priority of an idea of poetry over and against mid-twentieth-century versions of both cognitivist and dialectical philosophy – which is to say, over and against both instrumental reason and Communist 'science'.

---

18   Nancy 1991, p. 77.

There is a third layer to this American absorption of the idea of the per-
formative, though, which involves a rejection of the scientific pretensions of
literary post-structuralism itself – a residual urge-to-structure that, from the
vantage of the queer American 90s, seemed to tend towards political quiet-
ism. If the rise of student movements in the late 1960s gave non-Communist
Party, left-wing French intellectuals a way to outmanoeuvre what they took
to be the failings of a structure-dependent Marxism that yearned helplessly
for a working-class uprising that never arrived, American queer theorists of
the 1990s were able to draw on the then-insurgent energies of queer move-
ment politics to move even further away from a post-structuralist competition
between literary formalism and dialectical materialism, and to turn instead to
figures of the expressive body as the metonym for a different idea of perform-
ativity.

I think this is what enables Judith Butler, in her 1997 *Excitable Speech*, to
identify a too-abstract opposition between structure and style in her critique
of Pierre Bourdieu, and also to bat back at an allegory of structure-versus-
utterance in Derrida's work on the performative. Looking back, one can read
into her critique of Derrida a counter-allegory in which the merely 'semantic'
functions as a social energy that can actually influence the social 'structure'
that should, according to a Derridean scheme, work on an entirely other plane.
Reading Derrida's 1972 essay 'signature Event Context', she asks why his account
of performativity requires that 'the structural [always] exceeds and opposes the
semantic, and the semantic is always crossed and defeated by the structural?'[19]
As a way of leaving behind the political attitude embedded in this account –
be it defeatism, or resignation, or even a kind of theodicy – Butler argues, later
in the book, that 'No act of speech can fully control or determine the rhetorical
effects of the body which speaks'.[20]

This idea of the body as rhetorical re-situates 'performativity' twice, we
might say: first, by locating its political force in its medium, the body, rather
than in the separation between utterance and structure, *langue* and *parole*,
and second, by highlighting the power of the body as rhetorical rather than lin-
guistic. These shifts allow Butler, and much of the queer theory that followed
her, to do justice to the queer movement energies of the era – that is, to ima-
gine utterances that don't merely reply to structures, but to alter them. Later
in her career, this move will also allow her to link the performative to an idea
of 'doing justice to someone', as in her beautiful and heartbreaking essay on

---

19   Butler 1997, p. 150.
20   Butler 1997, p. 156.

David Reimer, the Canadian man who was forcibly raised as a girl after a failed medical procedure.[21]

In the 90s, though, to do justice to a queer body was more often than not to take into account that body's susceptibility to devastation, not least because of the AIDS epidemic. And so the American transposition of the performative to the zone of the body, and to the terrain of rhetoric, carries with it not only insurgent energies ready to shake off an earlier defeatism, but also a deep solicitude for the body's vulnerability. So the intertwining of militancy and solicitude we can find in Butler, for instance, finds cousin formulations in Leo Bersani's 1995 volume *Homos*, where the expressivity of the queer body at once re-writes deep psychoanalytic scripts but also opens onto new terrain for figuring humanity as the capacity to be tender. Take this passage, which utterly re-works the idea of the threat of paternal castration:

> We might imagine that a man being fucked is generously offering the sight of his own penis as a gift or even a replacement for what is temporarily being 'lost' inside him – an offering made not in order to calm his partner's fears of castration but rather as the gratuitous and therefore even lovelier protectiveness all human begins need when they take the risk of merging with one another.[22]

I can't recall another moment in 90s queer theory that so fully exemplifies the American transposition of 'affect' and 'performativity' into the militant, solicitous structure of feeling that takes up residence in the zone of the body – here, ferociously insisting in the specificity and worth of gay male sexual fantasy while ushering into the scene of its enactment a new universalism. Like Butler's transposition of the question of performativity from the terrain of structuralist and post-structuralist analogies to linguistics, and into rhetoric, here Bersani transposes the body's affects and its performative life into the realm of aesthetic experience: indeed it recalls the many places in Adorno's aesthetics where the body helplessly emblematises and enacts the origins of mimesis.[23]

Now, what does this all have to do with poetry? Well, for me, coming of intellectual age in the queer 1990s, the connections were clear. Since I witnessed a transposition of the great 'turn to language' from a French analogy between literary study and linguistics to an American insistence on the rhetorical and

---

21   See Butler 2004.
22   Bersani 1995, p. 112.
23   See, for instance, the astonishing passage on the shapes of the bodies of rhinoceri in Adorno 1973, p. 180.

aesthetic dimensions of any analogy to 'language', a transposition driven both by queer activism and by the AIDS epidemic, I felt licensed to begin reading poetry otherwise than I had first been taught – otherwise, that is, than the post-structuralist insistence on the *prima facie* political character of the lyric understood as 'language' *per se*. What if one began reading poems, even poems called 'Language', not as instances of 'performativity' and 'affect' pitted against linguistic structures, but as the rhetorical and aesthetic practices of particular poets in particular times and places?

∶

In the rest of this essay I will trace the local byways of a 'turn to language' in one influential poetic subculture of the 1950s and 1960s, the circle around Jack Spicer that was the scene of the Berkeley and San Francisco 'renaissances'. Like de Man, Spicer thought of poems as *events* in language; but he developed his ideas, not as a critique of dialectical thinking, but as a strategic response to the new forms of commodity, spectacle, and enclosure that took hold in San Francisco at mid-century. I will suggest that the meanings of 'language' generated by Spicer give rise to a second idea about the social function of poetic form, which is to hide and protect forms of experience that are endangered by the encroachments of capital on subcultural life. Indeed one of the reasons Spicer's profile in the literary academy has remained low since his death in 1965 is that he was so committed to poetry *as* subcultural. He was suspicious of East Coast literary life, the life of the prominent journals, even though he submitted poems to them; he would not sell his own books, sending copies only to those who bothered to write him personally to request a copy; and he urged others in his circle – you might say he policed them – to do likewise. Spicer's biographers Kevin Killian and Lewis Ellingham tell a story about how Spicer, on hearing that the poet Philip Whalen had been offered the then-significant sum of ten dollars to read at a poetry festival, said 'I'll offer him $11 not to read'.[24]

Spicer always insisted on a continuity between poetic form and what he took to be right social relations in a poetic subculture. Both things, he felt, are shaped by crisis, which itself took many forms, from a resistance to the commercialisation of the North Beach Bars where he and his cohort hung out, to a dread about the emerging possibility of nuclear war in the 1950s. Killian and Ellingham write about Spicer being terrified of the possibility of a Russian invasion

---

24   Ellingham and Killian 1998, p. 240.

during the Cuban Missile Crisis in 1962, to the point of advising friends to start saving water; they also recount his disgust with the music of the Beatles, whose songs began to displace the kind of noise Spicer and his crowd liked to generate in the bars of North Beach. Where the Spicer circle had once instigated a popular 'Blabbermouth Night', in which patrons were urged on to ever-greater feats of spontaneous hyperbole and nonsense, by 1962 the North Beach bars were ever friendlier to that music Spicer called 'devoid of form and color, but full of images'.[25] So when he writes, in the 1963 sequence he called 'Thing Language',

> I
> Can-
> not
> accord
> sympathy
> to
> those who
> do
> not
> recognize
> The human crisis.[26]

He is both trying to name something that takes many forms, and trying to preserve the boundaries between those who do and those who don't stay true to the medium he held so dear.

I say 'medium' rather than 'form' because it was a significant feature of Spicer's sense of poetry that it was part of language, intermixed with other kinds, but stashed away in it, liable to flash out at any moment, easy to miss, and important to protect. In his 1961 sequence *Lament For The Makers*, Spicer rehearses an anecdote about the corpse of D.H. Lawrence that gives a good sense of how he conceived poetic form as medium-based:

> Then Frieda [Lawrence, the writer's wife] told us an incredible story. Someone who wanted Lawrence – and Frieda named the possessive admirer – wanted him in death as well as in life. Frieda's house was invaded and Lawrence's ashes were stolen.

25   Ellingham and Killian 1998, pp. 99–100, 255, 306.
26   Spicer 2008, p. 379.

'You can believe', said Frieda, 'I had a hard time getting them back. But I recovered them. And I made up my mind that nothing of the sort should happen again. So I fixed it'.

'How?' we asked. 'What did you do?'

'I had the ashes mixed with a lot of sand and concrete. Now they are in a huge concrete slab. It weighs over a ton'. She laughed heartily. 'A dozen men could not lift it'.[27]

If we want a ready allegory for Spicer's sense of poetic form, there is none more illuminating than this one – 'form' is a simultaneous scattering and preservation of poetic language that is designed to prevent thievery or mis-use. It is designed to create a relationship of initiation between poet and reader, where the reader must work, not to become learned, or to assemble a whole out of fragments, as in the Pound tradition, but to catch the flash of the poetic before it is re-submerged in protective camouflage.

By these lights poetic form is minimally distinguishable from other linguistic strategies: Spicer's friend Jim Herndon recalls Spicer's relationship with his three-year-old son Jay, and how Spicer would tell the boy that the real name for his unwanted potatoes and broccoli was 'Child Psychology', or roar, when he left the Herndon's apartment at the end of the night, that he was 'Goin' to Texas!' As Herndon puts it:

> Children ought to be told a random combination of fantasy, outright lies and simple truth, all in the same tone of voice. The Giant's Garden, pigs can fly, cows eat grass. Correctly applied, this principle would keep the child's mind inviolate, curious, alert, and above all, wary.[28]

Years later, the poet and critic Bruce Boone would write about this insistence of Spicer's on the mixing – and the mixedness – of truth and untruth, 'The real and fake only make sense in terms of some always-seeming-to-be-impending disaster. You better be careful, is Spicer's advice – you might miss the point if you [aren't]'.[29]

So poetic language is meant to be only minimally different from its surroundings, though it is also different in kind. The worst fate for poetry is to have that minimal relational difference made absolute. Here is another parable of concrete, a gloss on the California poet Robinson Jeffers from 'Thing Language':

---

27   Spicer 2008, p. 113.
28   Herndon 1974, p. 57.
29   Boone 1983, p. 120.

A redwood forest is not invisible at night. The blackness covers it but it covers the blackness.

If they had turned Jeffers into a parking lot death would have been eliminated and birth also. The lights shine 24 hours a day on a parking lot.

True conservation is the effort of the artist and the private man to keep things true. Trees and the cliffs in Big Sur breathe in the dark. Jeffers knew the pain of their breath and the pain was the death of a first-born baby breathing. Death is not final. Only parking lots.[30]

Worse than death, here, is 24-hour illumination, the kind of brightness 'full of images' but 'devoid of form and color' that Spicer heard in The Beatles. Poetry, cicadian and respiratory, takes in and gives out its context; but the spectacle – and it's the spectacle we're talking about here, in Guy Debord's sense – the spectacle obliterates these rhythms and miscibilities. To fend off such flattening, Spicer always chose confrontation – ironically, confrontation with his friends and fellow writers. He kept a cordon, or a minor kind of counter-enclosure, separating those who did and those who didn't resist the 24-hour glare of the emergent spectacle. Anyone could cross over, if they proved true to his sense of poetry as more than aesthetic, but he did not hold back from denouncing those who lingered on the other side.

Spicer's companions resisted what they saw as his tests of loyalty, even as they admired his will to purity in writing. The record of their skirmishes is considerable; here is a piece of correspondence between Spicer and the younger writer Stan Persky, who published Spicer in his North Beach magazine *Open Space*. Spicer writes across town to the magazine (whose name, we should notice, speaks against exactly the enclosure of subculture):

July 30, 1964

Dear Stan Persky (I add the last name because I am sick of the tea-party first name business, my fault as well as yours, as if Open Space were a Turkish Bath of the imagination):

The only poem that interested me in the whole July issue (including my own) was the rhymed poem called 'Underwier' about half-way through the issue. Though the signature of it is given as Lew Ellingham, he tells me that the authors, in tandem, were you, Ron Primack, and Jim Alexander. The poem seems to me better than anything the three of you have written in the last two years and I wonder why you did not give your names to it.

Something happened. It isn't happening often enough now and I wonder if the accusation against Open Space is not that it is too homosexual but that it is too homogenous. Like cartons of milk.

...

I am, nonetheless, submitting poems in this August issue and will continue to even if things get worse.

Sincerely yours,

Jack Spicer

Persky replies:

Dear Jack,

This is the last 'Open Space' – like the end of part one; but not the end of the magazine – because as a poet my business is to do what's really real. The only point where you and I agree now is that people don't read poetry; hardly anymore.

Trying to figure out [...] how to be fair [to you] is hard, who have so often used unfairness for your way. Even in my dreams you confuse me by two of you: Dirty Jack and Radiant Jack. In one part I come into your room, your back to me, I see your elbows in the holes of your shirt, the oily glass, the back of you looms up big as a ship, and you growl and tell me to give it up. In Radiant Jack you yourself come to the warehouse where we're working, wearing clean sports-clothes, and you have tickets to the ballgame for me. It isn't that you've given little or withheld too much [...] but it seems to me you want a world small enough so that wherever you spit you'll hit something, a world you can control.[31]

At the time of this exchange, Spicer was 39, Persky 23. Persky senses that Spicer's resistance to the commodification of poetry, to its becoming-homogenous like 'cartons of milk', has resulted in its own form of enclosure, 'a world small enough' that 'wherever you spit you'll hit something'. Persky cannot experience the two practices – the serial quest for poetic purity, with its alluring integrity, and the stern, even cruel, rejection of friendliness, with its concomitant enclosure, its cordoned-off 'world' – as coming from the same person: hence 'Dirty Jack' and 'Radiant Jack'. But the two men of the dream – the grubby, cruel,

---

31   Ellingham and Killian 1998, pp. 302–3.

impoverished one, and the fresh, flush, generous one – are both bound up in what Persky renders as 'the warehouse', the scene of shared poetic labour that Spicer is willing to picket, as it were, if it threatens to produce commodities instead of poems. The young Persky senses the tension at the heart of Spicer's work, or its greatest challenge: it is a poetics of social relation, which implies at every turn that social relations must be managed as part of the poetic process. Spicer envisions that management as the keeping of his cohort clear of the market, but his friends experience it as volatile and ambivalent, both a form of integrity and an intimidating move toward cult-like fixity. The correspondence and the biography both amply demonstrate that the poets around Spicer felt a constant tension between the world-making possibilities of the poem, as Spicer expounded on it, and the world-enclosing strategies meant to protect 'poetry'.

So what *is* poetry? As I imagine you can tell by now, for Spicer it is less a thing than a relationship, a situation of language or an event in language where certain kinds of content flash out from camouflage and disappear. What that content might be is variable in Spicer's work, of course; it is less often rendered as image than as idea, conceit, or theme; and often, that theme *is* a theme of camouflage or interstitiality, as when he writes in the *Language* sequence

> Being a [poet] a disyllable in a world of monosyllables. Awakened by the distance between the [o] and the [e][32]

This isn't to say, though, that Spicer's poems are always 'about' poetry, that they are nothing other than a self-referential game. They are a game, I think, or a series of card tricks, designed to startle us, but part of the pleasure in reading them comes from beginning to sense an idea of language being hashed out that isn't reducible to a single theme. This is where Spicer's analogy to 'language' in the linguistic sense becomes important; oddly, it's also where his interest in folklore, legend, and balladry also assert themselves. Spicer studied as an undergraduate at Berkeley with the medieval historian Ernst Kantorowicz, who seems to have helped Spicer form a sense of poetry as part of a shifting corpus of textual matter with overlapping and different versions of the same story, like the different versions of the Arthur legend that comprise the multi-lingual 'Matter of Britain', or the variations of detail that mark different versions of songs in the ballad tradition.[33] A poetic fragment, then, has for Spicer the dual charge of being an event in language, and a piece of something like literary

---

32   Spicer 2008, p. 243.
33   Brief accounts of Spicer's work with Reed and with Kantorowicz can be found in Elling-
       ham and Killian 1998, pp. 19–21 and 122.

'matter', part of a set of concerns and 'topics' (to use the rhetorical term). This loose net of literary matter is kept fresh and alive by variation, substitution, and the transformation of nonsense into language, by a whole variety of activities Spicer called – almost certainly knowing the rhetorical sense of his word choice – 'invention'.

I'd like to close with a brief look at a poem from *Language*, the second of the poems from the series called 'Transformations', which begins with lyrics from the old English or Scottish ballad, 'Barbara Allen':

TRANSFORMATIONS II

'In Scarlet Town where I was born
There was a fair maid dwelling'.
We make up a different language for poetry
And for the heart – ungrammatical.
It is not that the name of the town changes
(Scarlet becomes Charlotte or even in Gold City I once heard a good
    Western singer make it Tonapah. We don't have towns here)
(That sort of thing would please the Jungian astronauts)
But that the syntax changes. This is older than towns.
Troy was a baby when Greek sentence structure emerged. This was the
    real Trojan Horse.
The order changes. The Trojans
Having no idea of true or false syntax and having no recorded language
Never knew what hit them.[34]

In linguistics a 'transformation' is the name for the operation by which the speaker of a language alters sentences from active to passive, or declarative to interrogative, forms. 'Poetry and the heart', here, are said by Spicer to ring syntactical transformations of this kind. But they also have an off-beat, ungrammatical language, like an extra syllable where there's no call for one. These two features of poetry, in this poem at least, Spicer makes different from a third kind of language change, the semantic variations and substitutions that the ballad accumulates over time. That accumulation, which can look like a collective unconscious, is what Spicer thinks will delight 'the Jungian astronauts'. And he likes that kind of language-change, too, as registers in his parenthetical aside.

---

34   Spicer 2008, p. 233.

But it's a fourth kind of linguistic variability, a set of rhetorical inventions, that gives the poem its movement. The leaps from part to part – from the ballad lyrics to the language of poetry, to town names to syntax to Greek to the Trojan War to an instance of shock – these are hallmark instances, not only of Spicer's poetry, which is always designed to keep us off guard, but of invention in the sense of the fresh arrangement of parts, topics, or tropes drawn from a received textual matter. And poetry, for Spicer, is the relation among parts of this matter that flashes out of it like the glint of a dead writer's bones in a ton of concrete, or unthieveable, uncommodifiable, because it cannot be separate from the strewn – nowadays we might say 'networked' – textual material from which it is drawn. From the safety of its recesses it reaches out to swat you, like Greek syntax charging on to the scene, or like a poem with an at-first inexplicable turn:

> Smoke signals
> [...] in the Eskimo villages on the coast where the earthquake hit
> Bang, snap, crack. They will never know what hit them
> On the coast of Alaska. They expect everybody to be insane.
> This is a poem about the death of John F. Kennedy.[35]

A poem like this shares with the post-structuralist language that bequeathed us the conjunction of 'affect' and 'performativity' an analogy to linguistics that turns out to be a cover for a return to rhetoric. To be sure, it is gleefully 'performative' – 'This is a poem about the death of John F. Kennedy', for instance, enacting the stated theme of 'never knowing' what will hit us. And in its attraction to rabbit's-hat games of invention it does not lie too far from Mallarmé's *Un coup de dés*. It even shares with the writing that interested de Man a focus on the linguistic 'violence' of its own composition and decomposition, on how the poet is 'Awakened by the distance between the [o] and the [e]'.

But I hesitate to make Spicer's poems into evidence for the ideas we find articulated in the Francophone affect-performativity nexus. This is because the poems are not an argument with philosophy: they are wrestling with other matters, not least the matter of capital, and it becomes hard to name that matter if the poems' performativity is taken up into the background narratives about the dialectic and its others that structure the critical feeling in post-structuralism. But the queer transpositions of 'affect' and 'performativity' into a rhetorical and aesthetic zone that includes the body may allow us ask what structures of feel-

---

35   Spicer 2008, p. 221.

ing are made articulate by the *performances* of the poems. For all the similarity between Spicer's recourse to the idea of poems as events in language and de Man's sense of writing as inducing events, that is, I prefer to see his 'turn to language' as a queer response to the work of capital in his time and place. I don't doubt we are enriched by a critical attention to how, in the interstices of any historical dialectic, linguistic making and unmaking occur behind the cogito; and I certainly think recalling the lightness of laughter in the midst of bleak absurdity can remind us that the dialectic hasn't captured everything in us. But that won't make it go away.

CHAPTER 5

Infinity for Marxists

... this is paradise
not for *people*
but paradise
regardless.[1]

•
•
•

In this short essay I'll try to identify some of the impulses guiding a recent turn to thinking about vastness in the critical-theoretical wing of the humanities, and to assess whether it might be put in dialogue with contemporary Marxist criticism. As readers of *Mediations* are no doubt aware, a wide variety of scholars in philosophy, literary criticism, and political theory are engaged in projects that re-scale their enterprise to suit what they take to be a larger world than the one we were able to study in the days of the linguistic turn. Two things in particular interest me about this interdisciplinary body of thinking: first, that its critique of 'the human' is all but interchangeable with a critique of textual interpretation; and second, that this critique seems to replace a critique of capitalism. The intellectual centre of gravity for this critique is in anti-humanist strains of contemporary philosophy, but I am less interested in a 'philosophical' critique of this infinity-discourse than I am in giving it just a touch of intellectual history, and in thinking about the very human perplexities and worries that may have led to its current allure.

The backdrop of this turn to the infinite is generally acknowledged to be the challenges posed by climate change, though many of the intellectual projects I have in mind express this only indirectly. More than a focus on climate or ecology as subject matter – though certainly some of this work does do that – the new infinity-scholarship shares across the disciplines an anti-humanism that is expressed as impatience with interpretation and with 'texts' – that is to say, an impatience with the residues of post-structuralism, which in its

---

1   Ward 2013, p. 37.

universalisation of critique as 'reading' was the last great trans-disciplinary paradigm shift.

This scholarly situation has led me to structure my thoughts here in something of a round-robin fashion, or at least a set of relays. What I'll be suggesting, below, is that this new anti-interpretive stance mistakenly equates Marxism with the deconstruction that critiqued it, rejects deconstruction while frequently repeating its key gestures, and swaps in ontology for epistemology in Christian language whose history it will not or cannot acknowledge. And it proposes as a method of (ana-)interpretation a stance toward reality that, in its insistence on the radical 'autonomy' of non-human objects and relationships, delivers a critique, not of capitalism, or anti-democracy, but of scholarly self-absorption. Against this presumptuousness, which it links to over-investment in texts, it proposes a limpid, un-rhetorical poetry of the world, which, when expressed as text, takes the form of litanies and lists that pale in comparison to the best actual poetry. So in what follows I'll be tracing how the new infinity-language both critiques post-structuralism in the language that post-structuralism used to critique Marxism, and implicitly repeats a second critique of Marxism also deployed by the post-structuralists, which worked by pitting Marxism against a certain idea of poetry. Then I'll turn to a poem that makes this opposition look shabby on both Marxist and poetic grounds. How this all plays out in the current idiom of infinity will take a little while to explain.

We might begin with its extent: this new language of the vast and the wide-open has touched several subfields, as we will see, but it is most immediately evident in literary ecocriticism. As the critic Cristin Ellis has pointed out, contemporary ecocritics have a strong anti-textualist bent. Ellis notes an overlap between critics as different as Lawrence Buell, who argues in his *Environmental Imagination* that theory served to 'efface the world', and Ursula Heise, who contends in *Sense of Place and Sense of Planet* that environmentalist discourse has overdeveloped a tendency to 'think locally', to the point where the latest eco-critics see their predecessors as having licensed what Ellis calls a 'parochial presumptuousness'.[2] The mark of this presumptuous parochialism is the environmentalist subject's projection of simple correspondences between herself and the wider world, which are made at the cost of investigating the alien variety of relations that are the wider world's moving parts.

More than any other contemporary ecocritic, Timothy Morton responds to this sense of literary theory's narrow gaze with a rhetoric of infinity. His 2010 book *The Ecological Thought* begins with a chapter called 'Thinking Big', which

---

2   Buell 1996, p. 5; Heise 2008, p. 12; Ellis 2012, p. 6.

concludes with an enthusiastic gloss on the mathematics of Georg Cantor, who conceived the concept of the 'transfinite' – a number bigger than we can count, though it is only the hem of the garment of infinity 'itself'.[3] The epigraph to the volume, from Emmanuel Levinas's *Totality and Infinity*, frames Morton's argument in Cantorian terms: 'Infinity overflows the thought which thinks it'.

Gestures like these have placed Morton in alliance with the loosely-affiliated group of philosophers who have taken to calling themselves, at times, 'speculative realists'. Several of these philosophers practice what has come to be known as 'object-oriented ontology', or OOO: a theory of being that, like Heise's 'sense of planet', is organised by the imagination of a set of relations among entities that do not place the human being at their centre. The best-known of these philosophers, Quentin Meillassoux, though he rejects affiliation with so-called OOO, nonetheless refers in his 2008 volume *After Finitude* to a 'great outdoors' in which the mind is at last able to free itself from the philosophical equivalent to the parochialism Ellis sees ecocritics rejecting.[4] The word the speculative realists have come up with for that parochialism is 'correlationism', by which they mean a narrowing-down of the project of philosophy to endless iterations of the subject-object problem. For the speculative realists, Kant is the great enemy: by focusing on epistemological questions, he shackled philosophy to what subjects could know, leaving us ill-equipped to grapple with the kind of mind-bending ontological problems we must confront if we wish to understand globalisation, the cosmos, environmental damage, or the deep time of the planet.

Not only ecocritics and young-turk philosophers, but literary critics and political theorists have made gestures that imply a vastness beyond textual analysis and after critical theory. Leah Price, in her recent *How to Do Things With Books in Victorian Britain*, opens by suggesting that 'the transactions that enlist the books stretch far beyond the literary, or even the linguistic', moving on to lambast recent critics of material culture for never getting down to the actual vastness of real books, and for clinging instead to 'theory' at the cost of a posture both overweening and far too cramped: 'the hermeneutics of suspicion has given way to a poetics of deflation … in the process, scholars change from the freest of associators into the most slavish of idiots savants'.[5] For the speculative realists, meanwhile, that hermeneutics is still a problem; praising the philosopher Alphonso Lingis, Graham Harman compares him favourably to what he takes to be the ongoing dominance of 1980s-style theory: 'where [Lingis] is

---

3   See Morton 2010.
4   Meillassoux 2008, p. 7.
5   Price 2010, p. 22.

engaged with the flesh and pulp of the universe, contemporary fashions have turned primarily to the interpretation and deconstruction of texts'.[6]

Not infrequently, these declarations of the outmodedness of deconstruction either encode or modulate into a similar claim about Marxism: Marx may have been able to explain the class formations and the methods of accumulation that emerged in the industrial era, the argument goes, but he could not have foreseen the planetary consequences of what capital unleashed, which extend far beyond what his original categories could grasp. There are more and less subtle versions of this argument; among the most clear-eyed is to be found in Dipesh Chakrabarty's 2008 essay 'The Climate of History', which adopts a pose of gratitude for how the 'hermeneutics of suspicion' allowed postcolonial theorists to critique universality, then moves on to suggest that it is exactly universality that climate change obliges us to conceptualise. Equating the poststructuralist 'hermeneutics of suspicion' with the critique of capital, he writes:

> Climate change, refracted through global capital, will no doubt accentuate the logic of inequality that runs through the rule of capital; some people will no doubt gain temporarily at the expense of others. But the whole crisis cannot be reduced to a story of capitalism. Unlike in the crises of capitalism, there are no lifeboats here for the rich and the privileged (witness the drought in Australia or recent fires in the wealthy neighborhoods of California).[7]

The problem here, of course, is that Marx's understanding of capitalism did not presume that the rich were immune to its effects. But the impulse to see Marxism as an outmoded vocabulary is too strong: so Chaktrabarty goes on to reinvent the wheel of the dialectic, as it were, suggesting that because humanity cannot conceptualise itself as a species, at least not yet, we are at 'the limits of historical understanding' and must make recourse to a 'negative universal history'.[8] The footnote in which Chakrabarty explains this coinage points right back to Adorno and Benjamin.

If the narrative of the obsolescence of Marxism is one side of the contemporary turn to deep time and infinity, then its other side is an anti-capitalism that has been entirely re-routed through philosophy. Speculative-realist thinkers like Reza Negarestani and Nick Srnicek have specifically thought through the question of whether contemporary philosophy might provide grounds for res-

---

6   Harman 2005, p. 61.
7   Chakrabarty 2009, p. 221.
8   Chakrabarty 2009, p. 222.

isting or overcoming capital. But though Negarestani refers to capitalism as 'the most recurring politico-economic figure of speculative thought', and Srnicek has written about it, they conceive of it in philosophical terms, as the great engine of 'correlationist' thinking: the problem with capitalism, for these thinkers, is that it creates an echo chamber that makes our minds small.[9] The capitalist problem that speculative realism seems best equipped to address, in other words, is not an actual dynamic of accumulation and exploitation, but the epistemological problem of capitalism's reduction of all phenomena to its own image. However revolutionary it may be in philosophical terms that these thinkers respond to capitalist epistemology not with a counter-epistemology but with an ontology, and however enthusiastically they may imagine subjects who think (or exist) entirely differently than the ones we know today, their anti-philosophical and anti-hermeneutic gestures are just that: anti-philosophical and anti-hermeneutic, not anti-capitalist.

To think dialectically, it seems, is not to think hugely enough, or infinitely enough. So how must we think, if we are to grapple with these unprecedented species-problems? As it turns out, in one way or another, the undialectical way we are urged to think, in this discourse, is *poetically* – but in a very particular sense, the sense that Archibald MacLeish was after in 1926 when he suggested a poem 'should not mean but be'.

In her recent *Vibrant Matter*, Jane Bennett champions the sheer alienness of the life of things: in their unknowability, especially in their unknowable relations to each other and not to humanity, things point to a universe wider that we can ever grasp. Bennett refers to this unknowability as the 'recalcitrance' of the object world; her language quite closely recalls what speculative realists and object-ontologists like Graham Harman and Ray Brassier refer to as the 'autonomy' of phenomena (including those it would be hard to call 'objects'). This recalcitrance is poetic for Bennett – it leads her to include, along the course of her argument, short lists and parenthetical asides that function as a 'poetry' that instances what she's after:

> one man's large black plastic work glove
> one dense mat of oak pollen
> one unblemished dead rat
> one white plastic bottle cap
> one smooth stick of wood[10]

9   See Negarestani 2011, p. 182; and Srnicek 2011.
10 Bennett 2010, p. 4.

Bennett calls these lists 'contingent tableaus' or 'assemblages': she shies away from calling them 'poems' straight out, I think, because that would suggest that they *mean* something, and the contemporary language of infinitude depends on a critique of 'meaning'. The tone in which this critique is delivered varies considerably: Morton affably turns to evolutionary theory for examples of non-teleological, non-adaptive features of animal life to argue on behalf of a big, raucous, non-meaning-intensive world.[11] He also turns to our experience of reading, which he suggests involves us assembling meaning out of patternless flux: as he puts it, 'meaning depends on unmeaning'. By the end of the passage in which he makes this claim, encountering texts has become like encountering people, and the unknowability and meaninglessness of encountering others is not hell, as Sartre had it, but endlessness. 'The stranger is infinity', he writes: not meaning-bearing per se, but not quite meaningless, either.[12]

Brassier, for his part, critiques 'meaning' in more Nietzschean terms. 'Philosophers would do well to desist', he writes in the preface to his *Nihil Unbound*,

> from issuing any further injunctions about the need to re-establish the meaningfulness of existence, the purposefulness of life, or mend the shattered concord between man and nature. Philosophy should be more than a sop to the pathetic twinge of human self-esteem.[13]

For Brassier, whose *Nihil Unbound* is subtitled *Enlightenment and Extinction*, the relentless auto-critique of philosophical Enlightenment has disenchanted the world to the point where we may finally be able to absorb the traumatic knowledge of our individual deaths as well as the inevitable extinction of humanity. As with Morton and Bennett, in Brassier's work the trap of 'meaning' in the sense of 'meaningfulness' is a result of a fixation on the human as the centre and the limit of our sense of scale.[14]

---

11   See Morton 2010, p. 73.

12   Morton 2010, p. 80.

13   Brassier 2007, p. xi.

14   In his turn to Freud's notion of the death drive as a conceptual resource for his argument about the unassimilability of the fact of our death and extinction, Brassier repeats the work of Leo Bersani, who in 1986 had already argued that psychoanalysis, in its inability to adequately assimilate the self-shattering aspects of sexuality into discourse, was a kind of 'epistemological catastrophe' that, in its attempt to 'coerce' the unassimilable 'into discourse', keeps us at a remove from 'any consciousness of being' (Bersani 1986, pp. 30, 40). Bersani's counterposing of epistemology and ontology, and his attachment of negative and positive values to the two, respectively, does not only predate the key gesture of the speculative turn, but grounds it in what would become a specific, anti-identitarian queer politics.

Given the Nietzschean aggressivity of language like Brassier's it should perhaps come as no surprise to discover that the new infinity-rhetoric frequently expresses itself in theological terms, particularly as (anti-)Christologies of one kind or another. Brassier, for his part, is a champion of the philosopher François Laruelle, whose 2011 volume *Future Christ* bears a strong resemblance to most accounts of Meillassoux's soon-to-be-translated *Divine Inexistence*.[15] In Harman's gloss on the French edition of Meillassoux's book, he suggests that Meillassoux develops an unprecedented attitude toward God, to be distinguished from agnosticism, atheism, and so on. This position, as Harman renders it, is 'believing in God because he does not exist'. The key, it turns out, is that God does not exist ... *yet*. This is the insight that Meillassoux claims to have uncovered in Stephane Mallarmé's 1897 poem, *Un coup de dès jamais n'abolira le hazard*.[16]

But even if we agree with this reading of Mallarmé's poem as encoding a secret Christology, we needn't see it as unprecedented: there have been Future-Christs for a very long time. Just restricting ourselves to the modern era, we can find this stance in Schelling's idea of the 'third age' of the world, the spiritual age, which describes a future dispensation in which a personalised 'Christ' will no longer suffice as the vehicle for the unfolding of the spirit of Christianity on earth, which will one day demand a post-personal, spiritualised 'Christ'.[17] Meillassoux's famous critique of Hume reads this way, too, as an effacement of religious arguments that predate his own: for Meillassoux, the failure of Hume's critique of causality is to back away from sheer 'factiality' (the possibility that anything could follow on anything else), which leads him to a watered-down probabilism.[18] But the Puritan preacher Jonathan Edwards, Hume's contemporary, got there long ago: read 'Sinners in the Hands of an Angry God', and you'll see that his exhortation to his congregants is based on dispelling their probabilistic sense of the likelihood of grace by recourse to arguments and figures whose force is to suggest that God could do *anything* next, at any moment. Take that, probabilists!

Alongside these Christologies, meanwhile, is an array of other gestures in this contemporary current that have Catholic resonance. In the conclusion

---

15   See Laruelle 2010.

16   Meillassoux claims to have uncovered this truth in Mallarmé (he treats it as a truth, not an interpretation) in Meillassoux 2012.

17   See Schelling 2000. Löwith 1957 provides a useful medieval back-history to Schelling's dispensational model in the passages on Joachim of Fiore. Joachim's sense of dispensational time as subject, moment-to-moment, to utter transformation, also forms part of the history behind Hume and Edwards.

18   See Meillassoux 2009, pp. 82–111.

to *Vibrant Matter*, Bennett writes that she would like to end with a 'litany, a kind of Nicene Creed' (the text of the 'creed' runs, 'I believe in one matter-energy, the maker of things seen and unseen. I believe that this pluriverse is traversed by heterogeneities that are continually doing things').[19] The video-game theorist Ian Bogost, too, is fond of the form of the litany, which like Bennett he owes to the work of Bruno Latour: in his recent *Alien Phenomenology*, Bogost describes writing a computer program that will generate what he calls 'Latour litanies' – arrays of what we are asked to take as incommensurably different things (weather patterns, cleaning products, theories of history, hair gel) that, he thinks, have a mind-expanding effect on the too-humanistic, text-centred reader.[20] And though he does not frame them as litanies, per se, Graham Harman, too, imagines the list of incommensurables to have strong anti-hermeneutic power. In a recent essay, he frames one such list in a way that's meant as a kind of encrypted defence of the theological language to which he and his fellow travellers make recourse:

> making human experience the homeland of all relations is no less out-landish than importing a theological concept of God into a philosophical sphere where faith no longer suffices as proof. In short, human experience has become the Almighty God of mainstream philosophy. Overmining has become the central dogma of our time: everything is relations, or language, or appearance to the mind. This dogma cannot be countered with an undermining theory that views the world as a partless, rumbling depth. What is missed in both cases is the autonomous reality of indi-vidual objects: dogs, trees, flames, monuments, societies, ghosts, gods, pirates, coins ...[21]

There are a few sleights of hand worth noting in this passage. One is the way a rhetorical equivalence – two equally 'outlandish' things, making God or humans the centre of everything – is treated as a philosophical equivalence, as if the relationship between secular humanism and deism is that they are 'opposites' in some formal sense, rather than positions with histories.

The second sleight of hand is related to the first: Harman reduces philo-sophy's relationship to the question of 'meaning' to two tidily opposed pos-itions, which he calls 'overmining' and 'undermining' (roughly overinterpret-ation on one hand, and a monist insistence on miasmic, predifferentiated

---

19   Bennett 2010, p. 122.
20   Bogost 2012, p. 94.
21   Harman 2011, p. 71.

arche-materiality on the other), and then, having performed this reduction, produces a Third Way – not 'overmining' or 'undermining', but the 'autonomous reality of individual objects'. But in order to enjoy the clarity and radicality of this third option, we've had to switch from a critique of 'meaning' to a celebration of 'autonomy' – that is, to a different question and vocabulary altogether. That switch elides the question of whether there might be 'meaning' in or around that radical autonomy. That the answer is 'yes' – and that therefore Harman has failed to get away from even the artificially narrow scheme he thinks he's demolished – is clear from his list. It is a kind of poetry, in which words don't distract us too much with meaning-play, but radiate, instead, both their own actuality and the actuality of the things they represent.

This anti-hermeneutic sense of poetry is old – perhaps as old as rhetoric. But for my purposes, it's worth noticing not its oldness but its lability: reading Price's testy denunciation of literary critics today as hidebound deconstructionists, obsessed with meaning and the critique of meaning, is not unlike reading the Derrida of 'From Restricted to General Economy', and watching him mock the Hegelianism of his day by characterising it as a huffing, puffing bourgeois habit of thought of assigning historical meaning to everything under the sun – a habit which he and virtually every other post-structuralist felt needed not the actuality of a Marxism but the unbearable lightness of a Mallarmé, to banish it from the scene.[22] So the insurgent anti-hermeneuticists of the 1960s have now become the navel-gazing hermeneuts of the new millennium, and along the way, the critique of capital has been replaced with a critique of *arrogance*. The poetry called forth to rectify the problem is still Mallarmé's (he is as beloved and exemplary for the speculative realists as he was for the post-structuralists they denounce): the poetry of being, not meaning; the poetry built out of words and not ideas; the poetry that limpidly presents us with an actuality, and spares us rhetoric, hermeneutics, and 'grand theory'.

But where is this poetry? It's not clear to me that we can find it in Mallarmé. Even if we could, his is only one location in a universe of brilliant twentieth-century poetry, much of which has struggled, not to replace thinking about some mere human bungle of capitalism with matters anterior to it, or more ontological, but to make poetry in and through the conditions the century gave us, not least the conditions of life under capital. Reading the post-war archive of anti-humanist thought, one wearies of the gestures opposing an arrogant,

---

22   I make this argument at greater length in Nealon 2011.

myopic criticism to a wide-open, ontologically pure poem-world; I find myself wishing for a critique of something other than arrogance, and for accounts of poetry other those concerned to ratify the ontological dignity of the art. This is why, though I fear it will seem abrupt, I want to introduce you to a great poem now.

In the title poem of his 2013 volume *The Crisis of Infinite Worlds*, the Cincinnati-based poet Dana Ward constructs a framework for comparing two distinct modes of infinitude whose significance, he makes clear, is not simply their vastness, but that they have come into play in his poem in a here and now. The poem is framed on one hand by Ward's misremembering the title of a DC Comics series he came across at the mall, a series called *Crisis on Infinite Earths*. That twelve-part series, published in 1985, was designed to establish retroactive continuity among the many and contradictory plotlines that had accrued to the heroes and heroines in the DC universe over the decades. Meanwhile, the poem is also structured by its opening address to Krystle Cole, the young Kansas woman who was party to the last days of a massive LSD-producing outfit run by the now-imprisoned chemist William Leonard Pickard. Pickard's facility was built in a revamped missile silo; in a subsequent memoir, *Lysergic*, and in a series of popular YouTube videos, Cole recounts experiences of intense LSD trips in the months before Pickard's November 2000 arrest. So the poem is playfully framed both by reference to the question of how long a 'pluriverse' of contradictory plotlines can last, and also by a sympathetic identification with the manner in which Cole describes the trippy, 'lysergic' mind-bending which, depending on how the poet takes her tone, she either enjoyed or endured. It begins like this:

> Krystle
> Krystle Cole
> you're all I thought about sometimes
> I watched you while our daughter slept
> your Sissy Spacek ways
> your laconic demeanor in relaying
> either ecstasy or trauma
> & the un-embittered empathy your voice conveyed
> on YouTube
> which is our loving cup
> the solution of butter
> & DMT you took
> anally that really made you
> freak the fuck out

> & your friends just stood there
> watching you
> as you hurtled alone through mirrored tunnels.[23]

What follows from this opening, already a richly articulated set of cross-currents of 'empathy' and dispassion – devoted YouTube viewing, beloved children sleeping under parents' gazes, friends looking away when they should attend to each other – is something like a super-compressed journey of the soul, not into Dante's heaven so much as into the nature-less 'universe' with which the ecocritics, object-ontologists, and speculative realists intend to beat back hermeneutics:

> It's that frictionless feeling
> the smooth & vacant course
> that lacks abruption, one wave
> the clinical mania undifferentiated
> whiteness
> contains when cylindrical cloud
> hard & plastic comes to represent
> the mind to the mind
> & thus describe a model
> of terrible momentum
> with unity of purpose
> toward nothing so much
> as cold, radiant nature
> stripped of Eros, of becoming,
> just the mainframe
> & its withering severity
> without any predicate
> of others, save perhaps their
> gazes, no walls,
> no nothing, completely
> white light & your name
> when your consciousness was
> splitting time was stopping
> you were going always into that.[24]

---

23   Ward 2013, p. 32.
24   Ward 2013, pp. 32–3.

Notice that the bare identificatory structure of address has not fallen away – that the poem is still, in the argot of infinity-theory, 'correlationist'. The 'you', Cole, has all but stopped being a self in her encounter with this lysergic vastness; but she is still the object of the poet's address. As we will see, this is not inadvertent, or a falling-away from some purer, more 'speculative' form of thought – the project of the poem is emerging specifically as the attempt to think personless infinity *through persons*. Cole is not only his object: as his subject, she leads him to make a further set of comparisons. 'You were always going into that', he says, a little in awe; then

> I was going always to the mall
> in those months,
> the young century's rainiest
> April & May, to walk the
> baby & to understand my art.
> I didn't understand.
> I would move the stroller
> through the halogen, over
> grooved tile & across those
> smooth marble expanses meant
> to simulate floating & gliding
> before that pure frictionless
> feeling was entire.[25]

Three time-scales – the centuries', the months', the time of reproduction – frame the poet's quotidian struggle 'to understand [his] art'. The problem of that art, it turns out, presents itself as the question of whether and how the 'frictionless' feeling of lysergic wildness, its 'terrible momentum', has anything to do with the mall's simulation of 'floating & gliding' and how those pseudo-sensations build into something 'entire'. It is tempting to say that the one, the mall, is a kind of bad totality, and the other, the trip, is its counterpart infinity, frightening but freer than that tiled enclosure. But the poem is not relying, as the theorists do, on a Levinasian frame, though infinity and totalisation are surely in play. After all, the mall's enclosure is a refuge, too, an infinity – well, he has more to say on that score.

Meanwhile, though, Ward is still trying to understand his art: pursuing the question of whether there's a similarity or possibly an asymptotic relation

---

25   Ward 2013, p. 33.

between the two kinds of frictionlessness he's describing, he finds himself
wanting to cease pursuit. The connections between departments in the Sears
he's wandering through, he writes,

>   ... felt
> besieged or like a mask
> for separation, they felt
> like connection between us
> in life but I didn't
> take my allegory
> further Krystle Cole, into your
> lysergic delirium later redeemed
> by a beautiful discipline
> of spirit & cosmography
> developed for praxis.[26]

It seems as though the question of likeness, posed as metaphor and meta-
morphosis – how is one thing like another? when does one space become
another? – it's as though this question of likeness fails before the *ars poetica*
of Krystle Cole, which is less a tracking of asymptotic mystery than a response
to situations. He likes her latest video, 'on candy / flipping hard & developing /
ESP with friends'; it suggested to him, he writes, that:

>   ... oneness
> was a leavened mix
> of random indiscretion,
> bruising wariness, & bliss
> obtained by synchronizing
> chemical encounter.[27]

This is the kind of array of 'objects' prized by Harman and others, when they
make their litanies and lists. But the items in this array are not dignified by
'autonomy' from us, or from each other. They are routed *through* each other;
they are mediations *of* each other.

Part of the attraction of the Krystle-method, though, seems to be that it's
more than the poet can muster. What he comes up with in the rest of the poem,

---

26   Ward 2013, p. 34.
27   Ibid.

instead, is a beautifully restless groping after ways to experience infinity and relation at the same time. Not all of them are nice; at least one of them depends on merging with capital.

> Krystle,
> there's a made up drug
> I wonder if you'd do it?
> Bradley Cooper, in *Limitless*
> takes this little pill, which
> in its candy dot translucence
> looks a lot like a tear plucked
> from the cheek in Man Ray's 'Larmes'.
> With it, he can utilize
> all of his brain, & so
> he un-riddles the patterning
> hidden in the ceaseless
> flow of capital, structuring its
> chaos in excess of any mortal
> with a terrible momentum
> & unity of purpose toward
> nothing so much as pure profit
> & complete subordination
> of the world.[28]

I have to say that, when I read critiques of 'correlationism' and how pinheaded it's supposedly made us all, how unequipped to think huge thoughts, I'm always reminded of the futurist meme that goes like, what could we become if we could use more of our brains? That the answer might be, 'better capitalists!' is the wry implication of this passage, just as it's one of the concerns of a theorist like Catherine Malabou, whose recent *What Should We Do With Our Brain?* keeps in play the possibility – one the speculative realists do not – that 'infinity' might be a mixed blessing.

Back at the mall, meanwhile, Ward has moved from the frictionless ease of illimitable surfaces to the junk-sundries of the smaller, less-profitable shops. It's here he encounters the comic book that makes the title of his poem, though, as he notes, he writes it down wrong, substituting 'world' for 'earth'. Wondering what the relation might be between the two forms in the closing mediation of

---

28   Ward 2013, pp. 34–5.

the poem, in which the poet tries once more to settle on whether the figure of the asymptote will serve him – is there a trajectory, he wonders, along which, after a certain point, 'earth' becomes 'world'? 'That same May', he writes,

> I had gone to Detroit. I saw
> the most wonderful graffiti, more
> a prayer, written on a wall
> in magic marker, it read –
> Two Things:
> 1) That we would grow closer & closer as time progresses.
> 2) That our ships would not crash.[29]

Ever closer, never crashing – a mystical union, and a Zeno's paradox, worthy of Dante. But at the end of the poem, as throughout, it's less infinity as math than as relation, that reveals itself as the subject of the poem; we can sense this in the way that, turning away from Cole and addressing himself in loneliness, he remarks on the medium in which the graffiti was rendered:

> Magic marker on a
> surface doesn't have
> much depth of skin.
> You move it smoothly
> on the wall & it stays smooth
> barely records the softest friction
> of two separate textures meeting.
> The wetness of its onyx
> dries quick or even quicker
> if you blow on it with circled lips,
> like clouds in old maps
> that blew ships across a flat earth
> to an edge I don't exactly
> not idealize.[30]

It's a textureless texture – 'magic', industrial – that recalls the frictionless floors of the shopping mall. But it can't help but be marked by how it renders: you can blow on it to make it dry faster. Does the image that the blowing generates,

---

29   Ward 2013, p. 37.
30   Ibid.

an image of the edge of the world, allow the ink to retain a trace of its sep-
arateness from us, its ontological 'autonomy'? Perhaps. But I think we would
misread the poem if we saw that breath as a ratcheting-down from illimitability
into myopic human meaning-making. The poem does not split the difference
between these two things, autonomy and solipsism, so much as upend the idea
that they are the relevant opposition. In the terms it sets up, infinity and rela-
tion are not opposites – they are shot through with each other, as much in
nausea and 'wariness' as in synchrony and bliss. They make and are made by
texture – by what we might call, in a more academic vocabulary, mediation.
This also means, of course, that the activities the poem describes are precisely
what we are urged, in this latest post-Marxism, to dismiss as merely 'human':
they are dialectical.

This seems to me the great error of the critique of humanism when it con-
joins with the critique of hermeneutics: the idea that scrutiny and attention are
somehow essentially englobing. This seems a displacement of a critique of the
social divisions that separate scholarship from politics onto the mechanics of
the scholarship. It is not reductive and parochial to read a poem closely, or to
read poems for a living; it is reductive and parochial to do so in a world where
that activity is cordoned off from the others that support it. In a world where
every professor was also a janitor, would we really find close reading so myopic?

Ward ends his poem with a fragment:

> That somewhere
> there's a precipice in this world & tracing
> my finger along those ardent lines
> I'd found the fault of it
> a little, in its boldness far too faint
> & not enough.[31]

He's been at the mall, thinking of a girl in a missile silo; he's wanting to find
a crack in the world that by way of enclosure separates us and pits us against
each other. But the opposition isn't between the mere human world and the
vaster universe that teaches us humility by ignoring us; it's between the quality
of paradise in the world that is and the hints of paradise in the world that might
be. Before the closing lines I cited above, the poet asks Cole a sinuous, twenty-
six-line long double question – one so long it doesn't conclude with a question
mark. It goes like this:

---

31   Ward 2013, p. 38.

Krystle, have you ever,
just standing around,
noticed someone smoking
in an older silver Volvo
& watched the comeback feelings
of a Tupac Easter Sunday
steep in their ambivalent features
until they are more radiant
than cinematic virgins
having lost it in the wake
of Saint Maria Goretti
whose patronage is lost
to the brutalized sweetness
of her charges
when depicted in the mind
& reconstructed
as a low-res simulation
by scientists the weekend
Wall Street's occupied & particles
are found to go
faster than light
then weirdly feel like
this is paradise
not for *people*
but paradise
regardless.[32]

This virtuosic query is built around a series of dazzling shifts of focus and scale. We begin with the becoming-auratic of a particular, anonymous face, which moves outward from the resurrection-discourse around the remembered person of Tupac Shakur into the traces of holiness in the unnumbered 'charges' of the Catholic saint and martyr Maria Goretti (who was raped and murdered in 1902). Then we're suddenly in a particular weekend, a here and now, in which advances in brain research and particle acceleration collide with the protestors in Zuccotti Park. The wedging of the occupation in between the technical advances seems to serve as a kind of spar: on one hand, sheer variety and juxtaposition propose a paradise, but the middle term in that variety sticks in

---

32   Ward 2013, pp. 36–37.

paradises's craw. And the 'weird' feeling the poet describes comes from a discovery that we are blocked from paradise, not by the way vastness makes us minuscule, but by how our social arrangements make it impossible to explore vastness except in technical terms.[33]

I've taken this time to walk through Ward's poem – which deserves much closer reading than I've provided here – because I think it gives the lie to the anti-hermeneutic anti-humanism on offer in the new discourse of infinity today. One reason for this, as I hope I've at least sketched here, is that Ward's poem does not rely on a false dichotomy between 'humanity' and 'infinity', working instead to co-locate life under capital with something like the varieties of infinite experience.

So can Marxists learn from this latest anti-humanist turn? Certainly we've had our day with language like this, not least by way of Althusser – whose youthful involvement with the organisation Action Catholique, and late desire for an audience with Pope John Paul II, suggests that more research is needed on the relation between secular and religious critiques of humanist presumptuousness.[34] And it's true that Marxist scholars in the humanities lag behind activists, and scholars in the social sciences, in thinking through ways to link environmental crises to the critique of capital without using the either-or vocabulary on offer in the infinity-discourse. The geographers and the sociologists are way out ahead.

But we'll catch up. Perhaps the lesson to be learned from the latest turn to infinity is that it would help to understand the need behind the desire to critique humanist hubris and textual interpretation. Is it just the confluence of a long Catholic tradition with the hangover from post-structuralism? Is it a way for Left-leaning liberals, grappling with feelings of powerlessness in the face of environmental destruction, to direct those feelings at themselves, in a masochistic anti-humanist discourse whose structure of feeling is something like species-shame? Or is it an attempt to import the wonder, if not the method, of the sciences into the life of the humanities? It is likely all of these. And as we seize the opportunity of the revival of interest in Marx to

---

33   The 'weird' feeling Ward describes bears some relation to a certain 'weirdness' prized by the speculative realists in the work of the horror writer H.P. Lovecraft, whose writing in pulp venues like *Weird Tales* gave to horror a specifically cosmic dimension: perhaps, many of the tales suggest, the universe is entirely indifferent to humanity. That Ward identifies this feeling, but also feels it differently, suggests that there is no necessary relation between the awareness of that indifference and the implications – generic, tonal, political – one draws from it. See Harman 2012 and Thacker 2011.

34   See Wolin 2010, p. 212.

learn and to struggle, we could no doubt incorporate a sensitive awareness of this latest turn's coordinates, even if it's not to incorporate the terms of that turn itself, which don't provide what Marxism needs today. No shame; more poetry.

CHAPTER 6

The Prynne Reflex

This essay is about a single poet, but also about a way of reading poetry. I'm focused here on the work of J.H. Prynne, but also on the ethical and historiographical presuppositions in which that work is embedded. I hope to describe, in this relatively short space, a way of appreciating the power of Prynne's poetry while backing away from some of its enabling premises – which have to do with literary modernism, on the one hand, and the idea of modernity, on the other. I'd like to do this because I think the time has come for us to begin questioning the ethical value of literary modernist form and technique, as well as our understanding of 'modernity' as a master category for understanding recent poetic history. I use the pretentious-sounding phrase 'the time has come' with a little embarrassment, but since so much of the critical conversation about poetry these days is about its relation to crisis – ecological crisis, economic crisis, the crisis of the university – I really do think that we would be better readers of poetry today if we identified capitalism, not modernity, as the engine of those crises, and distinguished capitalism as a struggle over the production of value from modernity as an allegory of historical stages. And, as you'll see, I think it matters which *version* of capitalism we emphasise in our conversations about poetry and crisis.

I think the dominant critical approach to poetry, at least in the English-language world, is centrally invested in a modernist narrative of the undoing of cultural damage, of getting back to lost origins. You might ask, how can such a desire for lost origins have survived the devastating post-modern critiques aimed at it in the 1970s and 1980s? That's a very good question; let's just say that the post-modern critique may have been more a lament for the failure of what modernism thought possible that a demurral from its goals. Already in the 1980s Andreas Huyssen had argued quite cogently that post-modern literary theory was in some sense primarily an excavation of the diminishing possibilities to be found in the innovations of literary modernism, not least innovations around the assembly of fragments into open-ended, non-holistic forms.[1] As more French literary theory of the period was translated into English, the centrality of Mallarmé's work to theorists as diverse as Julia Kristeva, Jacques Derrida, and Gilles Deleuze only drove home the point for American

---

1 See Huyssen 1986.

readers. As it turns out, Mallarmé remains crucial even for mutually antagon-
istic latter-day European theorists like Giorgio Agamben and Alain Badiou. So
we could say that an attachment to the value of open-ended assemblage offered
us by modernist poetry has outlived the popularity of the term 'post-modern'
itself.

Now, what's the link between the value of open-ended forms, and the desire
to use the notion of reversal as a model for undoing cultural damage? For a
recent example of scholarship that makes this link, we might turn to Susan
Stewart's book, *The Poet's Freedom*, which begins with an anecdote about Stew-
art seeing a young boy on a beach make a sand-castle, and then destroy it with
great glee. At first, Stewart says, she was dismayed by how casually the boy tore
down what he had so painstakingly created; but gradually, she writes, she came
to feel otherwise. As she puts it: 'Without the freedom of reversibility enacted
in unmaking, or at least always present as the potential for unmaking, we can-
not give value to our making'. This value, it seems, arises partly out of the fact
that destruction is impossible to regulate: 'there is no such thing as a precision
bomb, or even the precision destruction of a sand castle'.[2] At the end of the
book, Stewart includes a poem of her own, a *cento* called 'The Sand Castle',
made out of fragments from the book's introduction, scrambled so that the
original anecdote is both obscured and revivified. Open-ended form, here, is
explicitly linked to the return to what Stewart calls 'pure potential'.[3] It is the
poetic equivalent to a philosophical and political position Stewart sketches
out at the end of the prose portion of the book, in which she draws on Han-
nah Arendt to suggest that authentic political action, like poetic destruction,
involves a breaking-open, an undoing, of what has come before – a return to
inaugurality, or, in Arendt's word, natality.

One aim of this essay is to register my demurral from the premises of this
constellation. While I appreciate the importation of the language of vulner-
ability and precariousness into contemporary academic and poetic discourse
because it invites us not to take either the given or the made world for gran-
ted, I can't make the leap from that invitation to the formal premise that our
collective vulnerability to disaster, or the vulnerability of art to destruction,
is the result of an irreversible historical movement from simplicity to com-
plexity, or authenticity to hollowness, or religiosity to the secular. I also can't
accept the further formalisation of vulnerability into a result of the movement
of something like 'time itself', which is what Stewart pits against the reversibil-

2   Stewart 2011, 1–2.

3   Ibid., 2.

ity of art. Already, then, the tenderness of the position on vulnerability shades over into a formalisation that replaces a sense of history as the struggle over the value of time, 'modern' or not, with a truism about time's directionality.

My objections, though, are rather beside the point for now. Mostly I want us to begin to see some links between open-ended poetic form, and ways of reading poetry for its ethical value as a vulnerable tissue of fragments. But there's another piece of the contemporary conversation that's important here, also drawn from the modernist tradition, and it has to do with the ethics attached to difficulty in the modernism-modernity constellation. This piece will be especially important when we get to Prynne, not only because his poems are objectively quite difficult, but because he and his commentators have made 'difficulty' a central term by which to judge his work. In a 2010 essay for the *Cambridge Literary Review*, Prynne describes poetic difficulty in terms that link ethics to philology: as in the work of William Empson, Prynne champions the ambiguity of words, not least the complexities they derive from long use, as 'energy-promoting' for the reader, who is moved to do the hard work of inter-pretation by having to test out possible meanings from among the many a well-chosen word suggests.[4]

As I'll detail below, this ethics of poetic difficulty is linked to a critique of both commercialisation of language, and of the American language poets, against whose early emphasis on the 'free play' of signifiers he insists that there is no 'free lunch': that the play of signification, like everything else today, comes at a cost.[5] In a review of Prynne's 1999 *Poems*, Leo Mellor quotes Prynne's poetic fellow-traveller Ian Sinclair putting the case even more bluntly: 'Why should [poems] be easy? ... If it comes too sweetly then someone is trying to sell you something'.[6]

This notion that aesthetic experience is compromised by commercial ex-change forms the background for the persistent damage-language around Pryn-nian aesthetics. In the online journal *The Claudius App*, for instance, the poet and critic Keston Sutherland described the stanza form of his 2009 volume *Stress Position* in language that accurately renders one of the effects of a typ-ical Prynne stanza, too – as a 'metrical block whose reiteration as narrative would damagingly proscribe anything I could identify as my own fluency in poetic language'.[7] And in an early essay on Prynne, Simon Jarvis argues that the poet's work reminds us that poetry can only overcome a capitalistically-

---

4   Prynne, 'Difficulties', 2010, 159.
5   See Jarvis 1993.
6   Mellor 1999.
7   Sutherland 2011.

imposed division between truth and beauty by not overcoming it, but rather by writhing inside it: 'Only a poetry recalcitrant to exile from cognition, and a thought which admits its own artifice of articulation, can remain awake to the damage done and the capacities set loose by these formally free divisions of labour'.[8] This dialectical position nonetheless preserves the link between freedom and difficulty; I think it forecloses the possibility, not that the route to freedom is difficulty's opposite, but that freedom might not be an ethical category.

In the American conversation about poetry, we have our own touchstones for this particular ethics of damage and difficulty: the most obvious would be how key Language poets, who like Prynne came of age in the 1970s, built a critique of capital around a critique of the simplifications of thought engendered by the culture of commodification and by the rise of spectacular media – a critique whose central point was that capitalism made relationships thing-like, and reduced the complexities of political struggle and lived suffering to mere spectacle. Prynne has stated publicly that the early Saussurian commitments of the Language poets, their pursuit of generative arbitrariness and aleatory surprise, leave him cold; because he has a theory of the history of language that is built around the pressing of cumulatively deep meanings into the shapes and sounds of words, he prefers to tackle the problem of the commodification of language using older, Empsonian techniques that emphasise the historical treasures of ambiguity.[9] But both the Language poets in the moment of their most clarion poetics and Prynne in his recent essays make a link between an ethics of difficulty and a theory of damaged language. The idiosyncratic anti-capitalism they share has been eclipsed by formalist modernity-language: the U.S. poets have been construed as 'post-modern' and Prynne as 'late-modern' – the Americans the poets of the sharp break, and Prynne the poet of attenuated continuation.

Actually, as Anthony Mellors has suggested, the continuity of Prynne's work with the modernists may be less a technique *per se* than a *topos* or matter central to English-language literary modernism – the *topos* of the underworld, and of the cyclical return to life. Mellors points out that for the earliest modernists, this *topos* centred on the figures of Prosperpine or Kora; for later writers, not least Americans like Charles Olson, this vertical figure of *katabasis*, or going under and coming back up, was rotated 90 degrees, as it were, and given a new classical pedigree – the 'horizontal' arc of journeying and homecoming exem-

---

8   Jarvis 1993, p. 37.
9   See Prynne 1993.

plified in the wanderings of Odysseus.[10] In the early 1970s Prynne delivered a
beautiful, adoring lecture on this thematic of Olson's, which Prynne also exper-
ienced as a deep structure, a kind of boomerang arc, so that the short lyric
sections of Olson's *Maximus* added up to something like epic, and then col-
lapsed back into being lyric again, more beautiful for having been incorporated
for a while into a larger structure.[11]

Olson was a sometime friend and a great influence on the young Prynne;
Prynne's reworking of the Olsonian topos of exile and return, which has shaped
his whole career, involves re-inscribing that arc of homecoming in movements
of many different scales – not only the wide compass of the great Homeric
voyage, but the turning of one's head from left to right and back again, or the
movement of molecules back and forth across a membrane, so as to write a kind
of dream of the return to authenticity into even micrological space. As early as
1979, in an essay that remains among the very best on Prynne, Douglas Oliver
noticed that 'Prynne's work would reach, if it could, beyond the language condi-
tion where sub-microscopic events are mere metaphor for mental process to a
condition where they more closely become a description of the same, essential
process'; he calls it a 'sublime-literal'.[12]

Like Oliver, I think Prynne's ambition is toward a poetry that would stage
cognition's ability to reverse time and, in doing so, reach past mere metaphor.
I think this mostly because of how a belief in this ability organizes Prynne's
essays well as his poems. So let me give you three quick examples of how, in his
critical writing, Prynne has imagined pitting reversal or undoing against what
he takes to be the historical damage of modernity: one that addresses biology,
one that turns to economic history, and a third that thinks through poetry and
philology.

In a 1972 prose piece called 'The *Plant-Time Manifold* Transcripts', Prynne
imitates the proceedings of a scientific conference whose participants are
entertaining the possibility that at the level of cell membranes, plants could
be said to move both forward and backward in time. Indeed, given different
conditions of rot, compost, and generation, the scientists are interested in
how plants might be describable as being alive and dead at the same time:
as one speaker puts it, 'plant death is clearly a more complex event than in
other life systems'.[13] What's interesting about the piece is that it is not a lam-
poon of science but a kind of fantasia on it: Prynne is dead serious. And his

---

10   Mellors 2005, pp. 52–89, 58–9.

11   See Prynne 1999.

12   Oliver 1979, pp. 95–6.

13   Prynne 1999, p. 240.

readers have followed him: the poet and critic Justin Katko, matching this seriousness, calls the piece 'relativistic phytosophy'.[14]

In another piece from the late 1960s, this one called 'A Note on Metal', Prynne offers a sketch of economic history that tells a story of how stamped coinage emerged as the result of complex processes of social abstraction that began, at the dawn of recorded history, with simpler, more concrete measures of value, like weight. Interestingly, for Prynne, the rise of coinage is both a practical matter, involving the need for a medium of value transferable across ever greater distances, and a metaphysical one, since he imagines that stamped coins, unlike ingots or worked metal, are de-magicalised: their stamps over-write any trace of the resonance of the substance itself. It doesn't matter, Prynne believes, that a gold coin is gold so much as that it is gold whose value is backed by political authority, and for Prynne what's damning about the imposition of that authority is that it's an abstraction – an abstraction and a displacement from something magical, something alchemical, that was once evident to us when we first encountered gold. That poetry might help us remember this magic, and that such remembering is a leftist project, Prynne makes clear at the end of the essay: 'at this [late] stage', he writes, 'there is the possible contrast of an exilic (left-wing) history of substance'.[15] The triumph of the left, in this vision, would be measured less by justice or by liberation, whatever they might mean, than by a return to 'reality' or authentic life.

Finally, in a recent *Chicago Review* essay, Prynne imagines the lineation of the poem on the page, in its difference from prose in paragraphs, as a kind of machine for making time tremble and reverse: 'line-breaks or step ordering that override the unfeatured page space of normal printed language perform the overt function of continuity by versus and retroflex'.[16] That is, our eyes darting from the end of one line to the beginning of another create a kind of instability in linear time. Elsewhere he suggests that not only left-justified writing, but the etymology of English words, can be motivated or activated into reversing time, and to heightening painful, buried contradictions in the human history of violence, as when Wordsworth uses the word 'blessing' with beatitude but also, Prynne thinks, with an implicit awareness of the word's link to words like the French *blessure*, to wounding, to blood sacrifice.[17]

---

14   See Katko 2010. In the original version of this essay, I misidentified the date of publication
      of Prynne's text as 1968; it dates to 1972. Thanks to Ryan Dobran for pointing out this error.
15   Prynne 1999, p. 130.
16   Prynne 2010, 'Mental Ears', p. 140.
17   Ibid. p. 136; pp. 139–41.

All of these examples, I think, can make us better readers of Prynne's poetry. But they also make me feel my critical problem most acutely, and so I think I need to name for you the contradiction I experience between my keen interest in what Prynne's poems are capable of, on the one hand, and my rejection of the historical and ethical premises that generate them, on the other. It's not clear to me, for instance, that 'the unfeatured page space of normal printed language' exists in any continuous way such that we could say poetry stands out against it because of how it's printed – historically, the formats of prose have been as marked by conventions and surprises as poetry has, perhaps more so. And the stagist history of the rise of capitalist money, in which the problem with capital is that it's abstract and not concrete, has long since been disabled by a variety of scholarship in anthropology and economic history: I'd point to David Graeber's recent volume *Debt: The First Five Thousand Years* as the great synthesis and clarification of this scholarship. Finally, the intellectual strain behind the play-fulness of the *Plant Time Manifold* is all too evident. It is deflating indeed when a perceptive reader like Katko, glossing Prynne's piece for more than fifty pages, can only assert in the end that Prynne's insistence on our reading plants as mov-ing in more than one temporal direction is evidence of 'the poet's faith that his description bears absolute fidelity to the total logic of his own experience'.[18] Katko's use of the contemporary keywords 'fidelity' and 'logic' calls to mind the work of Alain Badiou, the arbitrariness of whose use of set-theoretical math to found a new ontology of 'infinitude' shares with 'relativistic phytosophy' an all-too willful hermetic 'fidelity' to its improbable cause.[19]

So what about the poems? As I've said, I agree with Oliver that Prynne is after a kind of 'sublime-literal' in which a poem can demonstrate that the activ-ity of the mind is like the activity of nature, that the movement of molecules is like the movement of the stars, that at some level erosion and continental drift and neuronal impulses and the etymology of words are all expressions of the same non-linear dynamism. At mid-twentieth century, the emergent dis-cipline that gave this belief a contemporary cast was cybernetics – a field of inquiry that presumed to find the structural commonality across psychological and natural disciplines by way of assuming an innate dynamism to all phe-nomena, which was to be understood via informatic keywords like 'signals' and

---

18   Katko 2010, p. 286.
19   For a devastating critique of Badiou's use of math, to which Badiou was only able to respond by huffing and puffing and bullying, see Ricardo Nirenberg and David Nirenberg. 'Badiou's Number: A Critique of Mathematics as Ontology', *Critical Inquiry* 37 (Summer 2011): 583–614, and Badiou's reply in *Critical Inquiry* 38 (2012), 362–87.

'feedback'.[20] Prynne likely picked up on such ideas from Olson, the opening assertion of whose canonical poem 'The Kingfishers' – 'What does not change / is the will to change' – finds its support in the cybernetic language that surfaces a few lines later: 'not accumulation but change, the feed-back proves, the feed-back is / the law'. While Prynne does not hew long or closely to this particular idiom – the first piece in his 1997 *Poems*, from 1968, begins with the language of signals, and it subsides shortly after – he retains his insistence on the non-metaphoric commonality of phenomena across scale. This seems important for understanding Prynne's career, since his belief in this trans-scalar commonality is what drives the wide reach of his reference, not least his famous juxtapositions of economic, scientific, and poetic language. This wide reach, as one reads across Prynne's volumes, is at least in part an expression of the sheer will to align seemingly incommensurate phenomena into a single cosmically coherent picture. Many of his champions see in this reach the measure of Prynne's genius; however true that may be, it is also an expression of his will to restore what C.S. Lewis mournfully called 'the discarded image' – i.e., a vision of the spheres.

Unlike Olson, of course, Prynne has never sought to restore us to the spheres by writing in the epic mode; indeed one suspects he actively rejects the attempt. In the place of epic, we find an ongoing engagement with a notion of lyric, expressed in the early work by the belief that attention to minutiae, given expression in shorter forms, can open space for human tenderness in a time of universally reified relations. This tenderness sits uneasily with the testiness that the cybernetic ambition breeds, so that, in the early poems, we are being spoken to by a poet who is both eager to show us the value of quiet attentiveness to what's small, and exasperated that we don't understand its significance (the first of the relatively few questions that dot his collected 1999 *Poems* is, 'How could this be clearer?'). Here is the penultimate stanza of 'Die A Millionaire', from the 1968 volume *Kitchen Poems*:

> And the back mutation is *knowledge* and
> has always been so in the richest tradition
> of the trust it is possible to have, to repose
> in the mysteries. The perversions which
> thrust it *forward*, as a new feed into the

---

20   A good survey of the trans-disciplinary ambitions of cybernetics, and of its reluctance to engage disciplines on anything like their own terms, is Jean-Pierre Dupuy, *On The Origins of Cognitive Science: The Mechanization of the Mind* (Cambridge: The MIT Press, 2009).

same vicious grid of expanding prospects
(profits) are let through by the weakness, now,
of names.[21]

There are three things in this passage that are resonant throughout Prynne's
career: the reference to knowledge as a 'back mutation'; the sense of forward
movement as a 'perversion' (rendered here in cybernetic language, as a 'new
feed'); and the sense that capitalism, in accentuating forward movement at the
expense of our ability to remain aware of the role of 'back mutation' in shaping
authentic perceptions, has done damage to language ('the weakness, now, / of
names'). The poem concludes with a mix of tender piety and teacherly curt-
ness:

> This is
> a prayer. I have it now between my
> teeth and my eyes, on my forehead. Know
> the names. It is as simple as the purity
> of sentiment: it is as simple
> as that.
>   P, 16

Later in *Kitchen Poems*, in a poem called 'A Gold Ring Called Reluctance',
Prynne invents another version of this elusive idea of literal continuity across
scale: that underneath seemingly irreversible phenomena is an endlessness,
both modestly un-metaphysical and quietly cosmic, bigger than linearity. He
discovers it while walking – walking slowly, in particular:

> As you drag your feet or simply being
> tired, the ground is suddenly interesting;
> not as metaphysic but the grave, maybe,
> that area which claims its place like
> a shoe. This idea of the end is a neat
> but mostly dull falsity, since the
> biologic collapse is violence reversed,
> like untying a knot.
>   P, 21

---

21   Prynne 1999, p. 16. Hereafter abbreviated *P* and cited parenthetically by page number.

The poet's interpretation of death ('biologic collapse') as 'violence reversed', and the body as a 'knot' awaiting its untying, makes a lovely bid for entropy as deserving our fondness. It also speaks to the career-long will to reversal with which I began. In a moment I want to sketch the way in which this matrix of concerns endures across Prynne's career, but before I do so, I want to turn to its one remaining element, which is the critique of capital in which that matrix finds its specificity. For Prynne, in the late writing as well as in the early poems, the critique of capital is to be conducted by pitting an actuality won of stillness against a frenzy of commerce that frays language. It is to be found in minutiae, and in something like un-velocity. Here are the last two stanzas of 'Gold Ring':

> And as the age or condition of this
> fact we call place grows daily more remote,
> the literalness thrives unchecked. The
> imbalance is frightening: the splintered
> naming of wares creates targets for want
> like a glandular riot, and thus want
> is *the* most urgent condition (e.g. not
> enough credit).
>   I am interested instead in
> discretion: what I love and also the spread
> of indifferent qualities. Dust, objects of use
> broken by wear, by simply slowing too much
> to be retrieved as agents. Scrap; the old ones,
> the dead who sit daily at the feast. Each
> time I hesitate I think of them, loving what
> I know. The ground on which we pass,
> moving our feet, less excited by travel.
>   *P*, 23

The critique of capital emerges here in the way two sets of words sift into opposition: on one side, the 'frightening imbalance' between 'fact' and the 'splintered naming of wares' (that is, something like advertising) produce a 'glandular riot' that overexcites something like a faculty of 'want'. To these are opposed 'discretion', the 'indifferent qualities' of minor, well-worn objects, and the 'slowness' that prevents them from capture in the circuits of commerce. All of this, along with a respectful nod in the direction of 'the dead', produces a lessened 'excitation' in which we are invited to rove and saunter, forsaking a presumably hyped-up, touristic 'travel'.

These oppositions are typical of Prynne's critique of capital, and they do not disappear in the later work. The pitting of one speed against another, but also the ethical commitment to personal refusal, and the sense that there is something 'glandular' in susceptibility to the solicitations of commercial life – that a central problem with capitalism is that it excites people's concupiscence – all these remain constant, as we will see. Indeed I believe they provide a template for the later work, despite the supposedly un-thematisable density of the more recent poems. The way to read the endurance of these concerns from the early to the later poems, I think, is to see them transposed from first-person statements of theme and belief, as we've seen above, to figures of reversible flow, and then to reversal-games at the level of the part-word. Rather than abandoning an early thematics of reversible damage, that is, Prynne in his later work saturates each poem with it. If reversibility stops being a 'theme' of the poems, that is, it isn't because it stops being a *concern* of the poems – indeed it becomes their formal principle.

Prynne's mid-career work bears this out. The 1983 volume *The Oval Window* is a good example: as Reeve and Kerridge note, the book assembles its matter from an array of seemingly incommensurable material, from the tropes of sixth-century Chinese 'Palace Style' poetry, to the ordering of cause and effect in computer programming, to the sloshing and cascading movement of the crystals in the inner ear that give us our sense of balance, and on to the Heisenbergian sensitivity to observation of data on financial markets ('Deaf To Meaning'). Once again, the poet brings that material into alignment (perhaps with the residual permission of those mid-century cybernetic ambitions), and frames the alignment with a proposition about the reversibility of time – here, in the volume's unattributed epigraph, which describes how computer languages operationalise the ideas of 'before' and 'after', and concludes that 'This condition says essentially that, / given the present, / the past and future / are independent / of each other'. But where in the volumes from the late 60s and 70s Prynne would have offered a first-person statement of programme or theme, pitting griddedness or spectacle (understood as perverse forms of relentless forward motion) against one or another micrological reversal of time, in *The Oval Window* we will come across it in small rhetorical turns and word-choices: the theme is in place, if miniaturised. Take the opening of this untitled poem:

> So: from now on too, or soon lost,
> the voice you hear is your own
> revoked, on a relative cyclical downturn
> imaged in latent narrow-angle glaucoma.

> Yet the snow picks up and infolds,
> a mist of gold leaf lightly shimmers
> as floating clouds go back to the mountains
> > *P,* 333

Here the thematics of un-damage are played out in the mini-structure, revoke-vs-infold: even as the 'voice' is made dumb and un-lyric in the 'revoking' movement of capital (the 'cyclical downturn'), the infolding 'snow', like the snowflake-seeming crystals in the inner ear, tumbles in upon itself and facilitates return to something less damaged: the clouds 'go back to the mountains'.

By the 1990s, Prynne has carried this theme of reversal down to the level of the morpheme and the grapheme. Take this poem from the 1997 volume *For The Monogram*:

> Tuck up tawdry attraction for the follow broken air
> > to separate yield and distort along the floor,
> moving flood in a pure scheme they have but them
> > selves alone flutter drain orphans in ultra wrong
> unit time set. Either dies young or lives (almost)
> > for ever trailing blab across some bad sequence
> of strides, seeking trim animal redress. For lifted
> > maternal protection slurping canny on a bundle at
> just one table in the entire universe, for him now
> > governed lazy just one it counts viewless torn lip
> chained. All possible out rankings flunk my presents
> > in ever hopeless profusion scattered grandly on
> sea-bed panegyric stipple. Brother set in both limbs
> > dismissed as a tort factor of age craning forward to
> counter stream cycle proof, invests its hatch cover
> > by orphan fragments reverting to current seed.
> > > *P,* 425

As usual, the word-hoard is organised as a blending of domains: here we get industrial agriculture (the 'flutter drain orphans') with a light dusting of computer-language ('stream cycle' and 'current seed') framed by a caution against finding something about the scene arousing (the 'tuck up' in 'tuck up tawdry attraction', being a way of hiding an erection by restraining one's penis with the elastic band of one's underwear). The 'orphans' in line 4, dying young or barely alive, are drooling as they move in a 'bad sequence of strides', on weak limbs with a 'brother set' in the bones, twisted into parallel from remaining mostly seated, their mothers replaced with 'a bundle' from which they suck, their lips punctured by the holes made for a chain, their worlds contracting to 'just one table in the entire universe', in stalls that are otherwise 'viewless'. As these poor creatures '[crane] forward' for sustenance, the poet notices the messy backwash of their suckling, or possibly their gag reflex, and imagines it violating the one-way motion of the flutter-valved tubes they are obliged to mouth at, producing a wet white counter-spray to the force-fed flood of milk that's all they have to gulp.

I've noted that from early in his career Prynne makes it possible to see, even in the flux of backwash, a metaphor for something like the great Homeric arc of exile and return (the backwash-sperm 'reverting to current seed' at the poem's close). What makes this poem typical of his later style is the way he also expresses theme at the level of the vowel and the dipthong – the poem is an extended play on 'u'-sounds in English, with 11 of 16 lines containing the letter either alone or as part of a dipthong, and a smattering of words like 'one', 'cover' and 'brother' that make a short u-sound even without the letter. I call this 'thematic' because the difference between the 'ou' in 'young' (line 5) and in 'count' (line 10) likely represent movements back and forth across a great vowel shift, a kind of perpetual miniature 'versus and retroflex' between what began as French and what ended up as 'English' pronunciations of the vowel combination – from *coup de foudre* to 'pound' and 'ounce', as it were. This play with dipthongs also raises background questions about the convergence and divergence of word-pronunciation across time, like how the 'er' in 'revert' came to sound like the 'ur' in 'current'. Whatever the actual histories of such convergences and divergences, it is more than likely that for Prynne they are meant to represent the time of the English language moving forward and backwards at once. This vowel and dipthong-play is one of the central elements of Prynne's late style, and once more I find support for my sense that it's thematic in critical writing by Prynne, not least his 1992 essay 'Stars, Tigers, and the Shapes of Words', which is a brief against Saussure and what Prynne calls the thesis of arbitrariness in structuralist linguistics. Against that thesis, Prynne suggests that there are deep cultural reasons why some, if not all, words are shaped the way they are – his main example, whimsically enough, being the 'twinkle' in 'Twinkle Twinkle Little Star' – a word whose terminal '-le', he argues, bespeaks diminutiveness on the model of the terminal '-le' in 'little', and brightness, on the model of the terminal '-le' in 'sparkle'.[22]

---

22   Prynne 1993, p. 9.

This may explain why, in the poem above, Prynne pairs his dipthong-play with a sustained attention to the shape and sound of the letter combination '-or' and its variants: notice 'for' (4 times), 'floor', 'distort', 'pure', 'orphan', and 'orphans', 'torn', 'profusion', 'tort', 'factor', and 'forward'. Meanwhile 'protection', 'profusion', 'brother' and 'proof' reverse the '-or' to make a series of 'ro-' sounds and shapes, making a kind of counter-current to the connotations of the 'or-' words. I don't know what Prynne thinks is the historical significance of this or-ro lability, except that after hearing the two sounds together they seem to call out to one another (and perhaps that, in things like the movement from the 'Orlando' in *Orlando Furioso* to the 'Roland' in the *Chanson de Roland*, which is modelled on the earlier Italian poem, we can see the transposition in literary history, too). But the point is, and this is a little astounding, that it's all done according to a thesis about modernity.

∶∙

In a 2006 seminar visit to a class taught by Keston Sutherland at the University of Sussex, Prynne referred to a conversation he had with one of his German translators in which, against the notion that they should work toward a German version that would transmit some English meaning, Prynne proposed that they simply translate 'the words'. A few moments later, he said that the infrequency of his live reading, at least in the UK, was due to a 'policy' he keeps to. With the audience chuckling, he joked that

> My policy ... is to read only to audiences that don't understand English. That sounds contrarian, but actually it works pretty well. It means I can read at liberty in China, I can read quite freely in Australia, I can actually read more or less in parts of the USA, and I can read quite widely in Canada, but not usually in Britain ... [laughter][23]

The serious part of the joke seemed to be that, in contexts where audiences aren't familiar with the meaning of the words or the phrases they congeal into, they can simply enjoy the play of sounds, instead of fussing about looking for meaning, or – worse – a 'moral': it's a joke, then, at literary Britain's expense. But this seems only partly serious. And the mere joke, the in-house British joke at the expense of the former commonwealth, seems only partly a joke.

---

23   https://www.archiveofthenow.org/authors/?i=77&f=922#922.

I mention these remarks because together they bring to a sharp point the questions I began with about the modernity thesis, and the ethics of difficulty, in Prynne's work. To read word by word, having given up the possibility of framing one's reading with prior assumptions, sounds to some ears like the very description of the way to read under conditions of what Adorno called 'wrong life' – eschewing interpretive presumption, avoiding the moral offence of being caught going *tra-la-la* next door to Auschwitz or in view of Fallujah, letting meaning, when it comes, thrust up from a two- or three-word sequence, dutifully reminding ourselves that all we have left now of a once-rich lyric tradition is a kind of infra-lyric beauty that is certainly ana- and possibly anti-hermeneutical. In this Adornian framework, the poet adopts (and presumably the attentive reader mimics) a position of 'damage' in which, as Simon Perril puts it, 'Utterance is more often maimed and wounded by a self-conscious sense of inappropriateness and inadequacy'.[24]

But there are problems with this framework. For one thing, it depends on a pun between semantic meaning and 'meaning' in the sense of 'the meaning of life' – the latter of which, indeed, Adorno critiqued mercilessly as a kind of country-club philosophical pursuit after the mass murder of European Jews. To read for a phrase or a sentence and attempt to gain from it local meaning is not to insist, like a mole-eyed bourgeois, that art be pretty and give us deep thoughts. To argue that those two things are the same is to reduce the critique of capital to a critique of concupiscence (which is, as we've seen, an old target of Prynne's).

The problem is broader, though, than a skirmish around how to read individual lines or phrases in poetry like Prynne's. It has to do with how to interpret his tone. To use the critique of damaged life as a background support for the unremitting *gravitas* of Prynne's work is to read Adorno undialectically – not, I don't mean to say, to mis-read the Adornian dialectic, since Prynne's best expositors are brilliant readers of Adorno, but to read his version of the dialectic as though it were simply correct. Certainly Adorno had a lancing critique of too-easy beauty, and of the homogenising force of mass culture, but he developed it in sentences that showed off his unmatched ear for that popular form, the aphorism. At the same time, he was never less persuasive than when critiquing the popular. This problem in Adorno, which is also a problem for Prynne and the Adornian reading of Prynne, stems from Adorno's own background reliance on an idea that, in its Heideggerian variant at least, he

---

24   Perril 2003.

opposed – the notion of reification. But he relied on it nevertheless, leading us decades later once again to the problem of a reductive critique of capital – here, the reduction of the critique of capital to the critique of abstraction and objectification. Adorno's defence of the qualitative and the non-identical as redoubts against the tendency to abstraction and objectification in systematic philosophy is far more persuasive than his critique of quantitative, homogenising mass culture, and that's because the qualitative and the non-identical live in the subject as much as in the object: unfortunately for the critique of reification, there turn out to be plenty of idiosyncratic and reflexive ways to love 'Oops I Did It Again'. My point is simply that, just as it is a pun to equate the desire for local meaning-making with the brute insistence that Life is Meaningful, so too is it a pun to construe the lyric as morally 'complicit' with capital because it has a price tag: the critique of capital is not the critique of price, but of *value*.

This matters, both for the critique of capital and for our understanding of the moral life of poetry (if it has one). Too much contemporary anti-capitalist theory depends on a linear understanding of both capital's operations, and its movement in history, as though the problem we face in the 21st century is that there is more capitalism now than there used to be, that it extends farther and deeper than ever before: this is the notion expressed in theories of 'affective' and 'immaterial labor', for instance. And certainly it's true that the forced politeness of a flight attendant, and the strokes of a keyboard at a console, are new capillary termini for capital. But this newness no more explains the history of capitalism than a critique of Autotune explains the history of blackface.

Capital works as a circuit, first of all, not a simple vector: in order to self-expand, it must move through phases, and it is beset with logistical, political, and financial obstacles at every moment of its metamorphoses from money into capital and back again. Marx didn't begin his critique of capital unidirectionally, or with a humanness that became commodified, a kind of H → C, so to speak. He begins with the movement of commodities in and out of the money form, over and over: M-C-M'. The relentless technological innovation capital compels is easy to interpret linearly, of course – we didn't have gas chambers in 1926, or iPods in 1987. But the linear interpretation fails to grasp the contradictory relationship between technology and the value produced by labour, which is that every innovation that frees capitalists from having to pay wages simultaneously moves them away from the source of the value – exploited labour – that in turn makes their profits possible. It also fails to grasp that not all money is capital, and that not all goods are commodities, at every moment, but only inasmuch as they are not lying around unused, or up for sale, and so on. This not to mention all the problems capitalists face in forming and maintaining stock, staving off wastage, gaining access to credit, enforcing labour discipline, securing a stable market, and surviving competition. That capitalists as a class have been so successful at solving (or deferring) these problems neither means that capital has simply triumphed over everything, as in the thesis of damaged life, nor that its perpetual vulnerabilities instantly suggest a route to its overthrow. It does mean that, if we are serious about understanding capitalism, or even just capitalism's relation to the impulses that lead to poetry, we can do much better than to bemoan 'reification'.

Without a sense of capital's beset metamorphoses, that is, we in the academy and in the poetry-world that's hitched to it end up telling ourselves modernity-stories about the Commodification of Everything instead of producing analyses of how capital is working today. And without a sense that it is participation in the capital-labour relation, not the existence of a market, that makes money and labour and commodities into bearers of capitalist value, our *ars poetica* tend to waffle between a thin hope that poetry, undercapitalised as it is, is somehow 'outside' capital, and a self-flagellating despair that nothing is. The 'dialectic' that tries to capture the movement between these two positions by producing negative art is less a dialectic than a practice of self-mortification with an older pedigree by far than capital. That's not to say that dark art cannot be anti-capitalist, or that there is a 'better', celebratory route to resisting capitalism via poetry. It's to suggest that the relationship between art and capital, whatever it will turn out to be, is not best understood – or practised – as an ethics.

So how do we read poetry like Prynne's, which has staked its claim to legibility on precisely that, on an ethical practice of self-ruining negativity? I think the answer is, by trying to historicise how he came to the positions he holds, and to the comportments those positions produce. This returns us, in closing, to the question of tone, and also to the arc of his career.

For all the praise given Prynne because he reads widely in the sciences, his poems feel less experimental than ascriptive, so that each new bit of scientific (or financial, or engineering, or programming) language comes to seem merely the latest support for Prynne's claim about the un-linear instabilities inside of seemingly linear time, and their capacity to model (if not actually enact) the undoing of the damage caused by linearity, grids, forward-thrustingness, and instrumentalisation. More consistent even than the absence of any lightness in the poems is the absence of the scientific emotions of perplexity and wonder. Early in the career, variations on the words 'hope' and 'hopelessness' come closest to that, and they carry the sweet residual erotic charge of the sonneteering lover's hopelessness; the poems of the 70s are full of them.[25] But along with question marks, exclamation points, and the first-person plural, they disappear in the early 80s, never to return.

This is perhaps to say that Prynne's late style is a victory for Margaret Thatcher. Looking back from the vantage of the later work, it is hard not to read lines like these from a 1971 poem, 'The Five Hindrances', and feel that a whole daylight world has been lost:

> The two friends
> Walk down the sandy track and we hold back
> The ends of the crescent. The future history of the
> Air is glowing, with amity beyond the path itself;
> Touched gently and brought to this stubborn wreck.
>
> 163

To be sure, the work that comes after is far more rigorous, more refusing, more minutely controlled: I can only imagine the compositional joy that must arise from the sensitivity to the relays among 'or's' and 'ow's' and 'ou's' that makes a poet able to shape a line like, 'undertow no more down, weak born to make allow fervent or you' (*Sub Songs*, 13). But that doesn't make the work better; it just makes it more stern.

∴

I have tried to suggest that perhaps the strongest argument for the value of the enduring thematics of reversal and anti-linearity in Prynne's work is an Adornian argument that, in the modern era, we live a damaged life. In the Prynnian version of that argument, the reversibility (or at least non-linearity) of patterns of everything from migratory drift, membrane salinity, and word-shapes can be pitted against the relentless instrumentalisation of time and persons demanded by capital, without actually being 'pitted against it' *per se*. But this argument

---

25   See, for instance, '... when so hopelessly / we want so much more' from 'Numbers in Time of Trouble' (*Poems*, 17); 'The qualities then area name, corporately, / for the hope they will return to us' from 'Sketch for a Financial Theory of The Self' (20); '... perhaps only the smell of resin // holds him to a single / hopefulness' from 'A Figure of Mercy, of Speech' (39), and so on. In some sense the early language of 'hope' is what the retroflex-trope grafts itself onto and then replaces, by way of the mediating term 'rise', variants of which ('rising', etc.) are used to describe moral, geographic, and meterological 'gradients' that are a kind of last pit-stop before the reversibility idea fully takes hold.

for the ethical merit of pitting reflex time against linear time, as the title 'The Five Hindrances' suggests, may be a better Buddhist than a Marxist one, since capital is a social relation and not a bad physics.

My argument, then, is not that Prynne's negative-dialectical poetry is too 'difficult', or too negative. It's that, by construing the dialectic in terms of physics and of ethics, his poetry is not nearly dialectical enough. The conditions of its legibility are not simply that we read word-to-word, staving off easy interpretation; they are also that we subscribe to a modernity-narrative that stakes everything on a notion of 'damage' that, in turn, depends on a very slender critique of capital as 'commodification'. I should be clear that I'm not wishing Prynne's poetry were built on a stronger critique of capital. Little of my favourite poetry is a product of 'correct' analysis, and I don't expect it to be. But since Prynne and his interpreters have made a claim for the force of his poetry on the basis of how its difficulty-ethics performs a compelling critique of life under capital, it becomes important to notice how and when that critique is not compelling. As an ethical comportment, this one is not. And the idea that Poetry and Marxism Are Serious Business, given warrant by the damage-thesis, is a damaging idea.

CHAPTER 7

The Price of Value

My essay, though it is meant to address the 'economic' dimension of literary value, approaches the topic at a rather steep rake. This is partly because the full-frontal approach, so to speak, has already been developed: there is a sturdy tradition of work that compares literary texts and economic ideas in analogical and homological terms, for instance – not least work in the vein of Jean-Joseph Goux and Marc Shell.[1] In this work it becomes possible to see long histories of overlap between how we have historically conceptualised words and coins, say, or householding and rhetorical economy. For a student of twentieth-century poetry like myself, such work provides an important back-history to the work of a poet like Ezra Pound, for whom matters of economics, rhetoric, pedagogy, and poetry all twined together in ways that continue to influence poets to this day.

More recent work has explored the intimate relationship between key elements of modern literary and economic *theories*. Tim Kreiner, for instance, has traced not only the similarities between Saussurean linguistics and marginalist economics, but also their historical co-emergence. Kreiner's work not only outlines the way Saussurean linguistics, which is built around the idea that the specificity and value of any given word is built out of a differential relation between that word and the words around it, also mimics marginalist economics, which imagines economic value to be produced in the price differences among commodities. He also situates Saussure's project, worked out beginning in 1907 at the University of Geneva, in the long shadow of Swiss marginalism, whose intellectual prestige ran high, through the renowned work first of Leon Walras, and later Wilfredo Pareto, both of whom were chair of political economy at the University of Lausanne from the late nineteenth to the early twentieth century.[2] There is certainly still a story to be told about how the literary theories built up around a Saussurean model of potential difference carry with it liberal-reformist politics of marginalism, whose focus on the way marginal-use values could afford the modern world a potential infinity of value was meant quite explicitly as a riposte to insurgent socialist theories of the economy that imagined a zero-sum game between capitalists and workers.[3]

---

1 See, for example, Goux 1990, and Shell 1978.
2 See Kreiner 2013, pp. 16–17.
3 In some of the important scholarship, not least in the work of Roberto Unger, the marginal-

But I am going to approach the matter of literary-theoretical 'values' and economic 'value' from a different angle, by way of a straightforward but idiosyncratic act of literary comparison. Such comparisons are basic building blocks of our work as critics, and I think they can make our values in this role visible quite plainly. I think the dominant historical frameworks we use to make such comparisons tell a value story, too. And I think that reshuffling which texts we tend to compare, as well as making comparisons that demand possible reperiodisation, can be useful tools for contesting dominant literary-critical values.

In my case, I have been interested for some time now in whether, for Marxist literary critics, such acts of comparison and reperiodisation might be of particular use. It seems to me that Marxist literary criticism has an odd double status in the profession: on the one hand, it is seen as a somewhat dated (if possibly resurgent) brand, or method, which limits critics to reading left-wing texts only, and constrains interpretation to the endless repetition of stale discoveries about the unacknowledged role of labour behind most literary production. On the other hand, Marxist criticism has an uncannily universal heritage in English-speaking literary academia: the very critics who would disavow it on the terms I described in the preceding text are nonetheless likely to tell modernity stories, for instance, that ultimately depend on an understanding that capitalism is the engine for most of what goes by the name of 'modernity' in the first place; or they turn to ideas like 'structures of feeling', which have a specifically Marxist provenance, whether or not they acknowledge it.

So in this essay I will be looking at portions of two historically far-flung poems in order to see if I can push back against this situation, not least by thinking about modernity and feeling. The first of the poems, Boethius's sixth-century *Consolation of Philosophy*, is, among other things, a Neoplatonic meditation on the sufferings of the body and the freedom of the soul. The second, a recent long poem by Jasper Bernes, is a more-than-realist account of recent anti-capitalist struggles that reflects on capital's ability to create persons and warp the very fabric of space and time. Both poems are prosimetric (that is, they alternate between verse and prose), and both take the occasion of a certain

---

ists not only passively facilitate a shift away from political economy to economics, but also do so in a pointed response to socialist critiques of capitalism. How precisely this is true is hard to determine, but we might see a latter-day measure of its plausibility in Robert Heilbroner's observation that modern-day economics, the economics marginalism helps create, has also created a blindness within the field whereby economists are so focused on the autonomy of 'the economy' as their object of study that they are unable to realise that they are in fact students of capitalism. See Unger 1987; and Heilbroner and Milberg 1995.

kind of human suffering to investigate whether, somewhere in the space-time we think we know, possibilities for salvation or political liberation might be lying in wait.

The aim of my comparing these two poems will be to suggest, first, that the prosimetric tradition they share, as well as techniques internal to the form, make the links between them much sturdier and stranger than a simple modernity story can explain; second, that we can profit from allowing ourselves to feel something more than scepticism about these poems' speculations on the cosmos, or on space-time; and third, that the philosophical framework to which we might turn in order to make a quick-and-dirty distinction between the Neoplatonic Boethius and the Marxist Bernes – that is, a distinction between 'idealism' and 'materialism' – tells us more about received ideas concerning religion and Marxism, respectively, than it does about the poems, or the problems that animate them. I will conclude, building on these three points, by suggesting that if we disrupt our first impulses to linear periodisation, clear feeling, and philosophical tidiness – that is, by questioning the literary-critical value we place on those things – we can see Bernes's poem in particular struggling to come to terms with capitalism in ways that actually improve our understanding of how capital produces so-called economic value.

So let's turn to Boethius's *Consolation of Philosophy*, famous not only for its exploration of the solace philosophy and poetry alike can bring to the suffering mind, but also for its mixed verse-prose structure. The moment most germane for my argument here is famously the central pivot of Boethius's text, the ninth poem of the third book in the *Consolation*. Readers will recall that Boethius has been imprisoned and sentenced to death after a mysterious reversal of political fortune under Theodoric, the Ostrogoth ruler of Rome. Though he professed to be a Christian, the 'consolation' of the title comes to the narrator not through religious doctrine, but through the figure of Philosophy, who appears to Boethius as a woman, and who leads him through a succession of prose dialogues, which are punctuated by verse interludes. The arc of the *Consolation* is from despair to enlightenment, and it follows a Platonic (and Neoplatonic) trajectory – which is to say that as Philosophy leads the narrator to let go of his outrage and his anguish, she does so by way of urging him to reflect more deeply, not only on the moral character of his suffering, but also on the evanescence and the insignificance of the material world.

This is consequential, believe it or not, for my reading of contemporary poetry: more and more I want to read it in light of the poetry that comes, not only immediately prior to it, but also long before it. So, when we read Boethius's Neoplatonic ode to the uncaused wholeness of divinity, and isolate this 'doctrine' from everything around it in the poem, we lose something important that poets today still tap into, not least the allure a certain kind of poem exerts when it invites us to meditate, not only on its propositions, but on the complex self-relation that is its shape, form, performance. In a recent study of the form of the *Consolation*, Robert McMahon argues that despite generations of careful modern readings of Boethius's text, its statements of belief about the nature of matter, the universe, soul have been taken as free-standing assertions of something like a Neoplatonic creed, whereas Boethius built the work to enable readers to experience such moments as part of an unfolding succession, a journey, in which statements taken as true in earlier parts of the work are altered in meaning by the exposition of the 'higher' truths that come after.[4] McMahon also goes to some length to demonstrate, not only the careful seeding of the *Consolation* with numerological significance, but also the way such numerology is meant to combine with the successive and retrospective structure of the work to facilitate not argumentative, but meditative reading. And in a compelling new examination of the political struggles over liturgy and literacy in late medieval England, Katherine Zieman pushes hard against the now-intuitive Althusserian notion, built in part around Pascal's remark, 'Kneel down, move your lips in prayer, and you will believe', that to sing, chant, recite, submit to the rhythms of a song or a text, even one organised around 'doctrine', is necessarily to be 'interpellated'.[5]

In addition to the isolation of 'doctrine' from its textual and literary surround, the practice of critique as critique-of-doctrine makes it harder to see the continuities between historically distant poetic stories about the value of matter and the meaning of suffering (and vice versa). There is hardly any scholarship, for instance, on how texts from the nineteenth and twentieth centuries that mix prose and lineated 'verse' are tapping into the long tradition of the prosimetrum. But as Peter Dronke has suggested in his study of the form, prosimetric composition establishes an extremely useful, flexible framework in which poets can signal shifts among degrees or kinds of reality, not to mention tonal shifts that embed or imply larger, looming modal ones.[6] But our narratives of 'secularisation', built around notions of doctrine rather than practice, and our exceptionalist accounts of literary modernism, which tend to afford it no longer historical story than one that looks back to the Romantics for contrast – these make it very hard to see contemporary mixings of mode in anything but a recent historical framework, or see them merely as 'secular' version of earlier

---

4   See McMahon 2006.
5   See Zieman 2008.
6   See Dronke 1994.

'religious' work. We thereby miss the full range of what such texts are doing, including the full range of how they are struggling with problems of value.

One way I think poetry struggles with problems of value – from 'value' in its most traditional moral and ethical senses to 'value' in a fully Marxist sense – is through the repertoire of techniques by which poems suggest that their forms are like the world, or that something about their forms is like something about the world. This is an ancient poetic practice, and a long-standing subject for criticism, including highly sophisticated, left-leaning contemporary criticism – as when Giorgio Agamben describes the rhyming structure of the sestina as 'eschatological', because, as a form of cyclicality, it is not linear, secular; sestina rhyme fulfills a temporal expectation.[7] Agamben, writing about the troubadour poet Arnaut Daniel, seems to 'believe' that such a device works, perhaps because he believes that Arnaut 'believed' it. But I wonder whether there is a slightly different way to approach the formalism that makes claims about how poetic form is like the material world, one less modelled on belief and faith (Agamben is writing about the cyclical time of the sestina in light of the writings of Saint Paul).

Take, for instance, the first seventeen lines of the 'invocation' that forms *Consolation* III.9. In these lines, which are sung by Lady Philosophy (possibly by the poet as well), the Lady and her companion appeal to the divine Creator to help them achieve the clarity it will take to comprehend the meanings of matter – which, in the Neoplatonic framework, is a first step toward understanding the meanings of suffering. In terms of their argumentative content, these lines have long been recognised as a straight-forward recounting of Plato's account of the origins and destiny of matter in the *Timaeus*:

> O you who in perpetual order govern the universe,
> Creator of heaven and earth, who bid time ever move,
> And resting still, grant motion to all else;
> Whom no external causes drove to make
> Your work of flowing matter, but the form
> Within yourself of the highest good, ungrudging; from a heavenly pattern
> tern
> *You* draw out all things, and being yourself most fair,
> A fair world in your mind you bear, and forming it
> In the same likeness, bid it being perfect to complete itself
> In perfect parts. *You* bind its elements with law ...

---

7 Agamben 2005, p. 79.

You, binding soul together in its threefold nature's midst,
Soul that moves all things, then divide it into harmonious parts;
Soul thus divided has its motion gathered
Into two circles, moves to return to itself, and the Mind deep within
Encircles, and makes the heaven turn, in likeness to itself.[8]

And so on. The question is, why sing the *Timaeus*? Why have two characters sing it? The Althusserian answer would be that, in singing, we are performing an action that makes us more susceptible to ideological imprintation (or, more precisely, that in dramatising two characters singing, the poet is inviting us to mimic such imprintation). In this light, it is a short step to claiming that the prosody of these lines is in service of the project of making the doctrine singable, unconsciously absorbable.

One might think this is a good or a bad thing, but it is certainly plausible. Even with a minimum of knowledge about Latin prosody, for instance, I can read the last line and a half of the invocation this way. In the Loeb Library English of S.J. Tester, it is rendered, 'And you [the Neoplatonic creator], alone and same / Are [to the blessed] their beginning, driver, leader, pathway, end'. In Latin, the last line reads, 'Principium, vector, dux, semita, terminus idem'. Why could we not see in the wide variability of end-sounds and end-letters of those last words the kind of allness the song is praising? M-sounds, r-sounds, x-sounds, terminal a's: like compass points of enunciative possibility. Bracketing the 'idem' (which, as the 'same' in the English, has the sense of 'alike', that is, of applying to all the terms in the list), could we not see in the 'x' of 'dux' ('leader') the chiasmus across which the last line pivots (it is, McMahon points out, something like the midway point of the *Consolation*)? Could we not read the 'x' as the crossover point for all the sounds and items on either side of it, two before and two after? Could we not see that 'x' as a miniature nadir of the Neoplatonic story of matter, created by glory, committed to being mere stuff, eventually returned to its creator? Can we read redemption into chiasmus?

Sure we could; we've been trained to. But how would we describe ourselves, doing so? As secular or anti-ideological readers who got caught up in an old way of having literary pleasure for a moment, a religious or mystical or ideological or demonstrably incorrect way? As readers who do not mind slipping up like that, every now and then? As readers who think it is just a game?

I am not happy with any of those options, especially because they depend on a narrative of either secularisation or modernity that presumes a break or

---

8 Boethius 1990, p. 273.

a declension from the past into the present. I would prefer to think of myself, at least, when I enjoy the experience and later the apprehension of the formal significance of a given range of sonic play and lability, as someone participating in an ongoing and ancient history that cuts across a stagist mythical-religious-secular history, is available to the right and to the left, and may be 'ideological' or not depending on the context in which it is deployed. I think of myself as visiting the literary history of engagements with the possible relationships between suffering and matter. I think of myself as being asked to imagine that understanding materiality more deeply might give me solace.

Much as a doctrinal reading of the *Consolation* seems to miss its motion, so too do 'secular' or 'materialist' readings of contemporary poetry, especially poetry on the left, miss the full scope of that poetry's engagement with capitalism. So let me turn now to the second of the two poems I'd like to read: Jasper Bernes's long poem from 2012, *We Are Nothing And So Can You*. The poem was written in the context of the resistance to the austerity policies brought to bear on universities after the 2008 economic crash. That resistance became militant and widespread in the San Francisco Bay Area in 2009–11, and one vector of that militancy developed along the axis of repeated encounters between protesters and the police – whose job, of course, is to protect things, in their guise as private property (not least the 'property' of the places protesters occupied, in this interval). It is the thing-ification of everything, and the reduction of humanity to thing-like status, that provokes the poem to meditations on matter and suffering and value – in this case, 'value' in a Marxist sense. Keeping the opening of Boethius's invocation in mind, take these lines from the middle of *We Are Nothing*. A microphone is tapped, thump-thump, and

> the thing is on, we're live from the
> server farm on the moon.
> Yeah, basically, humanity ... a caucus of depressed
> apes taped together by the boomerang
> of programmable matter, which moves either
> slower while the other moves faster, or faster
> while the other moves slower and therefore
> hurts less or more than bare being.[9]

We could certainly read these lines as a parody of the Neoplatonism of Boethius and others, or at least as its blunt negation. Indeed its demotic bluntness is a

---

9 Bernes 2012, pp. 9–10.

negative of the elevated rhetoric of the Boethian invocation. And the passage –
like the poem as a whole – is emphatically anti-humanist, if by 'humanism'
we mean belief in a humanity that has been guaranteed the kiss or destiny
of the divine. Finally, of course, the passage imagines matter moving at dif-
ferent velocities much like the way the orbits of the planets were imagined
in the Ptolemaic cosmos that came to accompany the Neoplatonic narrat-
ive of ascent. In this last instance, Bernes's 'programmable matter' is a secu-
larising, even Nietzschean, parody of the 'perpetual order' of the invocation,
one that swaps in capitalism where God or the pre-Christian 'creator' used to
be.

    Again, though, the satisfactions of such a reading are thin, to my mind. For
one thing, the 'humanism' of the Neoplatonic ascent that connects human-
ity to the divine is readily appropriable by church anti-humanisms that wish
to remind humanity, not of its continuity with divinity, but rather its depend-
ence on divine mercy. And the 'anti-humanism' of calling humanity 'a caucus
of depressed / apes' is too funny and too sad to be simply 'ironic'. The possib-
ility that capital takes charge of matter is being thought of in terms of human
pain. It is less anti-humanist than focused on dehumanisation. Something else
is going on, a deployment of literary techniques that certainly rework older tra-
ditions of poetic materialism, but depend on them, and acknowledge it. Here
are the next two stanzas:

>   The zoo is really just one big exhibit:
>   the *N. American Homo Artificalis*,
>   force-fed though the voluble casework
>   of habit, the simple bonds of the bourgeois family,
>   to which attach the foodstuffs and trinketized
>   feelings, the one-point perspective, light
>   brigade of virgin ontologies, our late display, its salad of malady
>   piled atop the great misshapen
>   happening of wealth where the sea was once,
>   shell-pocked, elective, civilized and critical.
>   Flames, too, are a form of literacy.
>
>   This is where we meet each other
>   once the cameras have been destroyed,
>   once the metering of time by hallways and workdays
>   by which we experience a change of ownership
>   has been destroyed, and the face deformed by things it has to say,
>   destroyed,

and the diagrammatic metals of combustible elsewheres, destroyed,
and the destruction, destroyed.[10]

In the first stanza, the poem moves with lightning speed through a series of
tropes for dehumanisation under capitalism – even our feelings are 'trinket-
ized'. What looks like 'family' is really just a feeding trough and a training in
appropriate emotion; what looks like 'light' is actually just 'late'. The sea has
been overcome by the accumulation of wealth. But with 'Flames, too, are a form
of literacy', the poem pivots over to its thematics of destruction – the destruc-
tion of surveillance, enforced productivity, the deformed comportments to
which we subject ourselves, the reduction of space to thoughtless, disposable
use ('combustible elsewheres'). These stanzas act out a chiastic movement that
the poem repeats on several scales, from the microswapping of the order of
letters and sounds from word to word (the l's and c's in 'shell-pocked, elective,
civilized and critical', for instance) to the way 'trinketized feelings' are reversed
by 'fire' into a place where 'we' can finally 'meet each other', to the prosimetric
alteration back and forth between verse and prose (more about which is in the
following text). These back-and-forth movements are not quite a 'theme' of the
poem, nor could they be said to constitute the entirety of its 'form', but together
they begin to sensitise the reader to a sketched structure in which, to be blunt
about it, capitalism keeps capturing time and space for the work of value-
production, but time and space keep failing it by becoming mere duration,
mere matter. Oddly though, it is in the area marked out by people becoming
mere matter that capital reveals its vulnerabilities, even as it exerts its greatest
power over living persons. Capitalist time and space form an X / Y axis in the
poem that feels as cosmic as anything in Boethius, but it is policed, militarised,
fully historical, and mortal. Note the x's in this summary passage, as well as the
poem's return to that lightly verb-like sense of 'matters':

Capitalism – how does it work?

a matrix of acts, inexact, x-ed out

and undercounted, overruled, compelled
to become a sum that never dawns

a sun whose blacks 'twixt past and future

---

10   Bernes 2012, p. 10.

> mount a series of tactical strikes
> in the precise place that body is no body
>
> and therefore matters, is the keep of the real, the reaper's keel[11]

In the poem's lineated verse, the opposition between capital and its opponents becomes mathematically stark – capital, immortal, the reaper, with time and space at its disposal; and its opponents, mortal to the core, mere matter, armed only with fire. And 'x', clearly, marks the spot. The spot is empty – 'that body is no body'; we are nothing – but the force of the emptiness is lost if we read it merely as a clever reversal of the achieved fullness of mystical union with God. This is because the poem is using chiasmus and reversal, not just to mock its earlier poetic deployments, but because those earlier uses have trained us to hear something about matter 'itself' when we come across them, and the poet wants to understand what is happening in contemporary capitalism by way of what is happening both to matter and to the category 'human'.

This is where the poem's outermost gaming with alternation – its movement back and forth between verse and the prose sections – becomes important. The prose sections are written, as Robert McMahon reminds us the medieval poetry of meditative ascent is implicitly written, in retrospect. Unlike in the Boethius, the retrospect is the least rather than the most 'real' thing about the poem, because what is being recalled has not happened yet. It is not mystical, quite, but it is italicised – and since Faulkner, at least, modulations into italicised prose have come to signal reverie, lyricism, a matrix in which anguish can be given shape, but not too rigid a shape. Here (again with a small ellipsis) are the closing two paragraphs of the end of the poem:

> We get an old city bus and give it the number of a line that doesn't exist – 47 or 810. Immediately we exclude all those sad characters who know where they are going and want to go there, who think in terms of means and ends, origin and destination, or who are compelled to do so by circumstances of class or bodily incontinence. This narrows our range of riders less than you might imagine ...
>
> Eventually we have so many buses running, so many constantly improvised lines, and so many partisans running into and out of the buses and grabbing provisions off the shelves of corner shops, with or without guns, and taking the gas that we need from the gas stations, with or without

---

11   Bernes 2012, pp. 22–3.

guns, with or without leaving behind the mutilated corpses of police, and getting off one bus and onto another, that the buses become like the rooms of a disarticulated mansion, whirling through space and crossing and recrossing, combining and disassembling in a stupid, manic dance ... There are sanitation buses and fully-armed bank-robbing buses and buses that hate all the other buses. There are so many of these buses spinning through the city that, eventually, it truly is as if they were themselves the only thing stationary in a crazy world jumping about in every direction, as if space had too many dimensions to be space but not enough to be time.[12]

This is not 'redemption'; it is not perfect peace. It is more like liberation, if the liberation of an immediately post-revolutionary moment is marked both by a sense of multiplying possibilities and unnerving disorientation (the 'stupid, manic dance'; the 'crazy world jumping about in every direction'). To put it more emphatically, the post-revolutionary matrix is more and less 'real' than the X / Y grid it has just supplanted.

By virtue of their merely possible futurity, the prose sections could also be said to take place in a less 'real' space than the verse sections. But they are also more 'realist': if in the verse we are given to witness letters and syllables reversing and unreversing, on the page, in the prose section in the preceding text we are given descriptions of whole buses engaging in that same movement, 'crossing and recrossing' as they grope to find the x-mark of a new world. I think this is one of the poem's great achievements – to write a description of a post-revolutionary moment that is not a utopia; to use techniques that orbit wider than realism, while looping through a descriptive realism nonetheless. This is beyond the resources of realist fiction when it tries to think about capitalism. The best dystopian science fiction, meanwhile, when it tries to extend capitalism into the future, tends to invite allegorical readings that, while pleasurable, tend to lose sight of the thing Bernes has kept our gaze on all the while: the conditions of production under capital, the ones that make us merely 'programmable', make us just sad apes.

What *We Are Nothing* does that realist fiction does not, though, is play brilliantly, and across scale, with reversal. I think that, when we tune into this reversal-play, and see it repeat itself – as technique, theme, form, key change, reality shift – we can also see how Bernes's rendering the fate of matter as a perpetual 'recrossing' rather than an ascent allows him to tap into older poetic

---

12   Bernes 2012, p. 35.

resources for thinking about matter without merely 'secularizing' them. I think it would be more accurate to say that in *We Are Nothing* the chiastic or orbital fate of matter in Neoplatonic poetics becomes, not profane, but epicyclical. It is as though the poem allows us to absorb, not only the ongoing literary practice of thinking about matter and suffering through poetic gaming, but a story about how the open-ended cyclicality of capitalist accumulation is both utterly new in history and also impossible to imagine without the capture and deployment of ancient capacities and humble, un-'modern' bodies.

Bernes's poem is also, if we care to notice, a caution about the limits of understanding Marxist anti-capitalist projects as 'materialist'. There is too much cosmos in the poem, too much reflection on what capital obliges us to become, for us to read simply as a 'materialist' poetic critique of some capital-ist reduction of 'spirit' to 'matter'. The poem is clearly suggesting, rather, that spirit and matter – whatever they are – find themselves yoked into the service of capital.[13]

This leads me to a final point that is, I am afraid, a bit terminologically twisty. One of the most wonderful things about Bernes's poem is that it performs a bafflement and dismay about the power of capital that nonetheless connects to a deepening resistance to it. I think this complex attitude – this poetic struc-ture of feeling, if you will – is possible in part because Bernes's anti-capitalism is not reducible to a philosophical 'materialism'. He clearly sees that, in order to reproduce itself on an ever-expanding scale, and in ever-intensifying ways, capitalism needs the perpetual nourishment of exploitable labour, uncapital-ised time, as-yet-unconquered space. It needs potential; it needs the 'ideal'. This is not just a point about how the poem gives the lie to unhelpful reductions of anti-capitalism to philosophical categories. It is about how a 'materialist' reading of contemporary capital tends to see it as an achieved thing, a 'cultural dominant', to use Fredric Jameson's term, whose greatest power lies in its sheer extent.[14] Sadly the situation seems to be much worse than that: it is not so much

---

13   As Erich Fromm argued more than fifty years ago, Marx was not interested in being a philosophical 'materialist'; and, as Z.A. Jordan points out, it was not Marx, but Georgi Plekhanov, who gave Marxist currency to the phrase 'dialectical materialism'. In the early twentieth century, Jordan reminds us, a wide range of thinkers friendly to Marxism objec-ted to the characterisation of Marxism as a 'materialism', because the philosophical bag-gage associated with 'materialism' simply looped it back into an ancient debate about transcendent causes and the metaphysical character of matter. Marx, of course, did not concern himself with developing a theory of ultimate historical causality, preferring to work outward from the dynamics of capitalism to explain its processes of accumulation and reproduction. See Fromm 2011; and Jordan 1967.

14   Jameson 1991, p. 6.

that capitalism has triumphed over every alternative – true enough – as that it *does* triumph over resistance, alternatives, the vicissitudes of the market, every day, again and again. 'Capitalism-has-won' is a modernity story. 'Capitalism-exploits-us-every-day' is an anti-capitalist one. *We Are Nothing* tells the second story, and in order to do so – this is the twisty part – it reaches past the false reading of Marxism as a 'materialism' in order to tap into the long *poetic* history of philosophical wonderment about matter, both 'materialist' and 'idealist'. That poetic tradition is what allows *We Are Nothing*'s unphilosophical anti-capitalism to shine with poetic and philosophical force.

I called this essay 'The Price of Value' so as to nod in the direction of what, for Marx, propels each cycle of capital accumulation, which is the transformation of value into price: the realisation of the values won from exploitation by sale in the market. Market exchange is, of course, only a moment in the circuit of capital; but while capital exceeds it, it cannot do without it. Sooner or later it needs to be vulgar, and let us know, not only what we are good for, but what, at any given moment, we are worth. More and more, in the university, we are told that the answer is, not very much. But there is a danger here for capital: what if the answer becomes, you are worth nothing? What if machines really *can* do your job, design your syllabus, teach your classes? What might being nothing free those who have been terminally devalued to do? *We Are Nothing* jokes about this – 'And now it seems / We'll have to discover something else to use / Our ration books for, like poetry?' – but it does not only joke. Toward the end of the poem, in its italic future anterior, the poets asks an ancient question about value in the only way still possible, the radically contemporary way:

> ... would the 500 years experiment find at its limits not just capitalism or class society but the human form, not just the speaking ape but all the carbonated sacs of self-reproducing logos that foamed out of that old, terrible constancy? ... The frequencies collecting in our forehead felt good – we understood it not at all at once, the bright reasons flashing like stairs in the dark. We drank it up. And then we fought as hard as we could.[15]

---

15   Bernes 2012, p. 32.

CHAPTER 8

The Anti-humanist Tone

This essay forms part of a project whose aim is to develop a clear picture of the sources and styles of contemporary anti-humanism. Though we tend to think of the critique of 'the human' as a project led by the French post-structuralism of the 1960s, it is both older than that, and more various. The sources of anti-humanism are as old as the classical rhetoric of misanthropy, and include an enduring strain of Christian theology that insists on an infinite, humbling difference between God and 'man'. And though the primacy of post-structuralism in the literary academy has long subsided, the anti-humanist rhetoric in which it took part has survived, even flourished, in recent years. In contemporary politics, anti-humanism shapes a whole flank of environmentalist discourse that bemoans humanity's supposedly innate rapaciousness, and it forms part of current anti-racist rhetoric, which includes 'Afro-pessimist' arguments that, because dehumanisation (or a structural position outside 'humanity') so centrally shapes the experience of Black people in America, they might best give up on the category of 'the human' as a staging ground for appeals to dignity. A similar argument can be found in queer theory, which includes a whole variety of arguments in favour of seeing queerness as monstrous or inhuman.

In contemporary philosophy, meanwhile, anti-humanism is at the centre of new 'object-oriented ontologies' that make much of how supposedly ego-driven, overweening human subjects get in the way of better understandings of the workings of everything from political life to the universe itself. We can even find a strange, triumphalist strain of anti-humanism in the techno-optimist rhetoric of Silicon Valley, not least in conversations about 'the singularity' – the projected future moment when robots surpass humans in every aspect of cognition, possibly including emotion.

As these different aspects of anti-humanist rhetoric blend into modern anti-humanism, they are also increasingly visible as arguments about how we should *feel* about being human. Though anti-humanism is generally framed as an argument about humanity, in other words – the claim, for instance, that cosmically speaking we are tiny to the point of insignificance – its claims may be most significant for the tone in which they are delivered (our insignificance, if that's what it is, can be described in tones both wonderstruck and baleful). Indeed I have come to think of anti-humanism less as a set of propositions than as an historically transmitted, and rarely questioned, repertoire of attitudes.

These attitudes, I want to suggest, are as much about the material condi-tions that structure human relationships as they are about the existential value of humanity. In the twentieth century, this meant that such attitudes were, however ontologically they were framed, also always attitudes about capital-ism. In the opening chapter on 'tone' in her pathbreaking 2005 volume *Ugly Feelings*, Sianne Ngai argues that 'tone's generality and abstractness should not distract us from the fact that it is always "about" something'.[1] For Ngai, the 'aboutness' of tone cannot be compassed by New Critical models of tone as a set of reader-writer relations, such as address; instead, she thinks closely through Adorno's struggle both to incorporate and hold emotion at bay as the prop-erty of art objects. Adorno's Marxism is of use to Ngai because his dialectical method continually points to a set of determining conditions that are contra-dictory products of social struggle, which makes it possible to read the strange way tone seems both to emanate from objects and to be created in response to them: there is no one 'subject' in the subject-object dyad favoured by theorists of tone. In a brilliant later essay, Ngai hones her sense of this elusive 'aboutness' by tracing the afterlife of Marx's concept of value as it produces the concept of 'real abstraction' – a way of understanding that no one commodity can fully express its capitalist value, since value-production under capitalism depends on the totality of the process of accumulation.[2]

This essay means to pick up Ngai's discoveries from a slant angle, by framing anti-humanist rhetoric in terms about a particular kind of 'aboutness' it never quite acknowledges – that is, its concern, not just with 'humanity', but with property and value-production, expressed in a set of imaginary class relations. I will try to convey the centrality of tone to anti-humanism by focusing briefly on some moments in English-language literary modernism, and then on a few moments in the history of critical theory. Reading these moments together, we should be able to see at least two of the key features of twentieth-century anti-humanist rhetoric: an insistence on an absolute gap between humanity and its others (God or nature, especially), and a critique of meaning-making, sym-bols, and metaphors as devices of false consolation that distract us from the hard wisdom of appreciating this absolute gap. I will close with a parenthet-ical gesture in the direction of exciting developments in contemporary Marxist scholarship that has no particular use for this comportment, and with a con-temporary poem that is part of a remarkable new literary anti-capitalism that doesn't depend on anti-humanist tropes.[3]

---

1   Ngai 2005, p. 87.
2   See Ngai 2015.
3   My pivot from modernist poetry to critical theory, then back to contemporary poetry, takes a

1   Modernist Anti-humanism

I'll begin with a 1916 essay by T.E. Hulme called 'Humanism and the Religious Attitude'. Hulme was a polymathic critic and poet who died young in the First World War, but who had a notable impact on a range of key modernist thinkers, not least T.S. Eliot and Robert Frost. His writing is blunt and polemical, so he gets very clearly at some key anti-humanist ideas – most importantly, here, the idea of an absolute gap between humanity and God. At the beginning of the essay, he asserts that his aim is to clarify problems in our perception of reality. 'Certain regions of reality differ', he writes, 'not relatively but absolutely'. He elaborates this way:

> Let us assume that reality is divided into three regions, separated from one another by absolute divisions, by real discontinuities; (1) the inorganic world, of mathematical and physical science, (2) the organic world, dealt with by biology, psychology and history, and (3) the world of ethical and religious values. Imagine these three regions as three zones marked out on a flat surface by two concentric circles. The outer zone is the world of physics, the inner that of religion and ethics, the intermediate one that of life. The outer and inner regions have certain characteristics in common. They have both an absolute character, and knowledge about them can legitimately be called absolute knowledge. The intermediate region of life is, on the other hand, essentially relative; it is dealt with by loose sciences like biology, psychology and history. A muddy mixed zone then lies between two absolutes. To make the image a more faithful representation one would have to imagine the extreme zones partaking of the perfection of geometrical figures, while the middle zone was covered with some confused muddy substance.[4]

This cosmology and its attendant theology are also an aesthetics. Critiquing the religious art of the Renaissance as not really religious at all, Hulme writes,

> When the intensity of the religious attitude finds proper expression in art, then you get a very different result. Such expression springs not from

---

distant permission from Andreas Huyssen's argument that critical theory can be interpreted as a post-facto speculative armature for the artistic avant-gardes that preceded it. See Huyssen 1986.

4   Hulme 1936, pp. 5–6.

a delight in life but from a feeling for certain absolute values, which are entirely independent of vital things. The disgust with the trivial and accidental characteristics of living shapes, the searching after an austerity, a monumental stability and permanence, a perfection and rigidity, which vital things can never have, leads to the use of forms which can almost be called geometrical.[5]

Hulme's essay is a dense crossroads for several aspects of anti-humanist rhetoric. There is a reason, for instance, that he keeps returning to geometry as his preferred language for aesthetics and cosmology alike: as Amir Alexander has argued, in seventeenth-century Europe geometry was the Catholic Church's preferred basis for mathematical inquiry, since it was easily interpreted as the study of the works of a maker with no contiguous relation to humanity. Alexander shows very clearly how geometry emerged as the math of church authority when it was confronted with an emergent calculus, whose language of differentials implied that the differences among things – perhaps even humanity and divinity – could be described in terms of slopes and gradients, rather than chasms. This math opened up a dangerous bridge, so to speak, between god and humanity, suggesting the possibility of a human arrogation of divinity to itself, if it were to be able to conceptualise infinity.[6]

Hulme's aesthetics also has what we could call a literary component, since in insisting on the unbridgeable discontinuities among zones of reality, he is partaking of a long hostility to metaphor that can be traced to Plato, but which reaches a polemical high point with Nietzsche. You may recall that in 'On Truth and Lying in a Non-Moral Sense', from 1873, Nietzsche regards metaphor as a pathetic human invention designed to keep us from recognising the puniness and the ephemerality of our life as a species. He begins by writing,

In some remote corner of the universe, flickering in the light of the countless solar systems into which it had been poured, there was once a planet on which clever animals invented cognition. It was the most arrogant and most mendacious minute in the 'history of the world', but a minute was all it was. After nature had drawn just a few more breaths the planet froze and the clever animals had to die.[7]

5   Hulme 1936, p. 9.
6   See Alexander 2014.
7   Nietzsche 1999, p. 141.

This is virtually a recipe for later Lovecraftian weird tales and horror stories about the insignificance of humanity, tales that are championed by contemporary 'speculative realists' as delivering hard truths about an absolute break between humanity and the cosmos.[8]

In its dramatic distance-taking from the dailiness, or even the historical character, of human life, Nietzsche's language here also partakes of the rhetoric of prophecy (which comes to fullest flower, of course, in *Thus Spake Zarathustra* [1891]). And there is something of the prophetic in much anti-humanist writing. Indeed the trace of the prophetic offers an important way to think about anti-humanism, since sooner or later the use of a prophetic tone or stance must produce the question, to whom is this prophetic language addressed? To reflect on this, I'd like to turn to a moment in literary modernism where the rhetoric of prophecy, given a broadly anti-humanist coloration, both indicates and obscures its origins in very concrete circumstances.

I'm thinking (you will not be surprised to learn) of T.S. Eliot's 1922 poem *The Waste Land*, which has not only been figured since its first success as a kind of prophecy of the particular alienations native to twentieth-century history, but also features a literal prophet, the mythical Tiresias of Thebes, as well as the Sibyl of Cumae. I am thinking of the poem, but also its title, which has received little scholarly attention. In English common law, the late-medieval definition of 'the waste land of a manor' begins as a category to describe land that is either unusable or not in use, and which, therefore, was traditionally available for *common* use. Later, however, the concept of 'waste land' becomes a political tool in the hands of capitalist landlords, who were given license by the concept to expropriate commonly held land that was 'waste' only in the Lockean sense that it was un-capitalised upon.[9] So we could say that one sense in which the tone of *The Waste Land* was able to be called prophetic was that it gestured, if broadly, at an earlier form of dispossession – the history of enclosure – that prefigures the later capitalist alienations of wage and commodity with which Eliot's early readers would have been intuitively if not analytically familiar.

This makes Eliot's poem sound anti-capitalist, which it surely was. We don't often think of Eliot this way today, because contemporary anti-capitalism is a language of the left; but a century ago it was still possible to be a right-of-centre, even an aristocratic, anti-capitalist. Eliot's writing, not least his influential essay-writing, falls squarely in this zone.[10] But *The Waste Land* itself bears

---

8   See, for instance, Thacker 2011, and Harman 2012.
9   For a detailed version of this argument see Wood 2012.
10   My sense of Eliot's conservative anti-capitalism has been shaped by the arguments made in Joel Nickels's *World Literature and the Geographies of Resistance* (Cambridge UP, 2018).

this out inasmuch as the content of its prophecy is not only about universal dispossession, but also about something like secularisation.

Eliot's poem, its readers know, makes inventive use of parallels between Greek myth and twentieth-century civilisation, generally so as to depict contemporary life as fallen, distorted, and pathetic by comparison to mythic antiquity. *The Waste Land* strikes anti-humanist postures, that is, inasmuch as it depicts humanity in a sorry relation to mythical divinity, or even just the dignity of mythic tragedy. That this is a political strategy as well as a literary one is clear in Eliot's 1923 review of James Joyce's *Ulysses* (1922), in whose similar techniques Eliot clearly found himself reflected: 'In manipulating a continuous parallel between contemporaneity and antiquity', Eliot wrote, 'Mr. Joyce is pursuing a method which others must pursue after him ... It is simply a way of controlling, of ordering, of giving a shape and a significance to the immense panorama of futility and anarchy which is contemporary history'.[11] Just a year earlier, the conservative German political theorist Carl Schmitt would argue, in his influential *Political Theology* (published the same year as Eliot's poem), that 'All significant concepts of the modern theory of the state are secularized theological concepts'.[12] The literary strategy Eliot describes as 'controlling' and 'ordering' a contemporary 'anarchy' is met, elsewhere in Schmitt, with a conservative political theory championing strong sovereignty over and against exactly such 'anarchy'.

Schmitt's theory of secularisation, and Eliot's depiction of the fall from mythic dignity, share more than a declensionary shape. In 1983 Hans Blumenberg wrote in *The Legitimacy of The Modern Age* that the history of the concept of 'secularisation' that helps shape Schmitt's theory of sovereignty, is criss-crossed by episodes of alarmed objection to the expropriation of church lands from Westphalia on. These expropriations, Blumenberg suggests, intermittently but persistently dog more contemporary, neutral-sounding concepts of secularisation. As we know, of course, the concept later becomes almost inconceivably broad, but – and here's what interests me most – Blumenberg suggests that it still carries something of the aggrieved *tone* attached to the dispossession of a propertied class.[13] So the prophetic, anti-humanist tone of *The Waste Land* may be tangled up in the political history of land use in more than one way: not only because it makes contemporary life seem sorry in comparison with myth, and distantly analogises that sorriness to the history of enclosure, but how it further analogises the dispossessions of enclosure –

---

11   Eliot 2005, p. 167.
12   Schmitt 1985, p. 36.
13   See Blumenberg 1983, pp. 18–22.

which devastated peasants – to the dispossession of aristocrats and wealthy monastic communities at the hands of strong, 'secular' states.

If we could say that the use of the rhetoric of prophecy is a way to give literary shape to the anti-humanist insistence on a wide or even absolute gap between humanity and divinity, we could also say that the 'humanity' placed on one side of this gap gains literary force in part because prophetic and secularising rhetoric erases the tracks of its class histories. This is ironic inasmuch as prophetic and secularising rhetoric are meant, as in Hulme, Nietzsche, and Eliot, to come across as clear-eyed, hard truth. This irony, meanwhile, can clarify for us the ways in which a rhetoric of negativity or criticality can come, by dint of its tone, to obscure what it is meant to be critical *of*. If in English-language literary modernism the persuasive character of prophetic anti-humanism had this effect, we can see a similar problem in modernist critical theory, which took up an insistence on absolute gaps by way of a critique of the symbol. Unlike the literary history of anti-humanist language I've sketched here, though, the critical-theoretical one tries not to obscure its class character, but to foreground it unambiguously from the left – at least at first.

2   Critical Anti-humanism

The critique of the symbol begins as a modernist reaction to an earlier, Romantic critique of allegory. Most commentators suggest that it was Goethe who transformed 'symbol' and 'allegory' from broadly synonymous terms into an opposing pair, writing in *Maxims and Reflections* that the symbol is the device by which writers express ineffable ideas, whereas allegory is the device by which they communicate specific concepts. Goethe argues that the symbolic technique is best suited for poetry because the symbol inexhaustibly excites our intuitions, whereas allegory is exhausted once it's de-coded.[14] In Coleridge, influenced by the German idealists, this difference in kind gets transformed into a difference in values: though Goethe did not impugn allegory *per se*, simply noting that it was most germane to kinds of writing he didn't count as especially 'poetic', Coleridge influentially pits the modes against each other – at this point they have gone from being devices to being modes – by aligning the symbol with a living organicism, and allegory with a reductive mechanism.

This is to say that the critique of the symbol has come down to us as a critique of organicism and of the idea of harmony. The lever by which pressure

---

14   Bell 1997 provides a compelling summary of these twists and turns.

is applied to the idea of organic harmony between humans and nature is the idea of time. The symbol is contemptible to its critics, because it factors out time and history, offering a momentary flash of an impossible union between humanity and nature, and hewing to that moment of insight as though it were continuously accessible to us, or as though it were true. In a much-cited passage from his 1928 *Origin of German Tragic Drama*, Walter Benjamin puts the distinction this way:

> Whereas in the symbol destruction is idealized and the transfigured face of nature is revealed in the light of redemption, in allegory the observer is confronted with the death mask of history as a petrified, primordial landscape. Everything about history that, from the very beginning, has been untimely, sorrowful, unsuccessful, expresses itself in a countenance – or rather a death's head ... this is the form in which man's subjection to nature is most pronounced and it gives rise to the enigmatic question not only of the nature of human existence as such but of the biographical historicity of the individual.[15]

Allegory, here, rather than being merely a mechanical writer's tool, is a mode of worldliness in which haunting emblems, rather than pointing at ineffable unity, keep us in mind of our scars, because it is narrative and durational rather than imagistic and instantaneous. It dispels our illusions of paradise with the hard truth and the cold water of lived human history. It is the hangover to the high of the symbol.

But there are problems with this rhetoric of demystification. For one thing, while it appears to be the case that Benjamin champions allegory against the symbol because allegory does not offer a vision of redemption, it is more accurate to say that in the *Trauerspiel* book symbol and allegory have different relations to it – symbol promises instant redemption, while allegory, far from refusing redemptive language, heightens the drama of redemption by expanding its compass from the individual to society itself, and by insisting that redemption will only happen when all are redeemed. The preference for allegory over symbol, here, is less the demystification it purports to be than a prolongation of the suspense around redemption.

So there is a crypto-optimism embedded in Benjamin's revolutionary pessimism; I think his readers can generally sense this. Perhaps more unexpected, though, is that the vision of redemption on offer in the *Trauerspiel* and else-

---

15   Benjamin 2009, p. 166.

where in Benjamin's work is a vision of *sovereignty* which he first built up in admiring response to the work of Carl Schmitt. As Horst Bredekamp has shown, in the *Trauerspiel* the young Benjamin polemically reverses the location of sovereignty in Schmitt from the ruler to the masses – a bravura move that nonetheless accepts the sovereignty-framework of the right-wing political theorist as the correct one.[16] This remains the case in his 1940 'Theses on the Philosophy of History', which pits a militant historical materialism against both Social Democratic politics and empirical historicism, both of which Benjamin finds wanting because they are expressions of an abstract, struggle-free concept of progress. Against these progressive forms of imagining time, Benjamin imagines it divided between a continuous flow and moments of dramatic arrest, akin to the Greek concepts of *chronos* and *kairos*, respectively. In Schmitt, it is the sovereign which is able to create or seize upon *kairos*; in Benjamin's theses, it is the revolutionary classes who are able to do this. But, as Bredekamp suggests, it is sovereignty, rather than capital, that is at issue, despite the bravura inversion. We can see this in Thesis XVI, when Benjamin aligns the revolutionary hatred of ruling classes with the militant clarity of the historical materialist, both of whom exercise a particularly masculine sovereignty over themselves:

> A historical materialist cannot do without the notion of a present which is not a transition, but in which time stands still and has come to a stop. For this notion defines the present in which he himself is writing history. Historicism gives the 'eternal' image of the past; historical materialism supplies a unique experience with the past. The historical materialist leaves it to others to be drained by the whore called 'Once upon a time' in historicism's bordello. He remains in control of his powers, man enough to blast open the continuum of history.[17]

This melodramatic vision of masculine militancy is built around the idea of absolute sovereignty as of a *fleeting* moment: the anti-humanism of this idea becomes clear when we see that it is purchased at the price of a theory, not just of 'homogeneous, empty time', but of oblivion. Benjamin owes this to Nietzsche: indeed, Thesis XVI has close parallels with passages in *The Use and Abuse of History for Life*, from 1874, as when Nietzsche writes of the 'man' who must come to terms with human insignificance this way:

---

16   See Bredekamp 1999.
17   Benjamin 1969, p. 262.

Then [he] learns to understand the words 'once upon a time', the 'open sesame' that lets in battle, suffering and weariness on mankind, and reminds them what their existence really is, an imperfect tense that never becomes a present. And when death brings at last the desired forgetfulness, it abolishes life and being together, and sets the seal on the knowledge that 'being' is merely a continual 'has been', a thing that lives by denying and destroying and contradicting itself.[18]

Benjamin inverts Nietzsche's use of the phrase 'once upon a time' – in Nietzsche it tears down the veil, while in Benjamin it *is* the veil – but he preserves the constellation of transformation, abolition, and history-as-'battle'. And Thesis xviii precisely recalls the opening of Nietzsche's 'On Truth and Lying', cited above:

'In relation to the history of organic life on earth', writes a modern biologist, 'the paltry fifty millennia of *homo sapiens* constitute something like two seconds at the close of a twenty-four-hour day. On this scale, the history of civilized mankind would fill one-fifth of the last second of the last hour'. The present, which, as a model of Messianic time, comprises the entire history of mankind in an enormous abridgment, coincides exactly with the stature which the history of mankind has in the universe.[19]

Benjamin's revolutionary anti-humanism, then, depends on a high-contrast binary between the masculine seizure of sovereign power and a vision of surrounding oblivion that, in its disregard for what today we might call social reproduction, is equally masculinised. This insistence on a model of militancy as tragic sovereignty directs attention away from opposition to capitalist accumulation, and toward a critique of false sovereignty – not least the false sovereignty of liberals and Social Democrats, who supposedly think they can benignly engineer human 'progress' with light taps on the steering wheel. And it is this critique of hubris, rather than an anti-capitalist or communist politics, that survives into the anti-humanist criticism that would follow on Benjamin.

Paul de Man, in his influential 'Rhetoric of Temporality' (1969), tacitly borrows from Benjamin's introduction of a chastening temporality into the symbol's cloistered playroom. He is blunter than Benjamin, referring at one point to the symbol's 'ontological bad faith'.[20] In a brief reading of Rousseau's 1761

---

18   Nietzsche 2015, p. 6.
19   Benjamin 1969, p. 263.
20   de Man 1983, p. 211.

Nouvelle Héloïse, he suggests that the realism of the lover's amorous feeling is in fact built around a highly literary reference to the allegorical *Roman de la Rose* of the thirteenth century. For de Man, this instance of literariness posing as realism points to the intertextual character of all literary writing, a feature of writing he then suggests is anterior to all pretensions to realism or to symbolic harmony: 'The prevalence of allegory always corresponds to the unveiling of an authentically temporal destiny. This unveiling takes place in a subject that has sought refuge against the impact of time in a natural world to which, in truth, it bears no resemblance'.[21] In the closing portion of his essay, de Man re-works his contrast between allegory and nature, which is rendered as a contrast between literariness and naturalism, into a contrast between fictionality and nature, where the privileged vehicle for fictionality is irony. As you likely recall, irony for de Man is a tool of self-objectification, by whose action we are reminded of our non-fit with the world, as when in Baudelaire's famous essay on laughter we see our innate clumsiness when we trip and fall. Inasmuch as literariness is like fictionality, de Man seems to suggest, allegory is like irony. Both are endless, and both, he says, are demystifying:

> Allegory and irony are thus linked in their common discovery of a truly temporal predicament. They are also linked in their common demystification of an organic world postulated in a symbolic mode of analogical correspondences or a mimetic mode of representation in which fiction and reality could coincide. It is especially against the latter mystification that irony is directed.[22]

These sentences describe a kind of baseline of shared values in literary theory and criticism that, if we disagree with them, require effort to dispel. In its language of nature's non-resemblance to humanity, and its use of phrases like 'authentically temporal destiny', de Man's essay partakes of the same spatialised domain model, and the same language of sovereignty, that we saw in Hulme and in the Schmittian aspects of Benjamin.[23]

But there are problems here. Why is intertextuality best characterised as abyssal, and why is its infinitude – if that's what it is – seen as 'inorganic'? Why

---

21   de Man 1983, pp. 206–7.
22   de Man 1983, p. 222.
23   I outline the persistence of this sovereignty-based aesthetic theory with Joshua Clover in Clover and Nealon 2017 (Chapter 10 in this volume).

is the inorganic seen as a tonic? What looks like a bracing demystification is actually the reappearance of the literary and philosophical *topos* we've seen already, in which human pretensions to omniscience need to be broken by contact with the infinite. Why is the literary equated with the fictional in the sense of the untrue? We have learned from the work of Mary Poovey that fictionality is not simply a Platonic truth-category, but a web of social relationships built up around the ability to trust in the reliability of a given fiction.[24] Why is reality, as de Man puts it elsewhere in his essay, 'empirical'? Frederick Beiser has shown that German philosophical debates throughout the second half of the nineteenth century, debates that follow on the same idealism to which Benjamin and de Man are responding, went far beyond a simple equation of reality with empirical fact.[25] What does it mean to say that humanity 'has no resemblance' to the natural world? The tradition of German philosophical anthropology, from Helmuth Plessner and Alfred Gehlen down to Blumenberg, persuasively suggests that our species-relation to nature is at least as well described in terms of a wobbly, contingent fit, in which we are niche organisms only ever partly suited to dynamic, unstable environments.[26] This view is borne out in debates in evolutionary biology, which Richard Lewontin, among others, has laboured to make clear to non-scientists.[27]

That it is so easy to dismantle the claims of de Man's essay suggests that its persuasive power lies less in its propositions than in its tone. Though the prestige of his variant of post-structuralism has subsided, the anti-humanist web of argument in which he participates continues to serve as a critical default for literary academics whenever we make arguments built around the 'demystification' of a text. We see this both in more avowedly left-wing Frankfurt School arguments that pit a despairing negativity against an all-devouring capitalism, and we see it in contemporary anti-humanist philosophy, which has made a sport of critiquing post-structuralism for a myopic focus on texts rather than on the cold immensity of the universe – a critique that repeats the very moves de Manian post-structuralists, relying on Nietzsche, once deployed against the humanisms to which they objected.[28]

---

24   See Poovey 1998.
25   See Beiser 2014.
26   Vida Pavesich outlines this conversation in Pavesich 2008. I am grateful to Chris Westcott
      for directing me to her essay.
27   See, for instance, Lewontin 2000.
28   I make this argument in a bit more detail in Nealon 2015.

3   Coda: Marxism without Anti-humanism, Poetry without Modernity

I am aware that much of what I have suggested so far might seem to dovetail with the widely discussed championing of 'post-critical' literary studies in the work of Rita Felski and others. But I am after something different. Felski's project, especially as summarised in her 2015 *The Limits of Critique*, is to pit one mood or attitude – the 'critical' one – against a provisional set of tonal, methodological, and ethical opposites: appreciative instead of glowering, nuanced instead of reductive, humble instead of arrogant. But her project is generalising, adjectival, and vaguely *ad hominem*: the book abounds in sentences like, 'Critique's fundamental quality is that of "againstness", vindicating a desire to take a hammer, as Bruno Latour would say, to the beliefs and attachments of others'.[29] Inasmuch as the book has its own theoretical framework, it is drawn from Latour, whose Actor-Network Theory (ANT) is remarkable for shadow-boxing with caricatures of Marxism, in particular: in ANT, Marxism is irrelevant as a critique of political economy; instead, it is just another form of methodological 'reductiveness' that can't do justice to sensuous particulars.[30]

I am less interested in championing positive or negative affects and attachments in criticism, *per se*, than I am in trying to unpack the histories of the class imaginaries that shape them. I have directed my attention to the anti-humanist comportment in particular because its rhetoric presents an interesting problem for the Marxist literary criticism that matters to me most: it remains our most fully elaborated model of a reading style whose affiliations are militant, but it seems to me to borrow too much from rightist political values to provide the tools a twenty-first-century Marxist criticism will need. Among those tools would be concepts and historical frames that do not oblige literary writing, or critical interpretation, to waffle between transcendent meaning or mythical wholeness and their utter absence. Outside the precincts of network materialisms and post-critical reading, there is a lively conversation in Marxist scholarship today that has focused on how capitalism not only demands exploitable wage workers to produce value, but also a whole range of relations to the wage – direct and indirect, readily available and forcibly excluded – in order to reproduce itself.[31] This focus on the production of different relations to the wage,

---

29   Felski 2015, p. 129.
30   For an incisive account of Latour's breezy dismissals of Marx and Marxism, see Noys 2014.
31   This scholarship cuts across studies of race, gender, and more traditional Marxist scholarship. See, for instance, Chen 2013. Chen's work, which tries to understand racialisation as a process that has historically included both compulsion to labour and exclusion from the labour pool, is in dialogue with a revival of the question of the relationship between

and on the vicissitudes of social reproduction under capital in general, suggests the possibility of a political framework in which race, class, and gender all play roles in capitalist value production in ways that invite us to think of aesthetic value, not in terms of sovereignty, or spatialised domains of authority, or high-contrast oppositions between lost or impossible fullness and tragic or ironic fallenness.

I can't compass this scholarship here. What I can do, very briefly, is to suggest that in tandem with this conversation in Marxist studies, contemporary poetry in English has achieved a remarkably fresh and flexible range of ways to address the capitalist conditions that gave rise both to high modernism and modernist critical theory. I will close with one poem from this foment, by Sandra Simonds. It would give me great pleasure to offer a 'close reading' of it – or, for that matter, a 'distant' one, since the conditions of its emergence are also of great interest – but instead I'll just suggest, by way of closing, that the poem is striking, but not unique, for how it thinks through a nexus of poetry-writing, teaching for low wages in the humanities, the property relations behind them, and the forms of social reproduction behind the property relations. The poem is evidence, I think, of the irony behind the project of post-critical reading – which, in con-struing militant styles of critique as forcing politics onto texts, is overlooking a great revival of militant literary writing. It is also evidence that, if we prise anti-humanist rhetoric apart from the longer and broader history of rhetorics of militancy, we can see contemporary forms of militancy that don't require the anti-humanist warrants of absolute gaps, natural indifference, or steep-grade

---

capitalism and slavery, one that explores both slavery's difference from, and facilitating of, emergent wage-based exploitation. For a good synopsis of this work, see Clegg 2015. Simil-arly, in their pathbreaking essay 'The Logic of Gender', Maya Andrea Gonzalez and Jeanne Neton extend a feminist tradition begun by Silvia Federici, who argues that wage labour emerges in medieval Europe partly by way of excluding women, and traditionally femin-ine forms of reproductive labour. See Federici 2004. Benanav 2020 develops an analysis of this dynamic around the post-World War II state's framing of the category of unem-ployment, whose porousness reflects Marx's own understanding of the labor market in Chapter 25 of *Capital*, Volume I, and elsewhere. What links these studies – not all of them yet in explicit dialogue with each other – is the possibility they offer for a political analysis of value production that unhitches Marxist scholarship from a hunt for a single revolution-ary class, and that opens it to a more capacious and coalitional sense of the relationships among patriarchy, racism, and proletarianisation. This political possibility has a literary-academic corollary inasmuch as it allows us to see how narrowly critical theory, working in a modernist vein, has conceived of the question of class composition, thinking of it in terms of sovereignty rather than in terms of differential relations to accumulation, and missing, thereby, any chance to grasp militant political energy or literary production that has 'humanist' characteristics.

languages of sovereignty. Compared to the declensionary modernity stories I have visited above, the poem is an exciting and beautiful alternative:

I Am Inside The Humanities And

if I step
       too far out of it,
          I'm dead. The figure
       at the top left corner is Securitas.
    No rent! No work! No wages!
      No more! For those thinking
 of disturbing the peace, let
    the hanged man be your warning.
In order to write this poem,
    I paid daycare $523
         for the week. Make sure you premix
       the bottles, bring diapers. Make it worth
            something, this time. Mayan
         countdown clock to Mayan
    countdown clock, two bodies,
 uncivilized, in a bed wanting
      the water of the world to
 give them back a pyramid.
       Also, the bronze head of Adam.
         Also, the world of children,
       their toys, the plastic imitation food – eggs,
       miniature cereal boxes, deformed mirror
       to the real. I could not keep working
    to make money for the people I despised,
       nothing is right, but I couldn't afford
       not to either. Late at night, Chris
          said 'I hate my job'. The hydro-geologists
          have to give permits to Gulf Oil
             for more water or someone
       will lose their livelihood. It was winter
       in Florida, the path to all principles
       of all inquiries led back to this
    one statement, like a recite
 from Publix: I was teaching
    the humanities again.

In the garden of the fallen
    aristocrats, where no one sits
on the lawn, it is as if heaven is on
    one side, hell, on the other,
and somehow I have slipped very far
    into the abyss between the two,
an abyss that contains suns
    the way black holes
do not give back the history
  of light, the way a galaxy
        turns like a clock
    into the desperate desire
for water and these flowers
     bloom like idiots,
     live as thieves.
  Chris' cryptic texts
from West Florida: 'No coffee.
  nuclear power plant' and a picture
    of some industrial
      map of rust.
O Apollinaire, eau-de-vie,
    in this garden, which is a mockery
      of all gardens,
  in this Bed, Bath and Beyond
of the intimate, remember me,
  I know what is real
  and I will remember how to steal
    back what is mine.[32]

32   Simonds 2015, pp. 87–8.

CHAPTER 9

Modernism, Critical Theory, and the Desire for Objecthood

This essay will give an abridged account of how proponents of two genres of writing, the critical theory of modernity, and the modernist *ars poetica*, thought about language in the twentieth century. In the later part of this period critical theorists, working in a broadly Marxist philosophical vein, thought about language in terms of how the historical and political transformations wrought by capitalism, especially technological and administrative changes, put pressure on a range of language practices from democratic deliberation to literary style. Earlier modernist authors of statements about poetry, meanwhile, did not always name capitalism as explicitly as their theoretical counterparts, but tended nevertheless to recommend poetic techniques designed to keep up with the technological changes driven by capital.

The concerns articulated by these two genres of writing touch on older concerns about rhetoric, namely the fear of excessive methodization in rhetorical teaching, and the risk of rhetoric becoming demagoguery.[1] In the theoretical writing I will briefly survey below, critics see capitalism posing problems of linguistic routinization that cut language off from its most vital sources. In the poetics statements I will track across the century, poets sense something similar, but they also push against what they believe is a creeping advance of the ego in the production of poetry. Across the course of this essay, I will suggest that the obverse concerns about rhetoric articulated by these two genres – about too much method, and too little self-control – also drove an attraction toward philosophical (rather than political) accounts of language under capitalism that hold out the promise of avoiding problems of rhetoric by being anterior to them or by being less methodological and more 'theoretical'. I will suggest that this attraction to the promise of a philosophical 'theory' has both limited critical theorists' ability to characterize accurately the operation of capitalism in the twentieth century, and, in its guise as anti-rhetoric, has produced a poetics that drifts from actual poetic practice, often including the practice of the poets writing the statements. At the end of the essay, I will turn to an early twenty first-century *ars poetica* that points toward both less

---

1 See Jost and Hyde 1997.

philosophical ways of thinking about capitalism and less skeptical ways of thinking about rhetoric.

Critical theorists tended to tell the story of what happened to language in the twentieth century as a story about 'modernity', an existential condition, derived from social, political, and technological changes under capitalism, in which received truths could no longer be relied upon. In the fullest version of this story, modernity is followed by a 'post-modernity' that either abolishes key features of modernity or transforms them beyond recognition. This story has proven persuasive across the humanities and social sciences; in the most renowned and well-elaborated literary-critical account, a 1984 essay by the American literary theorist Fredric Jameson, the productive capacity of capitalism outstrips our interpretive abilities so thoroughly that understanding basic relations like cause-and-effect or part-and-whole requires a multi-tiered hermeneutic system.

Jameson's essay, which was eventually turned into a piece called 'The Cultural Logic of Late Capitalism', brilliantly turned to the aesthetic theory of the sublime as a way of accounting for the difficulty of understanding the relationship of culture to industrial production in post-World War II capitalism. Drawing on the work of the historian Ernest Mandel, Jameson suggested that capitalism's sheer productive power in the second half of the twentieth century had obliged us to acknowledge a kind of capitalist sublimity, and he suggested that the cultural aspects of its latest phase, because they could not be captured by any single interpretation, might best be understood by a return to Thomas Aquinas's four-tiered system of Biblical interpretation, which moved outward from literal to allegorical to salvational and cosmic meanings. The distributing of literary analysis across 'levels' of historical meaning promised to make space for the too-muchness of a capitalism whose cultural products seemed otherwise uninterpretable in terms of older distinctions like those between high or low culture, authentic or inauthentic intention, and so on.[2]

The 'Cultural Logic' essay proved indispensable to left-leaning critics, not least because it established a firm foothold for Marxist literary criticism in a period of political conservatism. But the history Jameson drew on, from Mandel's 1972 *Late Capitalism*, came in for pointed criticism from Marxist theorists who felt that it made the advance of capital seem inevitable (Mandel described capitalism in terms of progressive stages and repeating 'cycles'). And the language of overwhelming sublimity with which Jameson characterised the aesthetic disorientation produced by capitalism of the 1980s tended to push Marx-

---

2   See Jameson 1991.

ist literary criticism in an epistemological rather than an explicitly political direction, since it focused on finding some stable ground on which to understand, rather than to shape, aesthetic experience.

But the epistemological worries shaping Jameson's project linked him to a key debate in critical theory. In the 1980s, the German philosopher Jürgen Habermas and the French theorist Jean-François Lyotard became involved in a prolonged exchange over the political and philosophical meanings of 'modernity' and 'post-modernity'. While that debate has receded today, at the time it was considered crucial for any left-political philosophy wanting to equip itself to describe the workings of capitalism in the twentieth century. And the modernity-into-post-modernity framework that the debate helped consolidate has still not been decisively replaced in humanistic scholarship. It is worth outlining, very briefly, how Habermas and Lyotard thought about the role of language in particular in their accounts of modernity and post-modernity.

For Habermas, European cultures since the Enlightenment had witnessed both a fragmentation of culture into separate spheres – drifting, in his most famous rendition, into isolated scientific, moral and artistic zones – and a further separation of each of these spheres into expert and everyday knowledges and practices. In his 1980 essay, 'Modernity: An Unfinished Project?' Habermas suggests that there are always hints of how these separations might be overcome, and briefly mentions Peter Weiss's three-volume novel *The Aesthetics of Resistance* (1975–81) as a momentary, partial success: the novel describes how a group of working-class German youth, through night classes that expose them to the history of art, begin to realise that, however they come to love the beauty in artworks, they actually need to give them a value quite different than those ascribed to the art by teachers and experts. Habermas hesitates here, cautioning himself and his audience by adding,

> However, a differentiated reconnection of modern culture with an everyday sphere of praxis ... will admittedly only prove successful if the process of social modernization can *also* be turned into *other* non-capitalist directions, if the lifeworld can develop institutions of its own in a way currently inhibited by the autonomous systemic dynamics of the economic and administrative system.[3]

For Habermas, language and rhetoric have a special role to play in facilitating the possibility that 'the lifeworld can develop institutions of its own'. This is,

---

3   Habermas 1996, pp. 52–3.

Habermas believes that the world of the everyday can cause forms of language and thinking to flourish in ways that reconnect, from below, the moral, technical and aesthetic domains into which he thinks the world has separated, as well as to overcome the separation of expert-elite and everyday values. Across many books and essays, Habermas outlines the possibility of a rhetoric aiming at ideal conditions of inclusiveness, equality, and non-coercion.

Like Habermas, Lyotard sees the condition of a certain modernity as the result of technical progress gone unchecked; but Lyotard's focus is on the post-World War II rise of computerisation, and on the reduction of all knowledge to its efficiency and potential profitability. 'Post-modernism', for Lyotard, is closely linked to a 'post-industrialism' in which the struggle among capitalists for profit must be conducted as a struggle to profit from ideas rather than objects. As with Jameson and Habermas, this presents an epistemological problem. As he puts it in his influential book *The Postmodern Condition: A Report on Knowledge* (1979): 'Our working hypothesis is that the status of knowledge is altered as societies enter what is known as the postindustrial age and cultures enter what is known as the postmodern age'.[4] But where Habermas sees technical expertise corroding the possibility of a unity between the everyday and the elite, or among the scientific, the artistic, and the moral, and sees a certain deliberative rhetoric as the channel for attempting to achieve that unity, Lyotard insists that the problem of capitalist technological development is that it papers over a human liveliness based precisely on incommensurable difference. One expression of this, in his work, is a capitalist rationality that poaches from, but denies, the 'libidinal' energy of the people whose lives it organises – that is, their pre-conscious, anarchic, rebellious, or unpredictable desires. The agents of this rationality, for Lyotard, have been modern 'grand narratives' or 'metanarratives' of humanity's eventual achievement of scientific truth and political emancipation, both of which dishonestly seek to 'totalise' inherently unruly histories and experiences by giving them a single, retroactively coherent, meaning. This tendency reaches a breaking point in the post-modern era, which finally achieves what Lyotard famously called an 'incredulity toward metanarratives'.[5] For Lyotard, the loss of grand narratives is a good thing, but capitalism's denial of the libidinal energies that give the lie to Enlightenment require a perpetual rebellion from within.

Astute observers of this debate wondered at the time what it meant for a conversation manifestly about the practice of capitalism to be so theoretical. The

---

4   Lyotard 1984, p. xx.
5   Ibid., p. xxiv.

American critic Mark Poster, for instance, asked whether Lyotard's celebration of 'difference' overlooked the concrete challenges posed by de-colonial and multicultural politics.[6] And the American philosopher Richard Rorty sensed in the debate a doubling down on that aspect of the philosophical tradition that was more concerned to find the grounds for understanding capitalist modernity than to articulate desires for improving or replacing it.

Rorty's thoughts on the modernity-postmodernity framework are of particular interest here because, in one crisp formulation at least, he likens a distinction between more theoretical and more pragmatic strands in the history of philosophy to a difference between the discipline of philosophy and the practice of rhetoric. As he put it in a 1984 essay,

> One can ... attribute Descartes' role as 'founder of modern philosophy' to his development of what I earlier called 'an overzealous philosophy of science' – the sort of philosophy of science which saw Galilean mechanics, analytic geometry, mathematical optics, and the like, as having more spiritual significance than they in fact have ... Had Bacon – the prophet of self-assertion, as opposed to self-grounding – been taken more seriously, we might not have been struck with a canon of 'great modern philosophers' who took 'subjectivity' as their theme. We might ... have been less inclined to assume that epistemology (i.e., reflection on the nature and status of natural science) was the 'independent variable' in philosophical thought and moral and social philosophy the 'dependent variable'. We might thereby see what [Hans] Blumenberg calls 'self-assertion' – the willingness to center our hopes on the future of the race, on the unpredictable successes of our descendants – as the 'principle of the modern'. Such a principle would let us think of the modern age as defined by successive attempts to shake off the sort of ahistorical structure exemplified by Kant's division of culture into three 'value spheres'.[7]

By turning to Hans Blumenberg's distinction between 'self-grounding' and 'self-assertion', Rorty allows his distinction between the theoretical and practical strands in the history of philosophy to double as a distinction between philosophy and rhetoric. For Blumenberg, those terms not only mark a difference between theory and practice internal to philosophy, between philosophy (which seeks 'grounds') and rhetoric (which 'asserts'), but between two oppos-

---

6   See Poster 1992.
7   Rorty 1984, p. 41.

ing attitudes to humanity that constitute a problem of 'philosophical anthro-
pology': a conversation about what humanity is or could be, frequently centred
on the question of whether as a species we are well or poorly suited for survival
on earth. In an important 1987 essay, Blumenberg describes this ambivalent
tradition of conceptualising the human to a prior ambivalence about how to
characterise rhetoric. Outlining the poles of this discourse, he writes:

> The varieties of what we now call philosophical anthropology can be
> reduced to one pair of alternatives: Man can be viewed either as a poor or
> as a rich creature. The fact that man is not fixed, biologically, to a specific
> environment can be understood either as a fundamental lack of proper
> equipment for self-preservation or as openness to the fullness of a world
> that is no longer accentuated only in terms of vital necessities. Man is
> made creative either by the urgency of his needs or by playful dealings
> with his surplus talents ...
>
> As far as rhetoric is concerned, the traditional basic conceptions of it
> can likewise be reduced to one pair of alternatives: Rhetoric has to do
> either with the consequences of possessing the truth or the difficulties
> that result from the impossibility of obtaining truth.[8]

Though it was not widely taken up in the English-speaking world in the 1980s,
Blumenberg's depiction of a split in conceptions of the human along this axis
of attitudes about rhetoric provides an interesting alterative to the modernity-
discourses whose political concerns so quickly became epistemological wor-
ries. As I will indicate at the end of this essay, his anthropology of rhetoric
has historiographical implications inasmuch as rhetoric, in his view, becomes
less a ruse for covering over epistemological limits than a tool for dealing with
historically situated struggle. Meanwhile, Blumenberg's more forgiving under-
standing of rhetoric will be useful to keep in mind as we turn to some important
twentieth-century *ars poetica*, because a distinguishing mark of the modernist
literary poetics essay is a strident realism meant to outmanoeuvre the ancient
Platonic charge that poets, as abusers of rhetoric, distract the *polis* from the
hard project of achieving wisdom.

When they wrote manifestos or poetics statements, practising poets in the
last century tended to lay greater emphasis on modern-*ism* than modernity,
though of course the modernist attitudes and techniques for which they advoc-
ated were aimed at confronting the effects of a modernity that philosophers

---

8   Blumenberg 1987, p. 429.

would theorise most fully in the century's last quarter. These modernisms run across the political spectrum, though they are broadly anti-capitalist, even when produced from the right (Ezra Pound's conservative-populist hatred of usury is a good example). They are also almost entirely anti-subjectivist and anti-rhetorical, where 'rhetoric' implicitly signifies unnecessary ornament, distracting expressivity, narcissistic personal psychology, and excessive sentiment. A whole range of modernist techniques – avoidance of too-easy iambic fluency; turning to the vernacular; the deployment of startling line breaks and enjambments; the introduction of white page-space as a structuring element of poems – were aimed at bringing lucidity and clarity to poetic language that was seen, correctly or not, as having been overtaken by sentiment and metaphor. But in an ironic twist, inasmuch as the poets of the burgeoning modernist 'tradition' worked off a very general sense of modernity, rather than a specific understanding of the capitalism that was driving it, their hard-nosed theorisations were generally too fuzzy to hit the mark. This produced an interesting and ongoing gap between what was championed in manifestos and poetic theory and what was practised in poems. In his pathbreaking study *Solid Objects: Modernism and The Test of Production* (1998), Douglas Mao has shown that poets in the early twentieth century were exceptionally tuned-in to the contradictions at the heart of objecthood – in particular how objects could at once seem free from human interference and also liable to a disappointing human projection.[9] In what follows I want to think through the modernist fascination with 'the test of production' in specifically anti-capitalist terms, and to link the modernist desire to be free from a humanness seen as tainted by sentiment with its sidelong attention to capital, which never quite names its 'object' as such.

The poet-critic T.E. Hulme's 1908 essay, 'A Lecture on Modern Poetry', though it did not circulate as widely as later work by poets like Ezra Pound and T.S. Eliot, was influential in key modernist circles at the beginning of the century. The essay has little to say about capitalism, but it articulates several key points that will preoccupy theorists of capitalist modernity later in the century. Hulme prefigures Lyotard's remarks about 'incredulity toward metanarratives', for instance, when the former writes

> ... the great poems of ancient times resembled pyramids built for eternity where people loved to inscribe their history in symbolic characters. They believed they could realize an adjustment of idea and words that nothing could destroy.

---

9   See Mao 1998.

Now the whole trend of the modern spirit is away from that; philosophers no longer believe in absolute truth.[10]

Hulme also sketches a narrative of separation of human capacities or practices akin to Habermas's – here, a distinctly modern separation of reading and singing or chanting:

> Starting then from this standpoint of extreme modernism, what are the principal features of verse at the present time? It is this: that it is read and not chanted ... We have thus two distinct arts. The one intended to be chanted, and the other intended to be read in the study. I wish this to be remembered in the criticisms that are made on me. I am not speaking of the whole of poetry, but of this distinct new art which is gradually separating itself from the older one and becoming independent.[11]

Like Habermas and Lyotard, Hulme describes an acceleration of production in his era – here, an acceleration of poetic production that he links to technology, specifically the newspaper.

Describing a process by which fresh linguistic images are born in poetry and then mature and decay in prose, he distinguishes between the way poetry and prose are produced, and notes that mass-circulated prose has obliged poetry to move ever faster to keep up:

> Prose is due to a faculty of the mind something resembling reflex action in the body. If I had to go through a complicated mental process each time I laced my boots, it would waste mental energy; instead of that, the mechanism of the body is so arranged that one can do it almost without thinking. It is an economy of effort. The same process takes place with the images used in prose. For example, when I say that the hill was clad with trees, it merely conveys the fact to me that it was covered. But the first time that expression was used was by a poet, and to him it was an image recalling to him the distinct visual analogy of a man clad in clothes; but the image has died. One might say that images are born in poetry. They are used in prose, and finally die a long, lingering death in journalists' English. Now this process is very rapid, so that the poet must

---

10   Hulme 2003.
11   Ibid.

continually be creating new images, and his sincerity may be measured by the number of his images.[12]

In Hulme's account, the reflex mental activity of prose is well-suited to mass production, while the special quality of poetry is both its font and its pillaged terrain. This *pas de deux* between something vital (poetry) and something rote (prose) also prefigures Lyotard's depiction of the dance between the unruly vitality of the players of various local language-games and the capitalist routinization of them.

For Hulme, the contrast between prose and poetry is cousin to a contrast internal to the history of poetry, between an older poetry driven by regular meter and a new, modern poetry driven by 'images'. In Hulme's rendition, an image is a hard-won form of instantaneous impression, as contradictory as that may sound, and it brings with it a special alertness that is the opposite of the effect produced by the old poetry:

> The effect of rhythm, like that of music, is to produce a kind of hypnotic state, … [but] the procedure of the new visual art is just the contrary. It depends for its effect not on a kind of half sleep produced, but on arresting the attention, so much so that the succession of visual images should exhaust one.
>
> Regular metre to this impressionist poetry is cramping, jangling, meaningless, and out of place. Into the delicate pattern of images and colour it introduces the heavy, crude pattern of rhetorical verse. It destroys the effect just as a barrel organ does, when it intrudes into the subtle interwoven harmonies of the modern symphony. It is a delicate and difficult art, that of evoking an image, of fitting the rhythm to the idea, and one is tempted to fall back to the comforting and easy arms of the old, regular metre, which takes away all the trouble for us.[13]

Hulme here revises the old Platonic prejudice against the un-rational anticlarity of poets by turning it into a prejudice against the unclarity of *bad* poetry. It is clear that he is aware of this when he writes, mischievously, 'Personally I am of course in favour of the complete destruction of all verse more than twenty years old. But that happy event will not, I am afraid, take place until Plato's desire has been realized and a minor poet has become dictator'.[14]

---

12   Ibid.
13   ibid.
14   ibid.

Regular poetic rhythm, in Hulme's essay, is figured not only as being like something mass-produced (or mass-induced), but also as something feminine and maternal: 'the comforting and easy arms of the old, regular metre, which takes away all the trouble for us'. This is, for him, the character of rhetoric, which he all but equates with musicality and femininity: 'Imitative poetry', he writes referring to poetry that clings to older styles, 'springs up like weeds, and women whimper and whine of you and I alas, and roses, roses all the way. It becomes the expression of sentimentality rather than of virile thought'.[15]

Hulme's dissatisfaction with the sentimentality he hears in the rhythms of 'metrical' poetry, and in the use of metaphors of 'roses', is more than literary. In his essay, 'Humanism and The Religious Attitude', he elaborates his critique of false comfort into a distinction between a human-centred view of the world, on the one hand, and another ('the religious attitude') that forces itself to come to grips with humanity's insignificance, on the other. In this essay, written shortly before his death in 1917, Hulme argues that

> When the intensity of the religious attitude finds proper expression in art, then you get a very different result [than in religious humanism]. Such expression springs not from a delight in life but from a feeling for certain absolute values, which are entirely independent of vital things ...[16]

It would be hard to overstate how archetypical the ideas about poetry and rhetoric Hulme develops here would become. To step outside the English-language world for a moment, Hulme's pitting of poetry and prose against each other, along an axis of alertness and susceptible wooziness, is replayed in mid-century France, when the writers of the *Tel Quel* group would face off against Jean-Paul Sartre, in an intergenerational, intra-leftist debate in which *Tel Quel* writers advocated for the complex reflexivity of poetry as a suitable tool for left-wing politics, while Sartre insisted on the political utility of clear, reportorial prose.[17] And we can hear clear echoes of Hulme's parable of the decay of a metaphor in the French novelist Alain Robbe-Grillet's 1965 essay 'Nature, Humanism, and Tragedy', when he writes,

> Metaphor, in fact, is never an innocent figure of speech. To say that the weather is 'capricious', or a mountain 'majestic', to speak of the 'heart' of the forest, of the 'merciless' sun, of a village 'crouching' in the hollow

---

15   ibid.
16   Hulme 2003, p. 188.
17   See Marx-Scouras 1996.

of a valley, is to some extent to describe the things themselves – their form, their dimensions, their situation, etc. But the choice of an analogical vocabulary, however simple it may be, in itself goes beyond the mere description of purely physical data ... In practically all our contemporary literature these anthropomorphic analogies are too insistently, too coherently, repeated, not to reveal a whole metaphysical system.[18]

Like Hulme, Robbe-Grillet sees metaphor as the vehicle for a rhetorical obfuscation of reality that contaminates and routinises language. The thrust of his argument in 'Nature, Humanism, and Tragedy' is an anti-humanist insistence that human persons are not, as they console themselves they are, at the centre of the universe. In fact, the universe is indifferent to their presence, just as 'The intensity of the religious attitude' in Hulme springs from an attraction to everything that is 'independent of vital things'.

It is not only the similarities that are striking here; it is the continuities across half a century, and across religious and political difference. Hulme's anti-humanist critique of metaphor and anthropomorphism is religiously orthodox, whereas Robbe-Grillet's is secularist; but they both partake of an earlier, Nietzschean critique of metaphor that can, by turns, be used either to demolish the idea of God (God is a metaphor that obscures from us our mortality and insignificance) or to support religious orthodoxy (our metaphors will always fail in the face of God's absolute character). Hulme's anti-rhetorical realism is politically conservative, even as it is meant to be aesthetically revolutionary, while Robbe-Grillet's anti-metaphorical realism has generally been taken as a left-wing position (his essay was originally published in *The New Left Review*).

Remarkably, we can find elements of this broadly anti-rhetorical, frequently anti-humanist attitude even in twentieth-century poetic manifestoes that are essentially humanist and rhetorical. Charles Olson's renowned 1950 essay, 'Projective Verse', is a good example. In that essay, Olson aims to pick up on excitement about new theories of communication, including emergent cybernetic theory, to suggest that poetry, if it freed itself from an old-fashioned attachment to meter and rhyme, might recover the lively relation to actual speech that it supposedly enjoyed in the Elizabethan era. The key element in this emergent poetics was the poet's breath – as a determining unit of sound, of rhythm, of ideation. Unlike Hulme's anti-humanist anti-vitalism, Olson's breath-based stance in 'Projective Verse' is deeply humanist. And the texture of Olson's essay is purposely oral, even when it is scholarly. Early in the essay, he writes, 'A poem

---

18   Robbe-Grillet 1965, p. 68.

is energy transferred from where the poet got it (he will have some several caus-ations), by way of the poem itself to, all the way over to, the reader. Okay'.[19]

At the same time, however, Olson's 1950 essay shares key traits with Hulme's piece from 1908. Like Hulme, Olson feels it necessary to steer poetry away from meter and rhyme; and as with Hulme, what Olson advocates for instead is a combination of speed, energy, and anti-egoic objectivity. The technological background has shifted: instead of the rise of a communicative medium, the newspaper, enjoying a heyday early in the century, here it's the rise of a sci-ence *of* communication and information, cybernetics, in the background. But as with Hulme, a relentless energetics is meant to displace the implicitly fem-inine and sentimental allure of rhyme and meter: 'I would suggest that verse here and in England dropped this secret [of sound being more than just met-rical] from the late Elizabethans to Ezra Pound, lost it, in the sweetness of meter and rime, in a honey-head'.[20] Instead of that 'sweetness', Olson argues for an energy-transfer that, like Hulme's laboriously wrought but instantan-eously communicated image, is lighting fast – 'it has the mind's speed', as he puts it – and the product of an implicitly masculine labour, which produces, as in Hulme, not feelings but objects. Olson calls this 'objectism':

> Objectism is the getting rid of the lyrical interference of the individual as ego ... that peculiar presumption by which western man has interposed himself between what he is as a creature of nature (with certain instruc-tions to carry out) and those other creations of nature which we may, with no derogation, call objects.[21]

As with Hulme, the philosophy of history that undergirds Olson's critique of sweetness, lyricality and the ego links him to the theorists of modernity and post-modernity with whom we began. Hulme's sense of poetic history was modernist inasmuch as it was anti-progressive, focused instead on a potentially eternal cycle of decays into rhetoric and rebirths into objectivity; Olson's sense of history is that of a vast arc that led into a technological modernity which needed to be overcome by a return to the kinds of oneness with nature that he sees in pre-colonial cultures, especially in Mexico: hence his critique of the lyrical ego, above, as a problem of 'western man'. Meanwhile, Olson was part of a generation that viewed advanced systems theory, and the technologies that

---

19   Olsen 1997, p. 240.
20   Olsen 1997, p. 241.
21   Olsen 1997, p. 247.

might grow out of it, as the route back to a communication un-muddled by lyr-icality and ego – un-muddled, in other words, by the kind of 'rhetoric' that, in poetic terms, is linked to rhyme and regular meter, and in political terms, to centralised state administration and dull parliamentary debate. The keywords of mid-century cybernetics – 'command', 'control', 'feedback' – are at the centre of Olson's canonical 1949 poem 'The Kingfishers'. That poem also quotes a then-triumphant Mao to produce a blend of revolutionary impatience (with bureau-cratic 'pejorocracy') and cautious hope that a new science of communication will foster a kind of second-take return to the 'primitive' knowledges and histor-ical rhythms embodied in the myths of rejuvenation attached to the bird of the poem's title. Writing in what seems to be an historiographical register, Olson declares, 'not accumulation but change, the feed-back proves, the feed-back is / the law', and continues,

> We can be precise. The factors are
> in the animal and / or the machine the factors are communication and /
>   or control, both involve
> the message. And what is the message? The message is
> a discrete or continuous sequence of measurable events distributed in
>   time[22]

This quantification of the idea of a poem's 'message' is anti-rhetorical in the sense that it is aimed at dispensing with the idea of a moral or spiritual content to poetry that lies beneath its forms or is separable from them. Olson's anti-rhetoric is consonant with the critiques of meaning and symbol that became second nature to the early cybernetic theorists, who were at pains to establish the plausibility of the idea that communication among elements in systems could take place without the psychological participation (conscious or uncon-scious) of individual actors.[23] That this anti-subjective – or at least anti-egoic – stance should have political dimensions may seem startling in an arguably 'lyric' poem, but it prefigures key attitudes developed outside of poetry too, not least in French structuralism, which would accrue significant left-wing cachet until the student revolts of the late 1960s.

   After the anti-colonial struggles of the later 1960s and 1970s however, aspects of these ideas were discredited. The valorisation of 'primitive' cultures over and against a neurasthenic 'modernity', for instance, came to seem implic-

---

22   Olsen 1987, p. 90.
23   See Dupuy 2000.

ated in a fetishism of those cultures, and the idea of 'structure' seemed too abstract as a ground or frame for revolutionary activism. As with the rise of post-structuralism, however, which preserved aspects of structuralist analysis while shifting its emphasis from deciphering systems conceived as finite and combinatory to understanding language anti-systemically as open and aleatory, the poetic statements that followed on Olson preserved key aspects of the anti-egoic tradition of which he was a part, even though their politics absorbed the energies of new social movements that Olson could not have foreseen.

Lyn Hejinian's 1983 manifesto 'The Rejection of Closure' is a good measure of these differences and similarities. On the one hand, Hejinian's essay (originally a talk) is more overtly political than Olson's. Hejinian, an American poet, makes explicit links to the academic French feminism of the 1970s and 80s, citing figures like Luce Irigaray and Hélène Cixous to argue that 'open' texts (as opposed to 'closed' texts) are anti-hierarchical and perhaps even anticapitalist:

> The 'open text', by definition, is open to the world and particularly to the reader. It invites participation, rejects the authority of the writer over the reader and thus, by analogy, the authority implicit in other (social, economic, cultural) hierarchies. It speaks for writing that is generative rather than directive. The writer relinquishes total control and challenges authority as a principle and control as a motive. The 'open text' often emphasizes or foregrounds process, either the process of the original composition or of subsequent compositions by readers, and thus resists the cultural tendencies that seek to identify and fix material and turn it into a product; that is, it resists reduction and commodification. As Luce Irigaray says, positing this tendency within a feminine sphere of discourse, 'It is really a question of another economy which diverts the linearity of a project ...'[24]

Elsewhere, however, Hejinian's distinction between 'open' and 'closed' texts draws on a critique of the lyric ego and a language of energetics that recalls Olson and even Hulme. She writes:

> For the sake of clarity, I will offer a tentative characterization of the terms *open* and *closed*. We can say that a 'closed text' is one in which all the elements of the work are directed toward a single reading of it. Each element confirms that reading and delivers the text from any lurking ambiguity.

---

24   Hejinian 2000, p. 43.

In the 'open text', meanwhile, all the elements of the work are maximally excited; here it is because ideas and things exceed (without deserting) argument that they have taken into the dimension of the work.[25]

As in statements by her predecessors, in Hejinian's essay 'things' should exceed other aspects of poetic composition – especially, here, 'argument', at least the kind of 'argument' to be found in a traditional poem. And while the anti-authoritarian and participatory language of Hejinian's essay marks its affinity with the social movements on which it follows, and its difference from the masculinist character of the *ars poetica* on which it draws, its rejection of the poet's authority is made on the same terms – a rejection of lyric ego and of rhetoric in its guise as excessively domineering language – that Olson uses to *establish* the authority of the poet. Finally, though her essay doesn't traffic in the kind of primitivism that makes Olson's politics of modernity founder on the question of race, the fact that her examples of open writing are drawn from the work of white writers returns us to questions of historical and geopolitical unevenness raised by the broad claims of the modernity theorists – that is, for whom might it be said that authoritativeness is best shorn? Throughout the 1980s, debates among poets ranging from the liberal to the left rehearsed versions of this question: were avant-garde techniques akin to advanced technologies that should be distributed more democratically among writers emerging from unevenly 'modern' historical trajectories, or were they like luxuries that the supposedly less 'modern' writers (usually, writers of colour) sadly could not afford?[26]

Fred Moten's 2015 essay 'Blackness and Poetry' takes as its point of departure the technologically and racially uneven character of the capitalist modernity against which the essays above pit themselves. For Moten, 'modernity' is most vividly expressed in the terrors of the Middle Passage that brought enslaved Africans to the Americas; he turns in particular to the now-famous historical episode of the slave ship Zong:

> In 1781 the captain of the slave ship Zong (a vessel of Dutch manufacture which earlier had been called *Zorg*, or *care*) ordered that some 150 Africans be thrown overboard so that the ship's owners could collect insurance taken out on their 'lost cargo'.[27]

---

25   Hejinian 2000, pp. 42–3.
26   See Kreiner 2013.
27   Moten 2015.

In this terrifying, demoralising episode, cutting-edge transport technology (trans-Atlantic shipping) and up-to-the-minute financial instruments (the insurance on the slaves) combine to make a mockery of the Enlightenment idea of the dignity of humanity. But the recording of this event also begs the question of whether there is, or can be, humanity. Moten's essay coordinates this vision of modernity with the question of humanism, and – in what will prove to be the essay's most generative idea – suggests that thought and sociability are indistinguishable from each other, at least where blackness is concerned: 'black thought, which is to say black social life, remains a fruitful site for inhabiting and soliciting the human differential within the general ecology'.[28]

This equation of social life and thought is the source of Moten's two examples of 'poetry': M. NourbeSe Philip's 2008 book-length poem *Zong!* – a multi-voiced poetic rendition of the existential wreckage caused by the murder of the slaves aboard the titular ship – and the improvisatory music of jazz composer Thelonious Monk. What they share, in Moten's essay, is a powerful poetics in which there is no humanity *without* sociability, without mutual dependence and mutual vitality. For Moten, these artworks share a poetics in which there can be no single voice, no purely solo performance, and, indeed, no 'artwork' in an enclosed, autonomous sense. They show up the disastrous character, for Moten, of the impulse to create a 'modernity' out of the idea of a possessive or 'sovereign' individuality that, because it was first predicated on some of us possessing others, can never be universalised except as a sham. As he puts it:

> we book passage on this transportive thought: that modernity (the confluence of the slave trade, settler colonialism and the democratization of sovereignty through which the world is imaged, graphed and grasped) is a socioecological disaster that can neither be calculated nor conceptualized as a series of personal injuries.[29]

What this means for poetry, in Moten's essay, is that

> Philip's heroism, which emerges as a radical disavowal of the heroic, consists in a deep and fatal sounding ... The one who dives, who falls, into the wreckage of the shipped cannot come back for or as or by herself ... *What remains is more than incalculable loss.* The logic of this supplement,

---

28   Ibid.
29   Ibid.

whose appearance as fade and induced forgetting is *terribly beautiful*, dictates that the next word be 'nevertheless'. Nevertheless, this deprivation is sung forevermore ... En masse, Philip realizes this inescapable and overwhelming truth: that insofar as the story of the Zong cannot be told, or sung, alone it isn't a story, it isn't anybody's story, at all. *Zong!* is the story of no-body and it cannot be sung alone.[30]

This irreducibly social, entirely choral, understanding of poetry, with its critique of the sovereign self, gives it a family resemblance with the other critiques of the lyrical ego we've seen here. It also pulls hard away from the idea, as in Olson, that the anti-egoic poet would therefore be A Great Poet, that is, still best grasped as an individual. This is a complex, inflectional difference that nonetheless suggests a stark re-framing of the anti-rhetorical aspect of the modernity-stories at work in twentieth-century statements of poetics. Indeed Moten writes,

> Even in Olson, whom I have been shamelessly and religiously chanting in my head this whole time, there's a massive problematic regarding the relations between genius, generative power, rule, concept, invention, concept, purposiveness and nature.[31]

Moten closes his essay by suggesting that (despite his ill-conceived, racist ideas about jazz), German critical theorist Theodor Adorno offers helpful descriptions of how a work of art, produced under the conditions of a modernity that is built from the outset on violence, gives itself a rule of form to obey, by disobeying that form:

> what if representation is the instantiation of a radical impropriety? What if truth is given in and by way of this dehiscence? This is something Adorno approaches by way of the notion of *Bewegungsgesetz*, which is usually translated as the law of motion, and by way of its relation to radical art's primary and necessary darkness.[32]

I end with Moten's essay because it both culminates and deviates from the twentieth-century habit of making the chastisement of the ego the pivot-point

---

30   Ibid.
31   Ibid.
32   Ibid.

of a story about modernity. On the one hand, Moten's essay doubles down on the utility of telling the story of the century as a story about modernity, since one version of the modernity-tale – it was built on dehumanisation, and has been a disaster – is never clearer than when counterposing the Enlightenment thinkers' supposed investment in what the political scientist C.B. MacPherson called 'possessive individualism' to the possession of human beings in slavery. In this light we can see Moten's attraction to the versions of post-structuralist theory that lay emphasis on the non-sovereignty of the subject who has built a sense of self on false premises, and also notice Moten indirectly suggesting that the possibility of post-structuralist critique may indeed be facilitated by the millions of persons whose subjected existence gave the lie all along to a possessive sense of stable selfhood. On the other hand, Moten's pulling the rug out from under the individual ego feels different from earlier manifestos that aimed to chasten the single lyric singer as too arrogant, too driven by the feminine sentiment of rhyme, or too metronomic; he wants, instead, to make the revelation of the non-sovereignty of the subject mark a recognition of our mutual dependency. Whatever its critique of the subject, the essay's tone is humanist, where the tone of the other manifestos we have looked at is broadly anti-humanist. Rather than rebuke those (bad poets, gullible readers) with presumptions to solitary, self-sufficient ego, it calls for them to lay down its burdens.

Moten's 'Blackness and Poetry' also points back to a whole other twentieth-century tradition of poetic manifestos, not least produced by black writers, that champions the social utility of poetry without making use of the anti-rhetorical framing devices I have been tracing. Walt Whitman's 1855 Preface to *Leaves of Grass* helps shape this tradition (when he writes that 'The United States themselves are essentially the greatest poem'), but it is given pointed and political voice in a range of poetic statements from Langston Hughes's 1926 essay 'The Negro Artist and The Racial Mountain' to Amiri Baraka's 1966 manifesto poem 'Black Art' and Audre Lorde's 'Poetry is Not a Luxury', published in 1985. Adrienne Rich's 1983 essay 'Blood, Bread and Poetry' forms part of this tradition as well – it is, indeed a counter-tradition, marked most clearly by its political explicitness and its generally non-academic production.

There is a final reason that Moten's essay makes a good ending or at least turning point for the tradition I've been describing. It has to do with two words he uses at key moments in his piece, and with their implications for how an understanding of 'rhetoric' as something more than excessive egoism also opens onto more complex historical understandings of capitalism. The words are 'nevertheless', and *Bewegungsgesetz*, or 'law of motion'.

Describing Philip's poem *Zong!* above, Moten writes that

The one who dives, who falls, into the wreckage of the shipped cannot
come back for or as or by herself ... *What remains is more than incalculable
loss*. The logic of this supplement, whose appearance as fade and induced
forgetting is *terribly beautiful*, dictates that the next word be 'nevertheless'.
Nevertheless, this deprivation is sung forevermore ...[33]

Moten is describing an unfathomable survival, any description of whose char-
acter must begin with a 'nevertheless' that marks a turn away from merely
aesthetic appreciation for the power or beauty of Philip's poem, and keeps in
play the slave-trade violence whose viciousness and scope deforms even a Yeat-
sian 'terrible beauty'. In this use of the word 'nevertheless', Moten is echoing
a similar use in German, where nineteenth-century debates about the philo-
sophical significance of new biological discoveries – including a discovery of
our species' dependence on highly specific and unstable ecological niches –
resulted in a sense that humanity's survival was a kind of low-grade against-all-
odds elaboration of viability.

For Blumenberg, however, the value of rhetoric is that it is the medium for
a kind of ongoing practical wisdom itself the product of both surplus *and* lack,
playfulness *and* necessity. This means that rhetoric is not only a practical but
also an historical tool, not least as a tool for history understood less as stages or
cycles, as in modernity theories or in the manifestos of Hulme or Olson, than
as a kind of struggle – a social and political struggle whose characteristics Blu-
menberg emphasises by a turn to Marx. This understanding of history leads
Blumenberg not only to a sense of irreducible sociality akin to Moten's, but
also to a use of that word, 'nevertheless', in a similar sense: the human subject's
non-sovereignty, however important it may be to point out as part of a critique
of Enlightenment notions of individualism, is more interesting for the way it
suggests a shared perplexity and a collective struggle:

> 'Men make their own history, but they do not make it just as they please;
> they do not make it under circumstances chosen by themselves, but under
> circumstances directly encountered, given and transmitted from the past',
> Marx writes in the *Eighteenth Brumaire*. The deeper the crisis of legitim-
> acy reaches, the more pronounced the recourse to rhetorical metaphor
> becomes – it is not inertia that makes tradition but rather the difficulty of
> living up to one's designation as the subject of history ... I am not cel-
> ebrating rhetoric here as in innate creative gift that man possesses. To

---

33   Moten 2015.

illuminate it anthropologically is not to demonstrate that it gives man a special 'metaphysical' distinction. As a behavioral characteristic of a creature that lives 'nevertheless' [trotzdem], it is literally a 'certificate of poverty'.[34]

This insistence on the practical nature of rhetoric links Blumenberg's essay to Moten's as a cousin form of demurral from an old critique of rhetoric, more recent examples of which we have seen above. It is also remarkable in that, as with Moten, Blumenberg's sense of rhetoric as the product of lack removes a key element of the philosophical tradition's similar characterisation: he sees that lack as most important for being a sign of vulnerability, rather than a source of duplicity. Finally, Blumenberg's slightly arm's length turn to Marx for clarification about the nature of the history out of which rhetoric emerges links his essay to Moten's in another sense. When Moten turns to Adorno's use of the idea of a *Bewegungsgesetz* or 'law of motion' in the artwork, he draws our attention to how Adorno is himself making an analogy between the compulsions under which art must operate, and Marx's characterisation of the compulsions under which *capital* must operate. The pressure of competition, of costly technological innovation, or worker resistance, of the tendency of the rate of capitalist profit to fall: Marx included all these in what he called the capitalist *Bewegungsgesetz* – not an eternal or cosmic law, but a tendential constriction of possibility reproduced each time capital triumphs – violently, and at a cost – over its obstacles.

Moten and Blumenberg work in tandem here because they both suggest ways beyond the impasses produced both by the theories that tell the story of language in the twentieth century as a story of modernity, and by the modernist *ars poetica* of the same century, which felt obliged to defend poetic technique against the possibility that poetry would be seen as rhetorical. To read Blumenberg against the history of the modernist *ars poetica* is to sense behind their manifesto-like aura another genre: the defence of poetry, which since the Renaissance has felt (in English at least), indeed, defensive – as though poets, responding to Plato over and over again across the centuries, have long felt they had to make the case for some version of realism to an imagined audience of the most sceptical people conceivable. To read Moten's 'Blackness and Poetry' is to see what the defence of poetry looks like with its guard down. And to read these two texts together is to sense the prospect of an embrace of non-sovereignty whose aim is not to 'critique the self', but to escape a philosophical

---

34   Blumenberg 1987, p. 452.

modernity-story whose origins can be traced back to philosophy's phobia of rhetoric. Blumenberg characterises that phobia as a resistance to abandoning the search for what one conservative journal of theology calls 'first things' in favour of beginning where we are. But in their desire to make poetry object-like, the modernists endorsed Augustine's *non verba res* (deeds, not words) at the cost of Horace's *in media res* (in the middle of things), where all poetry – including their own – begins.

To sum up: the anti-rhetorical impulse I've traced here in theories of modernity is linked to historical narratives that fail to describe capitalism accurately because they keep becoming histories of what happens to an individual self. Conversely, the poetic objection to rhetoric and ego, and the anti-rhetoric that champions thinghood over selfhood, are linked to capitalist dynamics more than the poets often realise, because they so frequently imagine egoless objectivity competing with capitalist technologies. But when we recognise the history of capitalism as involving more than problems of knowledge or selfhood, the limits of the critique of rhetoric as unseemly egoism (or routinising method) become extremely clear. The temptations to periodise according to modernity, and to proselytise against the self, proved equally irresistible in the last century; you might say that it was easier to advocate for the end of the ego than the end of capitalism. Still, the one is unlikely to depart us, while the other may yet be made to fall away, one day.

CHAPTER 10

Literary and Economic Value (with Joshua Clover)

Given the sheer variety of ways in which literature has been valued or defended, not to mention the universe of values literature has both championed and rejected, any attempt at comprehensiveness would be mad, and a linear history would either never arrive at its twenty-first-century destination, or arrive there at the cost of a vitiating generality.

Instead, this is a reflection on the relationship between literary and economic discussions of value, focused on later twentieth-century debates in each discussion that dovetail, implicitly or explicitly, with the question of whether literature, or the values it might express, can be said to be separate or autonomous from the economic and social system in which it is embedded – that is, global capitalism, limiting it, for the most part, to material in English and on translations from some European languages, and homing in on an even more particular set of conversations internal to Euro-American Marxism in the last several decades.

Why this highly specific, arguably presentist, and directly political approach? On the one hand, the intermingling of political theory, ethics, and the analysis of literature is ancient. Reading literature has long been championed as a medium for enlightenment or self-cultivation, that is, for its ethical value: but of course Aristotle concluded in the *Nicomachean Ethics* that ethical inquiry necessarily led to the study of politics. On the other hand, we are persuaded by the spirit of Karl Marx's remark in the *Grundrisse*, regarding a method that reads past history out of the most involute conditions of the present, that 'Human anatomy is the key to the anatomy of the ape'.[1] This metaphor of Marx's feels applicable, not only to the practice of reading backwards from the present, but of reading outwards from it. That is, if ethics is the study of how we might best live, and if global capitalism is, in the words of Susan Sontag's story of the AIDS epidemic, 'the way we live now', then the ethically focused tradition of championing the value of literature should welcome a new chapter that takes seriously the analysis of exactly how we live together, not least how we live together in a complex political-economic system. And since, as Robert Heilbroner has noted, the modern discipline of economics has been built around a refusal to name capitalism as the medium and object of its

---

1   Marx 1993, p. 105.

study of 'economies', the Marxist tradition has distinct advantages – not least its insistence that politics and economics are not separate domains, and that value is a constitutive feature of their unity rather than a virtue of one or the other.[2]

In other words, any attempt to answer the oldest question about 'value' – that is, what is the good, or what makes a good life? – must sooner or later be immersed, as it were, in the particulars of how we have ended up organising life so as to produce value. This means that all questions of value in the ancient sense must be thought through at least some of the particulars of value production under capitalism. Some of the Marxist debates have been absorbed into a 'critical theory' that has tended to deemphasise the economic origins of its criticality, because those traditions themselves have fallen behind more recent developments both in capitalism and its study. Conversations about literary value demonstrate the usefulness of thinking through the general question of value by way of particulars in twentieth- and twenty-first-century Marxist conversations about value, but also show that those conversations have tended to be more philosophical and less historical than they might best be. An irony is that, in order to press for a more historically focused study of how value production under capitalism shapes discussions of literary value, we skip over a lot of history.

A final idiosyncrasy is that we will also be bookending the specific question of literary value with discussions of aesthetic and economic value. This is because, whatever their specific interest, discussions of literary value have depended on ideas developed in prior philosophical conversations that eventually congealed into the category of aesthetics. Especially important is the way in which defences of literature in the modern era have deployed a language of mental faculties that is explicitly analogical to political relations of sovereignty. This is perhaps easiest to see in the run-up to Percy Bysshe Shelley's famous declaration, in 'A Defence of Poetry', that 'poets are the unacknowledged legislators of the world'. This declaration is framed by an extraordinary passage that makes a link between relations among mental faculties, and relations of material production:

> The functions of the poetical faculty are twofold: by one it creates new materials of knowledge, and power, and pleasure; by the other it engenders in the mind a desire to reproduce and arrange them according to a certain rhythm and order which may be called the beautiful and the

---

2   See Heilbroner and Milberg 1995.

good. The cultivation of poetry is never more to be desired than at periods when, from an excess of the selfish and calculating principle, the accumulation of the materials of external life exceed the quantity of the power of assimilating them to the internal laws of human nature.[3]

Writing in 1821, during the first heyday of British industrial capitalism, Shelley takes for granted that an inwardness marked by harmonious relations among faculties or 'principles' can serve as a stay against the predations of that capitalism. Shelley figures capitalism as a usurpation and a disproportion alike.

A political language of sovereignty and a spatial language of domain, in other words, shape Shelley's critique of nineteenth-century capitalism and serve as the basis for his counter-valuation of poetry. This literary-critical hinging together of intellectual faculties and social roles depends in turn on a prior philosophical history in which a key feature of the good life is the achievement of sovereignty over one's emotions. The championing of literary value depends on the philosophical framework that will develop into 'aesthetics' even more clearly in the history of defences of poetry in Sir Philip Sidney's 'Apology for Poetry', first published in 1595. In that essay, Sidney argues that poets are better moral guides than philosophers because poetry accesses a desire or motivation that is anterior to reflection:

> For suppose it be granted – that which I suppose with great reason may be denied – that the philosopher, in respect of his methodical proceeding, teach more perfectly than the poet, yet do I think that no man is so much *Philophilosophos* [a friend to the philosopher – ed.] as to compare the philosopher in moving with the poet. And that moving is of a higher degree than teaching, it may by this appear, that it is well nigh both the cause and the effect of teaching; for who will be taught, if he be not moved with desire to be taught? And what so much good doth that teaching bring forth – I speak still of moral doctrine – as that it moves one to do that which it doth teach?[4]

Indeed, Sidney continues, poetry allows for precisely the kind of moral education that the philosophers claim to value: an education that leads to the rule of reason over passion. This argument (along with many others in the same vein) allows Sidney to remark, a moment later, 'Now therein of all sciences ...

---

3   Shelley 2009.
4   Sidney 2002, p. 226.

is our poet the monarch'. The anti-capitalist pivot between faculties and social arrangements seen in Shelly finds its precursor in Sidney's argument among the disciplines, which, like Shelley's, is also an argument about the faculties. And literary value, in both these essays, is intimately linked to the idea of sovereignty, where 'sovereignty' is meant simultaneously to indicate hierarchical arrangements of human capacities and arrangements (hierarchical or harmonious) of social roles.

This mode of championing the specific value of literature by way of analogising relations among faculties to relations among social types, or social arrangements, is alive and well today. For instance, Martha Nussbaum's advocacy of a 'perceptive equilibrium' in novel reading, which she believes can create an ethically productive balance between fine-grained perception and impulses to universal moral laws: her argument is that ethically attuned novel reading can calibrate both emotion and cognition, and a harmonious relation between literary theory and philosophy.[5] This style of argument – the defence of literature – endures in literary debates.

While the separating of literary value (conceived as immanent to the text) from other modes (understood as imposed on the text by force and thus as instrumentalising literature for other ends) remains a persistent feature, such defences are varied in whether they purport that such an approach makes literature more effectively critical or happily 'post-critical'. Such approaches are so resolutely spatial in their conceptions that they cannot accommodate much in the way of thinking about time, expect perhaps as individual literary *Bildung*, or as a story of successive, quasi-mythological Ages (as in Shelley). Such defences also tend to remain locked in a disciplinary battle between literature and philosophy that can make very little room for other disciplines, such as history.

And, when this style of arguing for literary value does attempt to think historically, it tends to raise the question of economic relations, only to imagine them as yet another domain – separate from, or parallel to, history and politics alike.

There is however a more adequate way of thinking about value, one that is centred on the vicissitudes of value production in capitalism, rather than on a parable of the war of the disciplines, or a struggle among the faculties. We want to think about how forms of struggle that are simultaneously political and economic give the lie to such parables, while honouring the fact that they touch on desires that life under capital continually solicits and harries. As

---

5   See Nussbaum 1992, pp. 190–3.

suggested above, this departure from reading literary value out of the tradition of defences of literature will involve suggesting very different coordinates for thinking about the value of a poem or a novel, or of deep reading, or of joyous reading on the fly. But in order to maintain a sense that these coordinates, drawn from scholarship on the history of capitalism, might speak to literary-critical projects, we will take a look at a moment in literary theory and criticism that feels like a near miss, as it were – a moment in the 1980s when debates about the status of the literary canon provoked conversations about value that necessarily included reflection on the history of literary criticism, as well as the history of literature. Following that, we will turn to debates in so-called 'critical theory' that begin with a sense of the intimacy of economic and literary value, and therefore get much closer to the problem as we would like to see it reframed. We will suggest in closing, though, that critical theory has tended to fall into the same trap as the defence-of-literature tradition, in that it keeps trying to champion literature as other than capital, perhaps because it predates capital. This tends to bifurcate critical-theoretical positions into those that imagine utopian possibilities for literature, and those that can only imagine literary value as crushed under the weight of capital. These positions tend to gloss over the scholarship that focuses not just on the expansion of capitalism across the globe over the last few centuries, but on the vicissitudes capital suffers as it pursues its compulsion to expand forever. First, though, let us look at a literary-critical brush with thinking value and history together.

1   Literary Value and Literary Politics: The Moment of the Canon Debates

In his landmark 1990 study *The Ideology of The Aesthetic*, Terry Eagleton traced the history of an influential and primarily German discourse of aesthetic value that ranged from Alexander Baumgarten and David Hume to the work of Immanuel Kant, G.W.F. Hegel, and Friedrich Schiller, and on to the theories of Walter Benjamin, Martin Heidegger, and Theodor Adorno. Though the discourse Eagleton describes takes different shapes across a political spectrum, two of its features remain constant – it is a *philosophical* discourse, and it tends toward allegory. Writing about the first great wave of aesthetic theory, for instance, Eagleton turns to a formulation of Baumgarten's that is clearly meant to describe the political relations between a people and a sovereign through the idiom of the relationship between reason and sensory delight:

'science', writes Baumgarten, 'is not to be dragged down to the region of sensibility, but the sensible is to be lifted to the dignity of knowledge'. Dominion over all inferior powers, he warns, belongs to reason alone; but this dominion must never degenerate into tyranny. It must rather assume the form of what we might now, after [Italian Marxist Antonio] Gramsci, term 'hegemony', ruling and informing the senses from within while allowing them to thrive in all their relative autonomy.[6]

Eagleton's achievement was to identify, at the end of the 1980s, a common thread of political tropes around relative autonomy and hegemony in the complex and multifaceted discourse of aesthetics – a philosophical discourse about intra-cognitive capacities that, at first glance, would seem to have nothing to do with politics at all.

So Eagleton's work allowed scholars to see many of the twists and turns taken by an 'ideology of the aesthetic' on the left and right, especially in European traditions. In North America, things looked a bit different. At the same time Eagleton was writing about the political underpinnings of attempts to set literary value over and against politics or economics, the question of the political meanings of aesthetic experience was at the heart of raging debates in the United States over which texts should count as canonical in higher education. These debates were themselves downstream from the tumultuous political challenges to the global order posed by decolonising movements, by the rise of modern feminism, and by anti-racist activism. Major scholarship in English challenging the contours of the canon, and calling for altered ways of assessing literary merit, appeared throughout the period, from Elaine Showalter's *A Literature of Their Own: British Women Novelists from Bronte to Lessing* (1977) and Sandra Gilbert and Susan Gubar's *The Madwoman in The Attic: The Woman Writer and the Nineteenth-Century Literary Imagination* (1979) to Houston Baker's *Blues, Ideology and Afro-American Literature* (1984) and Henry Louis Gates, Jr.'s *The Signifying Monkey: A Theory of Afro-American Literary Criticism* (1988).

In the United States, this wave of activist scholarship was met with a forceful conservative pushback during the Reagan era, led by, among others, William Bennett, Allan Bloom, and Dinesh D'souza; but it also gave rise to a variety of critical and theoretical glosses on the concepts of value that, although not themselves activist, could be said to range from something like the centre-right to the centre-left. Work like Barbara Herrnstein-Smith's *Contingencies of*

---

6   Eagleton 1990, p. 17.

Value: Alternative Perspectives for Critical Theory (1988), Charles Altieri's *Canons and Consequences: Reflections on The Ethical Force of Imaginative Ideals* (1991), and John Guillory's *Cultural Capital: The Problem of Literary Canon Formation* (1993) attempted to summarise and give theoretical closure to these debates. By and large, however, this body of work demurred from the kind of explicitly class-based analysis developed by Eagleton, even though the question of 'canon' was quite clearly related to the question of 'taste'. In a definitive issue of *Critical Inquiry* devoted to the question of literary value in the age of canon reformation, where each of these authors first tested out the ideas that would lead to their monographs, Herrnstein-Smith, Altieri, and Guillory lean toward a broad pluralism: Altieri advocates a self-reflexive ethics of value that tests itself against the value judgments of others, Herrnstein-Smith pushes back against attempts to define axiomatic criteria of literary value, favouring instead a model of fluctuation and dynamic interplay among kinds of evaluation, and Guillory frames post-war literary-critical history in terms of a devolution from orthodoxies about literary value, in which a latter-day 'heterodoxy' of competing value claims and proliferating canons is to be neither lamented nor prized so much as acknowledged and studied as evidence of a play of differences that he takes to define culture.[7]

A notable exception to this demurral from pursuing the connections between economic and aesthetic value was Gayatri Chakravorty Spivak's 1985 essay, 'scattered Speculations on the Question of Value'. In that essay, Spivak attempts to historicise struggles of literary canons in the American academy by turning to the deep background of a longstanding international division of labour in which 'comprador countries' provided cheap labour power to 'advanced' nations: labour power kept cheap, most recently, by the subjection of poor women in the global South to the regime of the wage. Startlingly, even prophetically, Spivak counterposes these deep and recent histories with a critique of mid-1980s advances in telecommunication whose aim was to reduce the circulation time of capital. In contrast to capitalist futurists like Peter Drucker, who imagined the emergence of the 'knowledge worker' as the overcoming of the division between manual and intellectual labour, or Marxists like Antonio Negri, who predicted the machine-driven expansion of an anti-capitalist sphere of 'non-work', Spivak insists that under current geopolitical conditions, any overcomings of the divisions between mind and body, subject and object, fact and value, are not only provisional but extorted: whereas Solomon Brothers, thanks to computers, 'earned about $2 million for ... 15

---

7   See Altieri 1983, p. 58; Herrnstein-Smith 1983, pp. 11–15; and Guillory, p. 195.

minutes of work', the entire economic text would not be what it is if it could not write itself as a palimpsest upon another text where a woman in Sri Lanka has to work 2,287 minutes to buy a t-shirt.[8]

Spivak's point in bringing the gendered international division of labour to bear on the utopian prospects of computer technology is to argue that, inasmuch as canon debates in the literary academy had involved a 'materialist' desire to include histories of oppression and struggle alongside 'idealist' celebrations of genius and formal beauty, that 'materialism' was inadequate. It was inadequate because the 'material' and the 'ideal' in these usages were co-implicated expressions of a system of value production in which 'ideality' for some was achieved at the price of enforced 'materialisation' of others. Until that division of labour was overcome, she argues, and that regime of value production destroyed, the 'materialism' of adding Toni Morrison to a list of great texts would be subsumed under the idealism of a range of related ideas: that canons are finite lists, that mind and body are opposites, that the goal of the good life is to overcome the divide between them by sheer technological power.

Spivak's essay was in many ways years ahead of its time, but the sheer difficulty of her attempt to link questions of canon formation to problems of the geopolitics of value production may have limited its reception. It is also marked by a commitment to reading Marx's understanding of value production as an open-ended 'text' – in particular, as a textuality that is by definition, and before any history, recursive and aleatory. This effectively pre-decides the priority of text to value and undermines critiques (including its own) that seek to understand literary value in materialist terms. So the great wave of literary-critical self-scrutiny around 'value' came to an end without a deep transformation that work like Eagleton's and Spivak's might have inspired.

2   Value in Critical Theory

These transformations were happening elsewhere – and though they were multiple and contradictory, they were loosely gathered under the idea of the 'new economy'. As Robert Brenner has detailed, profitability in manufacturing, commonly understood to be the leading source of value able to drive capitalist expansion, waned decisively in the shift from the Long Boom (1947–73) to the Long Bust (1973–).[9] This was true not only in the United States but

---

8   Spivak 1985, p. 88.
9   See Brenner 2006.

across the leading industrial powers, and while this decline was uneven, it was a global phenomenon. Though some low-wage nations attempted to enter into the labour-intensive sectors grown fallow in leading economies, in general jobs lost from manufacture and ongoing losses from agriculture could not be fully absorbed elsewhere.

In the 1983 *Time* magazine article generally regarded as the origin of the phrase 'new economy', its authors wrote, 'Every industrialized country is looking to high technology for its salvation. But competitiveness, high productivity, innovation – or their lack – will be even more decisive in the New Economy than in the old; an inefficient chipmaker will suffer just as much as an inefficient steelmaker'.[10] This is, however, a somewhat misleading account; the force of information technology would not be that it provided a new line of leading commodities overseen by a comparable raft of producers. Rather, the new economy proposed to generate new value from greater coordination of both social and economic activity, a coordination enabled by advances in information technology. Notably, both critics and proponents of capitalism offered accounts of this change. For example, the theorists of the Italian workers' movement reasoned early on that, as all life (beyond the formal work day) was increasingly brought within the sphere of capital, value would come to derive from social relations as such:

> The more capitalist development advances, that is to say the more the production of relative surplus value penetrates everywhere, the more the circuit production – distribution – exchange – consumption inevitably develops; that is to say that the relationship between capitalist production and bourgeois society, between the factory and society, between society and the state, become [*sic*] more and more organic. At the highest level of capitalist development social relations become moments of the relations of production, and the whole society becomes an articulation of production. In short, all of society lives as a function of the factory and the factory extends its exclusive domination over all of society.[11]

Meanwhile, the prophets of what would be called Toyotaisation or 'Just In Time' production strategised to increase profits via a new integration of sub-contracted production and supply chains within an expanded global division of labor – logistics, in sum – to minimise any unused time or materials from the

---

10   Alexander 1983, p. 70.
11   Cited in Cleaver 1992, p. 137.

sequence leading from demand to production to sale. Further, as traditional production declined, the financial sector ascended, no longer an adjunct to industry but its replacement as a profit source. This offered a different but corresponding sense of 'social' value production, given that finance made profits from neither producing nor exchanging useful commodities but via a series of enchained beliefs about the future value of such commodities, beliefs themselves produced and propagated by communicative or discursive practices, emphasising the idea that information itself was able to generate new value.

The context for the 'new economy', then, was a shift in the early-industrialising nations away from a declining manufacturing sector toward service work and financial profit-taking, and an increased pressure on labour to conform to new conditions even as the work/life distinction was subjected to ongoing erosion. This dream of informationalised and 'socialised' value production was also, from the start, a dream of the conquering of labour: making it not just less expensive but more flexible, more fluid, more disposable, more 'efficient'.

In cultural and literary studies, these changes were noted early on, not least in Fredric Jameson's epochal 1984 essay, 'Postmodernism, or the Cultural Logic of Late Capitalism'. It is difficult to imagine a more influential periodisation of literary studies than Jameson's. Jameson's periodisation depended in turn on the work of the German economic theorist Ernest Mandel, whose 1972 volume *Late Capitalism* laid out a three-period scheme for the history of capital that ran from 'market capitalism' to 'monopoly' or imperialist-led capitalism, and on to 'late' or consumer-driven capitalism oriented by financialisation, that figure of value-from-discourse par excellence. This clean, schematic history lent itself well to a similarly bold narrative of cultural periods. As Jameson put it, 'my own cultural periodization of the stages of realism, modernism, and postmodernism is both inspired and confirmed by Mandel's tripartite scheme'.[12]

Jameson, like Mandel, was careful to avoid the implication that capitalist value is produced by technology; indeed, he insisted that even the greatest technological revolutions are themselves expressions of shifts in the relations between capital and labour. But Jameson's caution was largely set aside in the literary-theoretical discussions on value that were to follow – partly because, despite his own scrupulousness, his and Mandel's periodisations were built around the idea that capitalist technological revolutions subsumed what came before them – that is, they believed that each wave of innovation resulted in more capitalism, extensively and intensively. Jameson called it 'a prodigious expansion of capital into hitherto uncommodified areas'; regarding the value

---

12   Jameson 1984, p. 78.

of art, he argued that 'aesthetic production today has become integrated into commodity production generally'.[13]

This slippage wherein subsumption came to name commodification or marketisation was useful for thinking about the subjective conditions of making art – indeed, of thinking and acting – under the then-latest organisation of capitalism. But it blurred the difference between production and exchange, one organised by value and the other by price, in ways that would allow further confusions regarding value's relation to literature. For Marx, subsumption was a way to think about compelled transformations of particular labour processes, more than about periods in capitalist history, much less the making social of market relations; but the impulse to periodise according to a subsumption narrative – rather than one focused on the instability of capitalist social relations, for instance, or on capitalism's perennial need to stave off crisis – proved dominant in the literary-theoretical discussions about value from Jameson onward.

A confusion of price and value, and a drift in the meaning of subsumption, would have profound consequences for later debates about the relation between literary and economic value. Beyond liberal demands that literature should stand outside economic determination and thus serve as a repository for 'social' values, much of the critical discussion has drifted since the 1980s toward one of two poles: a broadly optimistic sense that technological advances and the unfettering of human creative potential would sow the seeds of the overthrow of capitalism, and a pessimistic sense that until some political force emerged to replace the defeated working classes of the mid-twentieth century, only minimal forms of existential autonomy from capitalist value production would remain.

The high point of the optimistic discourse on aesthetic value remains Michael Hardt's and Antonio Negri's 1999 volume *Empire*, which rode a wave of anti-globalisation protest to achieve a readership that extended beyond the academy. In that volume, Hardt and Negri leaned on Michel Foucault to argue that an earlier age of the disciplining of labour had been subsumed by an era of 'biopolitics', a concept applied now to their old colleagues' ideas of the 'social factory'. Now life as such and society were organized according to the demands of capital:

> Power is now exercised through machines that directly organize the brains (in communication systems, information networks, etc.) and bodies (in welfare systems, monitored activities, etc.) toward a state of auto-

---

13   Jameson 1991, p. xx.

nomous alienation from the sense of life and the desire for creativity ...
Power is thus expressed as a control that extends throughout the depths
of the consciousnesses and bodies of the population – and at the same
time across the entirety of social relations.[14]

But because capital has touched on life itself, Hardt and Negri argued, it has
unleashed life's own power with Pandora-like consequences that it cannot con-
trol:

> The analysis of the real subsumption, when this is understood as invest-
> ing not only the economic or only the cultural dimension of society but
> rather the social bios itself, and when it is attentive to the modalities of
> disciplinarity and/or control, disrupts the linear and totalitarian figure of
> capitalist development.[15]

Hardt and Negri, reinterpreting Marx's 'real subsumption' as a penetration of
capitalist social relations, not into artisanal labour processes, but into some-
thing like 'life itself', begin to imagine what they helped make famous as 'imma-
terial labour': work that purportedly adds economic value without newly mak-
ing a physical commodity. They elaborated 'three primary aspects of immater-
ial labor in the contemporary economy: the communicative labor of industrial
production that has newly become linked in informational networks, the inter-
active labor of symbolic analysis and problem solving, and the labor of the
production and manipulation of affects'.[16]

  In this narrative, the socialisation of labour – that is, its extension into realms
of existence previously not 'labour' at all, but part of social life – in this nar-
rative, the becoming social of labour is always a potentially Pyrrhic victory for
capital, since 'sociality' is taken to be unruly by definition: it is uncontainable,
excessive. The Italian Marxist Paolo Virno put it this way: 'It is enough to say,
for now, that contemporary production becomes "virtuosic" (and thus polit-
ical) precisely because it includes within itself linguistic experience as such'.[17]
Via small tags like the 'itself' in Hardt and Negri's 'the social bios itself', or the
'as such' in Virno's 'linguistic experience as such', literary and social value are
imagined as contrary to economic value *by definition*, as though the literary,
the social, and the economic were innately at odds.

---

14   Hardt and Negri 2000, pp. 23–4.
15   Hardt and Negri 2000, p. 25.
16   Hardt and Negri 2000, p. 30.
17   Virno 2004, p. 56.

This quietly tautological understanding of literary value reorients the discussion around literature and capital, rendering it more triumphalist but more ambiguous. Literature preserves a privileged claim on extra-economic value in these arguments. Moreover, because it now helps constitute value production, it takes on new potentials of opposition. Writing in 2012 about the same supposedly 'immaterial labour' identified by Hardt and Negri, Italian theorist Franco Berardi imagines its disruptive power as poetic:

> In order to accelerate the circulation of value, meaning is reduced to information ...
>
> But language and information do not overlap, and language cannot be resolved in exchangeability. Poetry [in particular] is language's excess: poetry is what in language cannot be reduced to information, and is not exchangeable, but gives way to a new common ground of understanding, of shared meaning: the creation of a new world.[18]

Berardi's celebration of literary 'creation' as a priori un-capitaliseable finds a strange counterpart in pro-capitalist narratives about the 'creative classes'. Management theorist Richard Florida, for instance, argues that the presence of a 'creative class' increases the possibilities for economic growth in a given area.[19] The implication is that, even if creative work does not directly produce economic value, its non-economic values – the social norms and arrangements it engenders – are economically desirable and will draw investment. This is the practical obverse of the argument, à la Berardi, that poetic thought and poetic uses of language can be a relatively direct source of anti-capitalist struggle.

3   The Breadth of Value Discourse and Its Limits

There is, however, a basic problem for these arguments, no matter their valences. Their validity rests on a misrecognition of capital's development of new sources of profit as a capitalist invention of new sources of value. However, there is only the most limited support for the existence of a 'new economy' that features a new kind of value production. While firms specialising in what is deemed immaterial production may themselves make profits – the sectors of finance, real estate, and insurance provide the clearest examples – this

---

18   Berardi 2012, p. 147.
19   See Florida 2002.

appears to be zero-sum redistribution of extant value. No new use values are produced, much less exchanged, and nominal price increases are subject to instant devaluation. In the era of the new economy, there is little indication of economic expansion either in the leading economies or at a global level in comparison to previous waves of industrialisation – a development outlined by thinkers as diverse as Brenner, the Marxist sociologist Giovanni Arrighi, and former secretary of the U.S. Treasury Lawrence Summers.[20] Thus the suggestion that literature has a new and privileged relation to value production via its relation to new modes of production seems more an ideology of the age than a truth; these new modes qualify as production in the sense of neither new uses nor new surplus value.

At the same time, it is inarguable that the form and phenomenology of work have changed in the face of deindustrialisation in ways that have had profound effects for literature. Increasingly, waged work begins to look like data entry and word processing. As Jasper Bernes argues, the forms of employment that post-Fordist firms offer resemble literary making far more closely than they do manufacturing labour.[21] The field of literature registers this clearly enough. New technology firms such as Facebook and Google, having become influential companies operating at the intersection of data, discourse, and affect, increasingly come to be site, source material, and model for literary production and innovation (suggestive examples of this include the early twenty-first-century 'Flarf' poetry, built up from the verbal detritus of blogs and comment boxes, or poet-artist Kenneth Goldsmith's project of 'printing out the internet').

While it can seem as though literature, under these conditions, is either a redoubt for some older form of artisanal value, or on some cutting edge of performing and critiquing an emergent, 'biopolitical' form of value, it is more historically accurate to understand these literary forms as responding to a secular decline in capitalist value production: whatever the 'value' of their craftedness, or their wit, or their critique of craftedness and wit, it is not an opposing *form* of value so much as a lively human activity that takes place in a powerfully shaping political and economic context. It is possible, in other words, to notice that the problems addressed by literature, and literary form, may shift in radical and startling ways, without taking this to imply that we have entered some new and qualitatively different phase in the relations of value. This is, however, what critical-theoretical discourse on capitalism and art has tended to do –

---

20   See, for instance, Brenner 2006, Arrighi 1994, and Summer 2016.
21   See Bernes 2017.

both in the optimistic Italian discourse of poetry as counter-value, and in the more famous pessimism of the Frankfurt School.

Arguments on behalf of the anti-capitalist potential of the aesthetic would seem worlds away from the pessimism of Theodor Adorno and Max Hork-heimer, for instance; but they share with the Frankfurt School a reliance on the idea of subsumption as the way to simultaneously mark epochs in capital-ism and describe them in terms of a new subjectivity. In the case of the work of Adorno in particular, subsumption and value are intimately linked, and the linkage has fostered recent arguments that attempt to extend his thinking into the era of so-called neoliberalism.

Though Adorno's writing has been steadily translated into English since his own lifetime, it was not until the 1990s that interest in his work expanded bey-ond German-studies contexts and into the Anglophone humanities at large. In the United States, this was due in part to the 1989 publication of Jameson's *Late Marxism, Or, The Persistence of The Dialectic*, which positioned Adorno as the preeminent thinker of political defeat on the left, and therefore perfectly suited for the tail end of a decade of Ronald Reagan and Margaret Thatcher. The revival was apt: for just as Adorno had witnessed the political defeat of the German working classes between the two world wars, so too was the end of the Long Boom accelerated by the rise of a right-wing coalition bent on destroying the power of labour unions.

In the English-speaking world, at least, Adorno is read most closely for his account of the negativity that any aesthetic experience must suffer if it is to have any integrity; he is best known as the theorist and proponent of self-cancelling, agonised reflexivity in art. But less attention is paid to the historical framework in which Adorno makes his arguments on behalf of negativity. It is a framework that depends on the idea of subsumption as a psychic and political experience, in particular the subsumption of the category of 'the individual' under the demands of capital. It is loose and flexible, more of a philosophical anthropology than a history per se, and its polemical aim is to invert Enlighten-ment narratives of universal human progress: in *Negative Dialectics*, he writes, 'No universal history leads from savagery to humanitarianism, but there is one leading from the slingshot to the megaton bomb'.[22] Earlier, in his *Minima Mor-alia*, he specifically analogised the transformations wrought by capital in the worker's bodily movements – the kinds of transformations stylised earlier in the century by Charlie Chaplin – to Marx's account of subsumption in the labour process. 'Only when the process that begins with the metamorphosis

---

22   Adorno 1973, p. 320.

of labour-power into a commodity has permeated men through and through', writes Adorno, 'is it possible for life to reproduce itself under the prevailing relations of production'. Then, in a nod to Marx's idea of the 'organic composition of capital' (OCC) – roughly, the ratio of the value of machine to human power in a given production process – Adorno adds,

> The organic composition of man refers by no means only to his specialized technical faculties, but ... equally to their opposite, the moments of naturalness which once themselves sprung from the social dialectic and are now succumbing to it. Even what differs from technology in man is now being incorporated into it as a kind of lubrication.[23]

This analogy between transformations in the labour process and deep existential transformations ('the organic composition of man') has proved costly. Of course changes in the character of work create corollary changes in people; but for Marx, OCC was a way to describe the ratio of means of production to living labour in the production process, and therefore part of an attempt to track the value productivity of different capitalist sectors and enterprises: it offered a glimpse of the different roles that cheap labour and cheap means of production had to play in facilitating capitalist profitability.[24] It can be understood as a ratio between the value of machines and labour inputs; and for Marx, its tendency was to rise over time, as inter-capitalist competition obliged ever-greater mechanisation to lower unit costs while reducing wage expenditure. Unlike the subsumption of 'life' to machinic regularity in Adorno's analogy, however, OCC is for Marx a way of describing the labour process in production, not 'life itself', and its tendency to rise is not, as for Adorno, an irrevocable loss; it is always met by various counter-tendencies (expansion of the labour market, lowered wages) that keep living labour profitable to exploit. So Adorno's figures of 'permeation', 'incorporation', and (widely used elsewhere) 'liquidation' take what in Marx is a description of the countervailing forces at play in producing value and transform it into a modernity story. In this story, 'life' has always aimed at 'progress' but found only snatched moments of happiness in a complex devolution. The concept of value in Adorno – expressed as anti-progress, as 'damaged life' – hitches a ride, as it were, on Marx's analysis of capital, but its aim is to articulate something that became a more generalised tragic sensibility.

---

23   Adorno 1996, pp. 229–30.
24   For an excellent discussion of Adorno's idea of the 'organic composition of man', see Tomba 2014.

This modernist anguish about 'subsumption' in discourses of aesthetic value has retained a great deal of power in the decades since Jameson's reintroduction of Adorno to the English-speaking world. But the discourse of subsumption still tends to end up thinking in terms of 'relative autonomy', much like the liberal, pluralist languages it meant to oppose. It drifts quickly into an ontology of social life, rather than an analysis of value production under capital, and this drift registers in its metaphorics of integration and penetration. Further, because 'commodification' rather than value production is its analytic lever, subsumption language gets caught in a game of determining which art objects are and are not fully commodified.

Even in work that expressly critiques ontologised narratives of subsumption, it proves difficult to escape a metaphorics of commodification as a kind of saturation or penetration of social reality, in a way that questions the over- or under-estimation of art's autonomy from commodification without questioning whether 'autonomy' is the best way to discuss artistic value. In his 2015 volume *Art and Value*, a high-water mark in the contemporary analysis of aesthetic and economic value, Dave Beech explicitly rejects languages of subsumption that are simply versions of modernity discourse: 'subsumption in Marx's economic analysis is never abstract or general but always refers to the subsumption of labour'.[25] Because commodities and markets existed before capital, he argues that the social relations *around* commodities, rather than commodification itself, should be the critical vantage point from which to understand the relationship between artistic and capitalist value. But his framework remains one of asking to what degree art is 'free' in the sense of freedom, and of imagining art and capital as domains. As he puts it,

> Throughout this study ... I will not ask whether art is or is not economic, or whether art is or is not exchanged as a commodity, but in what ways precisely art is subjected to or remains free from economic rationality and how exactly art enters or resists commodification.[26]

The arguments regarding literature and value are many and frequently offered in entangled conjunctions. They may suggest that literature (and the aesthetic more broadly) is increasingly subsumed by economic value materially and/or ideologically, or contrarily that its incommensurability with economic value is ever more distinct and pressing; they may suggest that as economic value pro-

---

25   Beech 2015, p. 243.
26   Beech 2015, p. 11.

duction has transformed, literature and the aesthetic offer an increasingly privileged role either against or in support of capitalist value production; they may suggest that literature and the aesthetic are, in comparison to other regimes and practices, ever more able and obliged to preserve other discourses of value.

4   The Unity of the Political and Economic

What all these arguments share is a domain model of 'economics' and 'art' that endlessly worries over their degree of separation or intermixed-ness, worries about the dominion of one over the other, without grasping that 'the economy' is not a *space*, virtual or otherwise, but a set of historical relationships. Even when this discourse acknowledges the relational character of capitalist value production, it tends to read history in linear terms: that is, it interprets the history of political struggles over capitalist value as a story in which there is simply 'more capitalism' now than there once was. This domain model, with its linear historiography, comes from the sovereignty tradition of Baumgarten, with a faculty-psychology apotheosis in Kant and a decline-narrative apotheosis in Eliot, and it fails to contend with the vicissitudes faced by capitalist expansion, which is never guaranteed beforehand, and whose victories are less 'subsumptions' of one domain by another than costly applications of force designed to preserve profitable class relations.

   This presents a final set of puzzles for the question of literature and value in the contemporary era. At the broadest historical level, this expansion of economic value is not just a core feature but the *differentia specifica* of capital against previous economic relations: its compulsion to expand at the peril of ceasing to exist altogether. Capital is, after all, defined properly as *value in expansion*. But mourning the expansion of capital after the fact, as the domain and subsumption models do, loses sight of how effortful and tumultuous it is for capital to expand in the first place. So narratives of economic and aesthetic value as separate modes, the former always threatening to impinge on the latter, also keep re-installing the economic and the political as separate categories, when they are entangled from the start.

   This attempt to distinguish politics and economics leads to a kind of ultimate – which is to say, an initial – confusion. One can certainly argue persuasively that value production is expanding or contracting, that commodification is expanding or (in very rare cases) contracting, and even that more and more labour processes are really subsumed in the technical sense. However, these expansions and contractions are not expressions of an opposition between two different kinds of value, two autonomous regimes locked in some ageless conflict. Rather, they are expressions of a dynamic that is immanent to capital itself. While *value production* or commodification may rise or fall, these developments are compelled by a *value relation* that is already generalised once the great majority of the population is dependent on the market for goods, and dependent on work for access to the market – and in turn once both goods and labour become value-bearing commodities, and once firms are compelled to reinvest profits and increase productivity to survive inter-capitalist competition. Insofar as these are compulsions that unify the totality of social relations behind the back of consciousness, they render a new unity of the political and the economic that provides the mutually constitutive development of political economy.

In this circumstance, an artwork is or is not a commodity, art making is or is not labour, aesthetic production does or does not take part in the accumulation process. However, it is not possible to conclude as a consequence of any of these that there is some kind of value external to capitalist value. Indeed, the division of the political and the economic into discrete domains is a fetish of bourgeois thought: for example, in the idea that we are politically liberated in the sense of formal freedom, while we are at the same time economically unfree. This might be understood by analogy to an equally implausible separation of use and exchange value, implausible because under capitalism use values will be produced only because they have exchange value, while things can have exchange value only if they offer a use value as well. This is their material basis. Use and exchange are part of political-economic value as a whole, just as the two initial values proposed are part of political-economic value as a whole. They can be separated only in the movement of the ideal. Modernity, to the extent that remains a term that reveals more than it obscures, is not the name for the asymptotic victory of one side over the other but of the era defined by their unity.

The basis, therefore, of the demand that we recognise, valorise, and produce other sorts of value existing beyond political-economic value is a demand that literature and the aesthetic remain a space where the idealist conception of the world is preserved.

Of course it is easy to be sympathetic to this forlorn desire for there to be an outside to the value relation. One might argue that our sympathy for literature derives precisely from the ways in which it provides an arena for this desire to move. However, there is little gain in confusing this pathos for real conditions. Until those conditions change – whatever the impressive range of new forms of profit-taking capitalism invents, and whatever the equally impressive inventiveness of the aesthetic responses to them – the form of 'value' under which we live will remain the same.

CHAPTER 11

Abstraction, Intuition, Poetry

at the stadium our seats are really high
two flags fly along the perimeter
one national, one rainbow

the supreme court decision came down
June 26th, same day same anniversary
we shared then broke it, yours with Bonnie

mine with Heather. I message *hi*
guess where I am congratulations.
she married Caitlin this summer

they have that way of looking in photographs
the right amount alike, of corresponding
like Catherine and Elliot and Lindsey and Steve

there is an excellent image of her
giving someone the finger. That thing
she whispered in your ear

when she showed up at the office
when it was going down
stay away from my lady, white boy

This poem, from Stephanie Young's recent volume, *Pet Sounds*, develops in unexpected ways.[1] It begins sounding like a straightforward celebration of same-sex marriage, possibly even a patriotic one – marking the anniversary of the U.S. Supreme Court's 2015 ruling in favour of a constitutional right to such unions in *Obergefell v. Hodges*, framing the anniversary at a sports event with the rainbow flag flying alongside the American one. But it ends up with something else to celebrate – or perhaps, to value. The story that unfolds across its eighteen lines is of unexpected twists and turns. The speaker texts an ex, a

---

1 Young 2019, p. 42. Hereafter abbreviated *P* and cited parenthetically by page number.

woman, with whom she used to have an anniversary that happens to match the one her current husband (a man, whom other poems tell us has been with men) shared with his ex-wife. And we see the affection evidenced by the message more deeply when we learn, not only that the speaker and her ex-girlfriend survived a breakup, but that the breakup was messy, involving a shift in affections if not actual cheating, as well as a shift in the gender and the race of the person with whom the speaker would eventually end up. More than that, we learn that for the white female speaker of the poem, her non-white ex-partner's possessiveness – '*stay away from my lady, white boy*' – is still a part of what she values about her; it's part of something not rigidly possessive, in fact, but something fierce, something punk, or butch, or courageous. Other poems in the volume flesh out this value. They also make clear that for the speaker and her current husband, both whiteness and heterosexual couplehood are deeply imperfect categories. We get a whiff of the speaker's dissatisfaction not only in the affective loop by which we see her accept that her husband is irreducibly 'white' in the sense of unearned privilege, as in, the kind of 'white boy' who claims possession of something, or someone, that isn't his to claim, but also in her mischievous depiction of appealing homo-likeness through two examples of *heterosexual* couples. And in a final twist for this poem about couples and coupling, the most vivid scene of intimacy – a sudden, fierce whisper in the ear – is actually between two people divided by race and gender who are not themselves a couple.

The poem does not go down as easy as it promises, that is, with its middle diction and its roughly self-sufficient tercets. But for me, the real glory of the poem is its non-self-sufficiency; it really shines as part of a volume in which the gestures I've just glossed take on richness that is partly historical (we learn more about all of these people), partly political (all the identity categories I've just mentioned are put under further pressure), and partly formal (the opening poem in the volume makes clear that the tercets, which structure many of the poems, are explicitly referencing Dante Alighieri's *terza rima* and a thematic of inaccessible paradise). It is primarily from the vantage of the whole that individual poems take on their greatest beauty. And that beauty, while of course expressed in the medium of poetic language, is also a beauty of something like value, a set of values insisted on, against steep odds, as tools for rethinking what possession means. The book as a whole imagines differential forms of *dispossession* as the perennial ground of a compassion that appears, by the final page, to need only the lightest nudge to mutate into solidarity – specifically, a solidarity against capital.

Poems like Young's don't especially need what we'd normally call theorising. But my excitement in reading them is bound up with a desire to set them in a context that will show them off at their best. They feel liable to various forms of categorisation – confessional poetry, poetry as memoir; the self-critical poetry of white allyship – whose truth doesn't quite name what animates the work. What does animate it, I think, is a sense of value that is a bit abstract at first, because its full articulation requires a reading of something like the book as a whole. If I don't feel like a theorist reading these poems, though, the beauty of their kind of abstraction – the compassion it both invites and gives out – does make me want to advocate for a way of thinking rigorously about value that would depart from poems, get down to the business of understanding value under capitalism, and return to the poetry refreshed. I think Karl Marx could use some Stephanie Young. Or: Marxism could. And that will be the subject of my essay.

•   •
•

I have taken the occasion of the English Institute's 2019 theme of 'Abstraction' to pursue the interest and the importance of a key abstraction in the work of Marx, the abstraction he calls *value*. I will try to suggest that 'value', for Marx, has more political potential than non-Marxists are used to crediting Marx with, since they tend to think of Marxist theories of value as restricted to the surplus-value produced by exploited labour, and therefore, in political terms, as an economic theory of society that privileges class above other identity categories. The reason I think Marx's theory of value does not do this is because it is a holistic abstraction, an abstraction that expresses itself through a differentiated totality, and so I think it opens up possibilities precisely for thinking *across* categories. To stake a claim for this way of reading Marx is to acknowledge Marx's debts to G.W.F. Hegel – an unpopular position among Marxists, and a counterintuitive one on the academic left, where Hegelian philosophy tends to be seen as subsuming particulars into a foreordained and monological absolute. But I try to argue below that opening the passage between Marx and Hegel has the potential to help us think more clearly about the possibilities for solidarity, and the steep barriers to it, with which we are faced today.

There is another aspect of Marx's debts to Hegel that bears on how we might expand our sense of the utility of the abstraction called 'value', and it has to do with the role of intuition in holistic thinking. In a recent essay on the role of abstraction in Marx's theory of value, Leigh Claire LaBerge has called *abstraction* a 'social intuition capable of leading to the concrete'.[2] There is a

---

2   La Berge 2019, p. 246.

long history of Marxists coming after Marx who have tried to downplay this intuitional aspect of his work by making it a quasi-mathematical science, but I am interested in how foregrounding the role of intuition in Marxist thinking might broaden the conversation between political and literary Marxisms. As I will suggest below, recent scholarship on Hegel has made it clear that his philosophy can be understood to champion a deeply social and linguistic picture of what abstraction is and does – linguistic, not in literary criticism's half-century long sense of language as a structure, but in the older philological and rhetorical senses of language as an evolving, contradictory medium for thought and expression.

This will allow me to suggest, in turn, that we can read literary writing, not least poetry, in fresh ways if we are willing to be friendly to a holistic sense of what the abstraction 'value' might mean. In a book I wrote in 2011 called *The Matter of Capital: Poetry and Crisis in the American Century*, it was important to me to show that in the twentieth century, even poets not categorisable as Marxist or even leftist were frequently writing and worrying about capitalism, and how its forms of value might deform or destroy poetic ones. In this essay, however, I will try to highlight the advantages of reading what you could broadly call Marxist poetry for the way it illuminates resonances between a holistic theory of economic value in Marx, on the one hand, and the linguistic holism that fuelled the Hegel Marx turned to, on the other.

The poetry I will read for you in the second part of my essay will make these links by way of some very beautiful meditations on how property and dispossession shape its intuitions of likeness and even solidarity. First, though, I'd like to suggest that these questions are not esoteric to the study of American poetry. They have shaped the reception of Walt Whitman's poems, for instance, almost since their publication. This is consequential: in recent decades the reception of Whitman has served as a kind of proxy for debates about similarity and difference in American multiculturalism. When it comes to questions of abstraction, Whitman is still seen, even by some of his champions, as a kind of bad (or typical) Hegelian, subsuming lived and painful differences among people in the name of a merely speculative announcement of their likeness: he means well, but his ego takes over. In this debate, Whitman generally comes out looking 'kinda liberationist, kinda settler colonial', to paraphrase a remark of Eve Kosofsky Sedgwick and Adam Frank's.[3]

In a pathbreaking recent essay, however, Tobias Huttner breaks from this debate by reading Whitman's universalism in terms of his Free Soil politics,

---

3 Eve Sedgwick and Adam Frank make this quip (Sedgewick and Frank 1995, p. 500).

which made him an anti-slavery thinker, but only to the extent that halting the westward expansion of slavery would afford white freeholders *their* westward expansion.[4] For Huttner, this allows us to reread Whitman's democratic vistas less as bad Hegelian subsumptions of difference and more as a tactical punting of the question of abolition down the road in the name of a type of property relation. Whitman's support for the westward expansion of free soil for white farmers, (instead of the westward expansion of plantation-style slavery) can look like abolitionist opposition to racial enslavement, but it simply deferred reckoning with the problem of white supremacy, and arguably only deepened it by further entrenching a racialised homestead model of relation to the land. In short, Huttner allows us to move from a reading of Whitman that sees his habits of likening as usurpations of property – the subsumption of the specific personhood of his various others and addressees into his ever-expanding ego – to a reading that sees the poems as wrestling with the contradictions of how property is politically constituted in the first place.

To track this tension in interpretations of Whitman's habits of likening, not least across lines of racial difference, is to see its continuity with a central political problem on the American left today, which is the problem of how best to relate anti-racism and anti-capitalism. This problem is as old as Reconstruction, but in the deindustrialised North America of the 2020s, there is no way around it. The secular stagnation bred by declining capitalist profitability since the 1970s has accelerated the proletarianisation of the non-capitalist white population of the U.S., and though it is generating real possibilities for cross-racial solidarity, it has been aggressively re-narrated by the capitalist classes, who have redoubled up their age-old efforts to signal to working (or unemployed) white people that they have a property interest in whiteness that places them above immigrants or, of course, Black people. The counter-hegemonic project of identifying commonality across racial divides – which are of course not static, or simply historical, but produced and reproduced every day, every fiscal quarter, every business cycle – this counter-hegemonic project is still a work in progress. It faces daunting obstacles, not least how to overcome the historical tendency of the white labour movement in the U.S. to compromise with capital rather than take up arms with non-white workers. This is a problem for theory, as well. Ruth Wilson Gilmore has famously called racism a 'process of abstraction' that vertically sifts populations: a 'death-dealing displacement of difference into hierarchies'.[5] An important question for the left today is, might

4   See Huttner 2019, pp. 642–90.
5   Gilmore 2002, p. 16.

a declining rate of profit create opportunities to think across those hierarchies, with the aim of cross-racial militancy, or has the left been outmanoeuvred for so long that downwardly mobile whites are simply more attracted to racist populism? Mainstream political discourse in the U.S. (as we know too well) tends to provide two ideological solutions to this problem: a conservative one that doubles down on naturalised racial hierarchies, in implicit acknowledgement that there is no longer a high enough rate of capitalist profit to share at a level that would benefit the so-called white working class; and a liberal one that insists on imagining that there is enough to go around, if only racists could overcome their prejudice, or the rich would pay their fair share of taxes. Both of these ideological programmes gloss over the history of property relations in the U.S., not least their racial character. I would like to suggest that the key work that has highlighted the importance of understanding the racialised history of property in the U.S., were it to add 'value' to its repertoire, would have a powerful resource for articulating the potential for deeper solidarity across race than we tend to feel is possible.

Black and decolonial thought has been at the centre of attempts to think about property in rigorous ways since at least the time of W.E.B. DuBois's *Black Reconstruction* (1935). But for my purposes, it is the projects devolving from the expansion of the Reagan-Thatcher rightward turn into full-blown Clinton-Blair neoliberalism – that is, the deepening of what Robert Brenner first called 'the long downturn' – that make most sense as coordinates for our rethinking our contemporary dilemmas of anti-solidarity.[6] So I'd like to turn to two Black intellectual projects dating from that period: an exploration of the racialisation of property, and a critique of the limits of Marxism as too focused on property. The second is most important to my essay, but let me mention the first, since it helps explain the second. To think about property this way will lead me away from the question of poetry, but only in order to return to it with fresh eyes.

∙∙

Cheryl Harris's landmark article 'Whiteness as Property' laid out a complex and thoroughgoing framework by which to understand the legal history that established and that reproduced a 'property interest in whiteness', one so ingrained by the late nineteenth century that Homer Plessy and his attorneys deployed it in their arguments on his behalf.[7] In a recent elaboration of the global implic-

---

6   See Brenner 1998.
7   Harris 1993, p. 1747.

ations of Harris's work, Brenna Bhandar has linked the ongoing reproduction of racialised 'property interest' in settler-colonial contexts to political abstractions derived from the mobilisation of John Locke's arguments about the capitalist right to any land deemed insufficiently 'improved'.[8] For Bhandar, crucially, these settler arguments also include the racialising claim that the populations inhabiting such supposedly 'unimproved' territory are themselves in need of what capitalist construe as improvement. Racialisation and abstraction are linked, in Bhandar's argument, by how the Lockean logic of 'improvement' views property not only for what it is, but for what it could be, that is, against the measure of its potential profitability.

A second development in Black thought that helps us see potential linkages between abstraction and property has proven even more consequential in the academic humanities. This strand of Black thinking has an obverse relation to the study of whiteness as property, focusing instead on the predominantly non- or anti-revolutionary politics of the white working class in order to demonstrate the limits of any Marxism that cannot think *beyond* the abstractions of property. The key work here is of course Cedric J. Robinson's *Black Marxism: The Making of The Black Radical Tradition*, first published in 1983. Robinson's meticulous and visionary history of radical Black political action and thinking culminates with a distinction between a Marxism unequipped to acknowledge the foundational role of Black enslavement in the history of capitalism, and a more encompassing Black radical thought that could see anti-Black racism as a deeper and prior political problem.

The marker of the distinction between the two kinds of political thought is property. Looking back on his research, Robinson writes:

> There was the sense that something of a more profound nature than the obsession with property was askew in a civilization that could organize and celebrate – on a scale beyond previous human experience – the brutal degradations of life and the most acute violations of human destiny. It seemed a certainty that the system of capitalism was part of it, but as well symptomatic of it.[9]

Robinson sees a distinction between the political thought limited by an 'obsession with property' and a more foundational thought that is also marked out by a distinction between different forms of abstraction. He elaborates this dis-

---

8   Bhandar 2018, p. 8.
9   Robinson 2000, p. 308.

tinction by way of an interpretation of the political thought of C.L.R. James. He praises James's *Notes on Dialectics* as a highwater mark in mid-century Marxist thinking, not least for its early recognition of the political disaster of Stalinism. But he argues that James over-optimistically imagined a radical proletariat dialectically overcoming Stalinist authoritarianism. For Robinson, this was a pitfall of James succumbing to abstraction, its Hegelian form specifically: 'The most obvious problem stemmed from James's fascination for Hegel's mode of argumentation: the distillation of history into rich concentrates used solely for the grounding of abstract discourse'.[10] For Robinson, the irony is that had James set aside dialectical abstraction, he would have seen both the actual property relations that tied the radical Russian intellectual class to the bourgeoisie they hated, *and* the limitations of using 'property' to understand those intellectuals' eventual betrayal of the working classes they had once imagined leading. Implicitly, for Robinson, this betrayal is rooted in the history of racialising workers and peasants that ultimately took its most world-shattering form in the enslavement of Africans and in anti-Black racism.

To think past where he felt James had been able to go, Robinson turned to Richard Wright, who, he argues, 'was not entirely rejecting [Marxism] but was attempting to locate it, to provide a sense of the boundaries of its authority'.[11] One key boundary, again, is property. Robinson suggests that even in the 1930s, before his break with the Communist Party, Wright was pushing past this boundary, citing Wright's remark in 'Blueprint for Negro Literature' that '[l]acking the handicaps of false ambition and property, [Black proletarians] have access to a wide social vision and a deep social consciousness'.[12] Robinson tracks Wright's idea of a generative, negative Black relation to property forward to the 1950s of *White Man Listen*, where Wright would re-mark the boundary between Marxism and Black thought in similar way, revising the pairing of unpropertiedness and social consciousness into a contrast between class conflict and a political, existential search for meaning born of sheer annihilating violence:

> I maintain that the ultimate effect of white Europe upon Asia and Africa was to cast millions into a kind of spiritual void ... The dynamic concept of the void that must be filled, a void created by a thoughtless and bru-

10   Robinson 2000, p. 284.
11   Robinson 2000, p. 304.
12   Robinson 2000, p. 299.

tal impact of the West upon a billion and a half people, is more powerful than the concept of class conflict, and more universal.[13]

Through the reading of Wright that culminated *Black Marxism*, Robinson establishes a distinction between Marxism and Black radical thought that on the one hand feels categorical: Marxism is epistemological, and focused on abstractions of property and class that it mistakes for concretions, while Black thought is existential – today we would say ontological – and focused on a racialised world-making that is anterior to class and property, or deeper than them, or categorically different than them. On the other hand, inasmuch as Robinson sees Wright giving Marxism a necessary if subordinate place, the distinction between Marxism and Black thought seems to be more about different kinds of abstractions, or different media for it.

To contrast the existential alertness and agony of Black radical thought with a Marxism that, on the one hand, is 'obsessed with property', and on the other, follows Hegel in boiling down the richness of history to mere philosophical abstraction, is to leave Black thought and Marxism quite separate. But there remains a question of the door Robinson thinks Wright left open by putting Marxism in its place – locating it – rather than merely rejecting it. How far apart are the two locations?

They may be closer than is suggested by the sad history of the racism and anti-solidarity of European and American labour movements. For one thing, the critique of the limitations of a body of thought for its fixation on property – this is Marx's critique of Hegel. Hegel lays out his *Philosophy of Right* of 1820 on the foundation of a concept of property that, though it is unlike Locke's, is also grounded in the self-possessed individual. As Wright does with Marxism, so too does Marx do with Hegel in his 1843 critique of the *Philosophy of Right* – not rejecting Hegel's concept of property, but historicising it, and arguing that the form of private property that began as individual self-possession, already a stunted form of human freedom, serves as the basis for a deeper violation of the potential for freedom as it in turn forms the basis of capitalist social relations. Later on, in *Capital* itself, Marx will begin his analysis with a specific form of property – the commodity – whose basis turns out to be *dis*possession, that is, the commodity called labour power. One cannot come to be in the proud, self-possessed position of having the ability to exchange this commodity, Marx argues with irony, without having nothing else to survive by.[14] Marx does not

13   Quoted in Robinson 2000, p. 301.
14   See Marx 1970.

negate or invert Hegel's idea of property so much as give it a long history and a deep irony. And he did not reject Hegel's abstractions for his own concretion, though he sometimes boasted that that's what he had done. When he was in a more serious mood, he acknowledged that he had given Hegel's abstractions their place in an expanded frame.

So Marx puts Hegel in his place, as Wright does with Marx. But Wright leaves open a door by which we might think of Marxism itself as capable of more than a simple 'obsession' with the concept of property. What does Marx leave available in Hegel? And does it matter?

I think it does. When Robinson sees James meeting a political and theoretical limit because James succumbed to the Hegelian habit of reducing history to abstractions, he is placing himself in a lineage of critiques of Hegel that begin with Friedrich Schelling, and which distort Hegel. This would not matter much if it weren't the case that critiques of Marx as reductive of all political analysis to the question of waged exploitation did not themselves depend on the template of Schelling's critique of Hegel, which, as Stephen Houlgate argues, have gradually produced a false picture of Hegel as the ur-reducer of lived particulars to inward abstractions.[15] This is the template, in turn, for the main line of philosophical critiques of Marx. We know this critique of Hegel and Marx, in the English-speaking world, by the negative associations attached in the literary academy to the word 'totalise'. But to read *Capital* is to see that the framework of thinking from the whole that Marx takes up from Hegel and recontextualises, that is, the framework of totality, is less like a boiling down of diverse particulars into a flattening ur-concept ('the wage', or 'class conflict') and much more like the unfolding of a concept embedded in a social relation ('the commodity').

Critiques of Marxist thought that derive from Schellingian critiques of Hegel suggest that dialectical thought fails to think outside its categories – to think outside the wage, outside class, outside exploitation. But Marx's emphasis was always to examine how categories come into social being in the first place. The tragedy is that the history of communism and the labour movement in Europe and North America licenses the categorical critique. Those political formations embraced what Marx saw early on was capital's own strategy of sifting labour into hierarchies – even as it deskilled labour – and they allowed race, sex, and national identity to gird those hierarchies. But if we accept that we cannot get out of the mess of American history without grasping it as the history of racial capitalism, then it could be productive to follow Robinson's implication that

---

15   See Houlgate 1999, pp. 99–128.

Wright saw something worth holding onto in Marx. I think it would be espe-
cially useful to revisit what Marx meant by 'abstraction' – which has less to do
with property, *per se*, than to do with *value*.

⠂⠂

When Marx discusses 'abstract labour', he means the abstract character of a
total social labour whose individual expressions make no sense until they are
grasped as part of a whole – specifically, a whole that is the product of a history
of dispossession that allows different kinds of labour to be equated with each
other, because the dominant social meaning of the objects they produce is that
they were produced in order to make money; their actual use is secondary.[16]
Marx also calls the condition for this kind of abstract labour 'socially necessary
labor time'; it is what distinguishes his theory of value from David Ricardo's.
Unlike Ricardo, Marx does not calculate value in terms of individual physical
inputs that become commodities, but in terms of a total production of surplus
value that is distributed among competing capitalists as profit. As he puts it in
the first volume of *Capital*: 'socially necessary labour-time is the labour-time
required to produce any use-value under the conditions of production normal
for a given society and with the average degree of skill and intensity of labour
prevalent in that society'.[17]

In what follows, I will to try to flesh out the implications of this shift from
the quantitative to the qualitative, which is also a shift from Ricardo's famous
labour theory of value to what Diane Elson has usefully called Marx's 'value
theory of labor'.[18] In order to do so, I'm going to revisit some of the means
by which academic and political readings of Marx in the twentieth century,
whatever their merits, got in their own way. I will contrast these readings with
what I take to be more promising ways of interpreting Marx, which restore
to his work the importance of non-inevitable readings of capitalist accumu-
lation. This feels urgent in light of the looming possibility that capitalism has
reached a terminal period of secular stagnation, that is, a long-term decline
in profitability that cannot be permanently counteracted, even by the most
frantic measures. Oddly, it is the very possibility of a kind of terminal velocity
to capital accumulation that forces the question of its non-inevitable charac-
ter.

---

16   Marx 1990, p. 174.
17   Marx 1990, p. 129.
18   See Elson 1979, pp. 115–80.

The Marxist economist Michael Roberts, drawing on data stretching back a century, has recently shown that it is possible to calculate a long-term decline in capitalist profitability that corresponds to Marx's argument that under capitalism there is an inescapable tendency for the rate of profit to fall.[19] In Marxist circles this argument is referred to as 'the law of the tendency of the rate of profit to fall', or LTRPF. It is worked out in part three of Volume III of *Capital*, and built around the observation that inter-capitalist competition drives innovation in production, but also undermines its own conditions of *re*production. This is because, once capital has confronted the limits of absolute exploitation, that is, the limits of its ability to reduce wages, capitalists must turn to machine-driven efficiency gains in order to survive. Machines offer the advantage of reducing the number of workers required to maintain profitability, but the problem is that workers are the source of surplus value, and therefore of profit.

Unlike exploitable labour, that is, technological innovations cannot produce value; they can only buy time. So the expulsion of labour from the productive process produces short-term, sector-specific gains, but at a cost. What Marx suggests is that at a systemic level, the ratio of technology to labour – what he calls the 'organic composition of capital' (or the 'OCC') – will inevitably rise, and the risk of system-wide crisis increases.[20] But Marx also details the range of ways that capitalists can bat back at this tendency. The recipe can shift, but when Roberts lists some of the tactics deployed between 1982 and 1997, for instance, a time when profitability rose in the U.S., they are all versions of those Marx himself outlined in *Capital*: 'the greater exploitation of the U.S. workforce (falling wage share), the cheapening of constant capital through new high-tech innovations, the wider exploitation of the labor force elsewhere (globalization), and speculation in unproductive sectors (particularly real estate and finance capital)'.[21] These counter-tendencies to the tendency of the rate of profit to fall are where the action is – they are the means by which capitalist classes attempt to make over the social world to fit its need for endlessly expanding accumulation. These means are not guaranteed success, and they require a range of violence to mobilise.

Unfortunately, this framework of tendency and counter-tendency is still a minority interpretation of Marx. It got sidelined by the mechanistic view of history among political Marxists in the orbit of the Soviet Union, which claimed

---

19   See Roberts 2016.
20   Marx 1990, p. 571.
21   Roberts 2016, p. 21.

the mantle of Marxism after World War I. For those Marxists, capitalism would need to fulfil its full productive potential before its contradictions made a transition to socialism inevitable. This is the early-twentieth century version of contemporary accelerationist arguments about how advanced technology will inevitably undermine the logic of capitalist accumulation.

Another inheritance from the early and mid-twentieth century has gotten in the way of thinking about capitalism in terms of the vicissitudes of accumulation, and it bears more closely on the work of humanistic scholars on the academic left. This is the legacy of the Frankfurt School. Joshua Clover and I have argued elsewhere (and we are not the first to do so) that whatever the brilliance of Theodor Adorno's dialectics when it comes to aesthetic experience, for instance, his use of political economy is far less dialectical.[22] Indeed it is built on a linearised idea that, in his era, the processes of mass consumption had led capital to saturate every pore of modern life. The key term is 'modern' – what looks like a background of Marxist political economy in Adorno is more often than not an allegory about lost promises for freedom, more a moral declension than a set of economic tendencies and counter-tendencies. As he puts it in *Negative Dialectics*, 'No universal history leads from savagery to humanitarianism, but there is one leading from the slingshot to the megaton bomb'.[23] The sentence is dialectical, but the history is inevitable. Martin Jay long ago pointed out how the Frankfurt School's critique of progress was built on a rejection of sunnily optimistic socialist and liberal political theory, and hardened by the capitulation of German workers to military nationalism in the run-up to World War I; but the points scored by rejecting the idea that modernity has an upward trendline are lost in the capitulation to the idea that the problem is modernity rather than capitalism in the first place.[24] This is even more true of Walter Benjamin than it is of Adorno or Max Horkheimer. Frankfurt-style analysis produces brilliant accounts of aesthetic experience, but it reduces capitalism to a modernity that is linearised even as its products are interpreted dialectically.

The Frankfurt School problem of linearising the movement of capital has roots in exactly the Second International theories that its members rejected. For the intellectuals and strategists of the International, Marx was read as suggesting that capitalism had to reach peak capacity in order to trigger a

---

22   See Clover and Nealon 2017.
23   Adorno 1973, p. 320.
24   See Jay 1986.

transition to socialism. Instead of questioning the premises of this idea, they accepted it and inverted its conclusions: instead of peak capitalism producing a revolutionary consciousness in the working classes, it produces universal atomization. But capitalist accumulation is still understood as a kind of saturation – rather than, say, a movement from one set of contradictions to another.

It is possible to show, however, that the idea of a peak capitalism, or a capitalism that saturates the social field, is not to be found in Marx. This is not just because Marx lived in an earlier moment in the development of capitalism. In his 2015 study *Marx After Marx*, Harry Harootunian demonstrates that for Marx the idea of a completed capitalism is more a heuristic device than an historical prediction.[25] Harootunian's argument turns to another text of Marx's, 'Results of The Immediate Process of Production', that shared the fate of the *Grundrisse* notes and the *Theory of Surplus Value* in remaining unpublished until the 1930s, and that is not as widely read as the body text of *Capital*. For Harootunian the 'Results' helps deepen distinctions made along the course of *Capital* Volume I between different stages of capitalist takeover of the production process. In the 'Results', Marx distinguishes between what he calls the 'formal subsumption' and the 'real subsumption' of the labour process by capitalist imperatives to produce for value rather than utility.[26] For Marx, formal subsumption describes the initial encounter of capital with a preexisting labour process, which it takes over intact and begins to incorporate into larger enterprises. Real subsumption, meanwhile, designates a later moment in that same labour process in which its organisation is altered to comply with competitive pressures, thereby becoming what in broad terms we would think of as more fully capitalist.[27]

Thinkers across a range of Marxist tendencies have tried to construe the movement from formal to real subsumption as a gesture of periodisation, but this is not what Marx is suggesting. In the 'Results' and in chapters 16–18 of *Capital* Volume I, Marx closely correlates that first moment of formal subsumption with what he calls absolute surplus value, which is extracted by extending the working day, and he correlates the second moment, real subsumption, with his concept of relative surplus value, in which additional surplus value is obtained by technological means, especially through the addition of machines to the production process. What's lost in turning this sequence of moments internal to a given production process into a large-scale historical sequence is that Marx is describing inter-capitalist competition. This matters: no competitive advant-

---

25   See Harootunian 2015.

26   See Marx 1990, pp. 1019–38.

27   Ibid.

age lasts forever, and all competitive advantage is bought dearly. Higher wages in the white-collar tranche of the high-tech sector, for instance, are made possible by brutally low wages elsewhere in the value chain. Once we scale up to see capitalism as a totality – not a social totality, as in the Frankfurt School, but a totality of value-production specific to capital and labour – we can see that the 'real' in 'real subsumption' isn't an intensifier – like, shit's getting real in capitalism now! – but rather a marker of the contradictory entailment of all capitalist enterprises with each other. This is what totality means, as a circuit of accumulation: every wage relation needs an elsewhere.

So there is a non-linear way to relate the forms of accumulation to the development of capitalist history. In chapter 25 of Volume I of *Capital*, which is called 'The General Law of Capitalist Accumulation', Marx stresses that the revolutions in productivity driven by inter-capitalist competition have a contradictory effect on the labour pool. This is because the rhythms of large-scale industry are cyclical, and at different moments in that cycle capital both dragoons workers into waged labor, and expels them from it. Furthermore, because machinery lowers the cost of production if it is adopted quickly, it creates the possibility of paying fewer workers to achieve the same level of productivity. But because underpaying labour is the source of profit, this reduction in the number of workers must be compensated for by an increase in the *amount* they produce, regardless of any logic of what mainstream economics thinks of as supply and demand. This heedless expansion of production, in turn, lowers the value of each commodity, at the same time as it has created competition for scarcer jobs. Eventually, the relative advantage of new technology is equalised among capitals, and for a moment, hiring workers becomes relatively advantageous again, compared to investing in yet another round of new technology. But the workers called back into production are not the same as those who'd been expelled from it – they are younger, fresher – or, if they are the same, they are called back on worse terms.

The rhythm of accumulation therefore produces what Marx calls a 'reserve army of labour' stratified by age, health, working conditions, and skill level. And this reserve army expands continuously, drawing ever more people into the wage relation, then expelling them, and only ever partially reincorporating them, if at all. This stratified reserve army produces what Marx calls 'surplus populations' meaning they are superfluous to the needs of capital. What this means is there is also a tendency, as capital pits itself against itself, to pit workers, and classes of workers, against each other.

This dynamic does, though, provide an opportunity to notice that accumulation depends not only on the forced migration of labour into the wage relation, but on walling people out of it, as well. The logic of surplus population described in chapter 25 of *Capital* becomes the retrospective vantage by which to view the dynamics of what Marx referred to in the more famous chapter 26 as 'so-called primitive accumulation' – the name given to the expropriations of land and means of production in early modern Europe, which created the conditions for the spread of the wage relation. For a feminist scholar like Silvia Federici, the story of the enclosure of the commons and the rise of the wage relation is also the story of the establishment of a gendered division of labour by which women's work and women's knowledge are forcibly separated out of public life, as what congeals into public life includes both waged work and political activity.[28] It is also what Robinson is describing in *Black Marxism* when he writes that the 'tendency of European civilization through capitalism was thus not to homogenize but to differentiate – to exaggerate regional, sub-cultural, and dialectical differences into "racial" ones'.[29] If chapter 25 of *Capital* focuses on the business cycle to highlight the ways in which lives are shaped by exteriority to the wage, then chapter 26 expands the frame to direct our attention to a similar dynamic unfolding across centuries. Taken together, the two chapters allow us to think about not only capital's dependence on exteriorities to the wage in any given cycle of accumulation, but its production of those exteriorities across time, and downstream from the limits reached by previous cycles.

This conjunction enables a political viewpoint with the capacity to link workplace struggles with others that, to eyes trained by liberalism or by the politics of difference, still look separate. And political discourse on the left today has begun to reactivate these links: more contemporary anti-racist activists, prison abolitionists, water defenders, anti-austerity militants, and feminists have all become explicitly anti-capitalist. But we are a long way from the kind of universalism that might serve as the theoretical assist to linking these struggles. I have tried to outline, above, aspects of the Marxist tradition that have gotten in the way of such a project, and I've sketched another path from Marx to a robust holism that might help us reconceive the intraleft differences the capitalist classes surely enjoy observing us rehash. I have wanted to suggest in particular that when we look at how Marx understood what he called 'the general law of capitalist accumulation', we can train ourselves to see the commonality in all the different relations to value-production that have been entailed by absorption into wage labour, expulsion from it, forced exclusion from it, and degraded reincorporation into it. I think it is helpful to consider

---

28   See Federici 2004.
29   Robinson 2000, p. 26.

how the production of surplus value depends on a shifting recipe of all these relations to the wage, at any given moment, and how that recipe of stratification depends on prior cycles of accumulation. I think there are other ways to act on our intuition that we're all in this, some horrible 'this', together.

∴

Intuition – we are getting closer, once again, to poetry. Earlier in this essay I suggested that the anti-Hegelian critique of Marx as reductive of difference dated back to an influential critique of Hegel himself, Schelling's critique, and that that Schelling's influential view had shaped a reception history that equated totality with the elimination of difference. There is another twist to this critique, though, which is that the critique of totality is premised on a model of thought that specifically delegitimates intuition. Houlgate argues that Schelling is so committed to the Kantian framework that equates thought with judgment, partition, and categorisation that he faults Hegel for failing to abide by it, without realising that Hegel has in fact rejected that model of thought at the outset. Houlgate puts it this way: 'The principal difference between Hegel and Schelling is thus that Hegel understands thought to be a form of intellectual intuition, whereas Schelling understands thought to be primarily discursive. Like Immanuel Kant, Schelling takes thought to be essentially the discursive activity of judgment (*Urteilen*) or of forming propositions'.[30] In 1984, Gillian Rose began her *Dialectic of Nihilism* with a sustained analysis of how deeply Kant's conception of thought as *Urteil* (judgment) committed him to a conception for judgment that was itself historically saturated with arguments from property law that imagined possession as absolute, and difference as categorical. Intuition, in this model of thought, is an unwelcome guest, which sees likeness where there is none, or where none can be permitted.[31] Houlgate persuasively suggests that these are the terms through which Schelling saw the Hegelian idea of a concept: failing to respect property, imagining everything belonged to it.

Recent scholarship on Hegel suggests that we are missing something if we conceive of him as a philosopher of judgement rather than intuition, however, and that what we overlook has to do with the deep historical sociability of human language. In two different studies across the last few decades, John McCumber has made this case in great detail, arguing for a 'linguistic ideal-

---

30   Houlgate 1999, p. 119.
31   See Rose 1984.

ism' at the heart of Hegel's thought, one in which intuition is the source, not of the illegitimate traversal of domains that are separated by a categorical abyss, but of an ever-revising social activity in which our conceptualisations cannot be separated from our idioms. As he puts it,

> [for Hegel] the individual things we experience exhibit manifold distinctions, similarities, and relationships. Some of these – a tiny fraction – become semantic, that is, are given names and thus made universal. Which these are depends, as linguistic, upon the needs and capacities of the community whose language it is ...
>
> From a linguistic perspective, to have [true] existence thus means to have significance to a community; for only things which have such significance will find their way to semantic significance, and only in virtue of such significance can we talk to one another and become a community. The universals produced by our minds are thus the 'true' essences of things, not in that they are responsible for the existence of those things but *in that they are what matter to us in those things*.[32]

Timothy Brennan takes up a similar argument in *Borrowed Light*, pushing it in a more explicitly political direction. For Brennan, the linguistic Hegel is the Hegel of philology in its broadest sense, the centre of a *project* launched by Giambattista Vico, where the stakes of philosophical truth-seeking are shaped by the rhythms of the vernaculars in which the truth is sought. This is the great source, Brennan argues, of a Hegelian Marxism that placed its faith not in the inexorable march of historical laws, but in people: 'Both Marxism and philology adhere to historical forms of knowing, to the sedimentary traces of a past that happened, to the ultimate creativity of the unnamed, unheralded, popular elements of society'.[33] For Brennan, this is not merely a shared temperamental inclination, but the root orientation of Hegel's philosophical project, running all the way up to its apical concepts, not least the Absolute. As he puts it,

> The term 'absolute' has led to misconceptions. 'Absolute knowledge' for Hegel is not omniscience – not final, complete, or total knowledge – but knowledge absolutely given over (reconciled, one might say) to the collective nature of knowledge, to the contingency of any personal appre-

---

32 McCumber 2014, p. 108.
33 Brennan 2014, p. 10.

hension of it. The term is about the necessity of superseding the self in the recognition of the other, yielding a shared understanding of knowing as that which all humans have the capacity to possess.[34]

There is an opportunity here. When Robinson concludes *Black Marxism* by championing Wright's distinction between Marxism and Black thought, he attends not only to Wright's political writing, but to Wright's novels, the two of which Robinson describes in something like the philological terms that McCumber and Brennan make visible as part of a Left Hegelian legacy:

> In the syncopations and the phrases, the scamp and the beat, the lyric and melody of Black language, Black beliefs, Black music, sexual and social relations and encounters, Wright's work reconstructed the resonances of Black American consciousness in its contests with reality. The quests pursued in his novels and essays were set to the improvisational possibilities obtained in that Black culture's collisions with its own parameters and those prescribed by the market forces and labor demands of capitalism and by a racialist culture.[35]

What I have been trying to establish is that there is a way of reading the intellectual history of abstraction through the lens of property that allows us to rethink what it means to think about similarity and difference. I have been trying to suggest that thinking oriented around property as possession tends to imagine difference in categorical terms, whereas the Marxist starting-point of thinking property through *dis*possession leads to thinking difference in conceptual terms, that is, as a thing in motion, shaped by history but liable to revision. I have been suggesting that capitalist accumulation has a will to the categorical in its attempts to affirm and reaffirm the property relations that sustain it, as in Harris's and Bhandar's expositions of the racialising and endlessly re-racialising work of property law, but that it needs to be studied conceptually in the sense that dispossession, which is invisible in the eternal present-tense of the law, is historically variable: both path-dependent and unpredictable. I have tried to suggest, further, that capitalist history becomes clearest when we see its 'absolute', its drive to accumulate without end, as also endlessly producing elsewheres to surplus-value, both as its preconditions and as its waste. I have suggested that this conception of capitalist history might help us see solidarity

---

34   Brennan 2014, p. 76.
35   Robinson 2000, p. 315.

where it has been hard to see. And I have suggested that improving our vision would depend not only on getting a clearer sense of Marx's conceptual work, but of the aspect of intuition facilitating it. To that end, I have tried to suggest that Marx's relation to Hegel is neither a replication of dialectical thought in some sense of dialectics as the key to all mythologies, nor a triumphant materialism that inverts a mentalist Hegel. I have tried to suggest that Marx sees in Hegel the opportunity to think out of a specifically *social* intuition. And I am inching us toward thinking about how, if we conceive of intuition in linguistic terms – where human language is both tendential and inventive, not simply categorical or structural – then the 'improvisational possibilities' Robinson saw in the rhythms of radical Black thought may be part of a heritage of vernacular creativity whose full extent the widening disaster of contemporary capitalism makes it urgent to explore.

I hope to show in the rest of this essay that to think this way, and to use language this way, groping for similarities, is to risk a range of vulnerabilities, and to suggest that the risk is worth it. Some of those vulnerabilities we might think of as emotional – part of the glory of the Black thought Robinson identifies in Wright is its courage to risk articulating joys liable to destruction, or griefs liable to being weaponised. Some we might think of as political – like the potential overreach of imagining solidarity when there may not have been enough work to establish it: popular anti-racist discourse has good language for unearned allyship, for instance.

Back in the academy, we can see other vulnerabilities in terms of method. One resonant mood in literary criticism and theory today, broadly post-critical, is organised around advocacy for epistemological modesty: not making overbroad claims, not totalising, not appropriating; stay in your lane. The vibrant conversation around 'weak theory' in modernist studies explores the range of possibilities that spring up when one adopts this modesty about method.[36] But I am thinking less of the humanising vulnerabilities that can be disclosed when one reduces the ambit of one's observations – method as epistemological modesty, a heritage of Kant – than of the vulnerability entailed in discovering how powerfully a strong theory can describe the world, only to feel unequipped to change it, at least alone. The chastening limits I feel are not to what we can know, but to what we can do with how *much* we know. This is not to say I am not concerned with method – just that my own sense of where its vulnerability might lie is not epistemological, *per se*, so much as rhetorical; a matter not only of knowledge but of attention. Take, for instance, the risks I run by racing

---

36   See Saint-Amour 2018 and the engaging online forum it inspired.

through a long history of thinking about abstraction, only to place its burdens on a single book of poems.

∷

Pet Sounds blends and rethinks abstraction and intuition, possession and dispossession, likeness and unlikeness in memorable, beautiful ways. It is not a metaphorically dense book of poems at the level of the phrase, but it meditates on whether categories can successfully describe lives in ways that provoke Young's speaker to seek commonality with others whom she knows are different than her, and to distinguish such commonality from possession, likeness from subsumption. It is full of playful private names and in-jokes between couples, full of the deadening categories of the state, full of a wish for solidarities that may not yet have been earned.

The book's long title poem is structured as a sequence of untitled pieces that gives each individual poem its own integrity while drawing its greatest poetic power through the complex and cumulative connections among them. In their demotic language and personal candor, the poems take part in a recent period style that has reactivated the energy of earlier feminist and New York School poetics (Bernadette Mayer is a key background figure for the book). Young's work emerges from the collective energy of the San Francisco Bay Area poetry scene (she teaches at Mills College in Oakland, and edited a volume called *Bay Poetics* in 2006), which is remarkable for its history of fostering collaboration, for its deep connections to West Coast histories of anarchist, Marxist, and queer politics, and for its unpretentious affection for popular culture.

These qualities are signalled by the book's three epigraphs, which come from Marx (a quote distinguishing the pinprick-sting of money from the unbridled gore of capital), from Federici ('The family is essentially the institutionalization of our unwaged labor'), and from The Beach Boys ('God only knows what I'd do without you'), whose 1966 album *Pet Sounds* gives the book its title. Together they establish terrain for the title poem, which is a kind of memoir that attempts to make sense of the arc from adolescence to midlife by charting the course of two relationships, first with a non-white woman (Young is white), then with a white man, who'd been with a woman but who also identifies as queer. At least as important, they move in a world of semi-stable, lower middle-class employment (her teaching and his work as an actor, supported by office work), where families, chosen and unchosen, are both porous and determinative. The poems express a constant awareness of an outermost political horizon that would be something like revolution, but that awareness only takes on meaning through the poems' vernacular. And by 'vernacular' I mean both its diction and what turn out to be its concepts, which we can piece together only by reading the sequence as a whole, and which have to do with how initially circumstantial encounters – with their sudden loyalties, inevitable misrecognitions, and material limits – bequeath enduring attachments regardless. 'Pet Sounds' tells a story in which concepts, realised through words, can be mobilised to put pressure on categories like whiteness, and maleness and femaleness, as well as on the forms of possession that make them so inhospitable to liberation. It keeps intuiting likeness *across* categories, sensing regimes of possession as barriers to its realisation, and countering possession with a curiosity about the potential significance of lived similarities that moves between humour and elegy.

The first poem, just four three-line stanzas, begins with a description of metaphor-making, specifically of a metaphor the poet makes and then demurs from:

> in the dark I say you are a kitten
> and I am a kitten and this makes us
> homosexuals. it isn't true
>
> we are mostly straight
> old cats. it's the closest I can get.
>> *P*, 15

So we start with sameness, likeness, homo-ness – or, not quite. It negates itself. But the desire to 'get' to likeness, and queerness, will not be dispensed with by self-negation. The poet immediately questions her choice of category – not 'homosexual', but

> what is a kitten anyways?
>
> a younger woman who dates older men
> something we have done
>> *P*, 15

So the man in the partnership has dated older men, too. This doesn't help much, it seems, because the next move in this short opening poem is to conclude by re-booting the metaphor entirely, moving in the last line of the penultimate stanza from kittens to insects:

stout, furry, gray and white moth

totally dependent
the caterpillar of which resembles
highly social animals
    P, 15

Maybe it's the man's body hair that triggers the shift in metaphor; it's impossible to say for sure. And only the subsequent poems will make clear that the shift is typical of the roving, self-negating intelligence of both the poet and the couple, whose private language – their pet sounds – keeps even the poems' most pro-bative language close to the bodily production of sheer shaped sound. What we do know is that the poem's curiosity is most evident in the pressure it applies to the last lines of its first three stanzas, where 'it isn't true', 'what is a kitten anyways?' and the shift to 'stout, furry, gray' establish the difference between its formal units (the poem's categorical aspect, you could say) and its intellec-tual mobility. Through negation, critique, and the induction of new material, the poem's ideas keep walking out the stanzas' back doors.

This living tension will express itself across the book as something like a mat-ter of language colliding with categories, especially around scenes of care and social reproduction. The web of relationships depicted across the poems' sec-tions is built out of ever-shifting, often-lopsided caregiving relations, between the poet and her partner Clive, first of all, but also between each of them and their siblings and parents, or between them and friends and neighbors. Young pushes the language against different categories, not least 'woman', but also, toward the end of the volume, against the category of the 'household', at least as the state defines it. 'The US government says you and I are a household with two members related by birth, marriage, or adoption', she writes in unlineated prose, but only after having made clear that the category can't capture the tex-ture of the rhythms of care:

your mom lives in the cottage behind Bonnie
Randy stays with Bonnie most of the time

we take care of your mom some of the time
she takes care of Mark by letting him care for her

most of the time, the hardest parts
getting in and out of the shower

Randy and Mark don't speak

Michael visits Joanie's sister in the nursing home
calls his roommate partner, it sounds like business partner

we transfer money to your mom's account
for rent she pays Bonnie
    P, 76

Plain actions, simple phrases, rotating names: the language isn't poetic but its movement is. It's a kind of rondelé of tending that gives the lie to the idea that the categories of the state can capture all the work it takes to nourish collective life.

    This work, though it is shared in the world Young describes, is also always unevenly distributed, not least according to gender. In a short poem describing the overlapping but non-identical ways she and her partner care for each other's needs, Young writes:

I'm writing this [poem] in my office at work
because you're home sick. I knew
if I worked there I'd take care of you instead.

maybe you also meet your own needs
by meeting the needs of others. I think so.

that I do may or may not mean anything
about how far we haven't come. I am not
every woman. every woman is not in me.
    P, 53

If patriarchy encourages women to care for others at their own expense, and makes that self-sacrifice a central part of the category 'woman', Young suggests, then Clive may be feminine, too, inasmuch as he is other-directed in a similar way. Obversely, Young suggests that perhaps her own willingness, even her desire, to care for him may not emerge entirely because of the patriarchal pressure to validate herself though that care. But she knows she's too small a sample size, all by herself, to use that possibility as a measure of the success of what feminism has sometimes fought for: not only the freedom from compulsory care work, but the freedom *to* care for others. And in any case, she concludes, whatever the size of 'woman' as a category, as a concept it's internally riven: she can't join the party – 'I'm Every Woman' – that Chaka Khan kicked off in 1978.

Today, of course, the redoubling of collective efforts to uncover the history of the specifically racial differences internal to the category and the concept of 'woman' makes Khan's exuberance (and its mighty early-90s afterparty continuation, by Whitney Houston) feel distant and bittersweet. Young tracks this, too, by self-marking as 'white' throughout the book. What's so interesting about the category, though, is that it retains the instability of something conceptual, something you might want to avoid or rework, if you're liable to whiteness. In one poem, after she and Clive knock heads in bed before they're fully awake, Young wryly describes the embarrassment of going out in public after, knowing cultural codes will make her look like she's been abused:

> I walk around like that all week
> with a kind of jelly smeared on top. it takes a while
> to heal. don't be that guy, either of them.
> don't become that white woman artist.
>   *P*, 29

'Don't be that guy' seems to refer both to her and to Clive – don't be the abuser, abused; 'don't become that white woman artist' seems to indicate a cliché where the woman pays the price in abuse for refusing or neglecting her responsibilities to the man or men in her life. The light touch of cross-gendering opens space to imagine that, if she's not literally a 'guy', Young might also not quite fit into 'white woman artist' either, if she is able to outmanoeuvre the ghost-word 'tragic' haunting the epithet.

She is less able to avoid its comic aspect, which is what emerges from her inability to simply escape the label 'white'. Sitting on the stoop with her older friend Michael while they wait for the police and medics to arrive – his wife Joanie has just died – she looks back on their friendship:

> it wasn't until he introduced me to someone else
> as Jennifer that I corrected him and hurt his feelings
>
> I didn't say anything before because I didn't want to
> hurt his feeling or make either of us uncomfortable
>
> plus tbh it amused me

> Joanie, Jennifer, Stephanie
> white girls
> white girl names
> > *P*, 49

Excerpting limits what I can convey of the tenderness in those lines, the ease
Young feels with the comedy of the inescapability of her race, which emerges
in part because of Michael's own gentleness. But it matters for the greatness of
the poetry. It matters because it emerges out of intuitions of likeness that aren't
categorical but experiential – not, we are the same, but: we've been through
things together.

Young's are songs of experience, you could say – most importantly, in 'Pet
Sounds', the experience of love and affection across and inside the categories
created by racial ascription and gender hierarchy. In the case of gender, Young is
constantly swapping positions out of choice or necessity – going out dancing
with Clive and thinking, 'go ahead honey / let your femme flag fly' while she
leans against the wall and 'casts her chin' like a man, or remembering her father
being 'interested in me as a son' (P, 70–1). In the case of race no such swapping of
positions is possible, however, and aside from moments of wry or gentle com-
edy – 'don't be that white woman artist'; 'white girl names' – the ascription of
whiteness feels like a gravitational pull that is all but impossible to fight off,
but which it is imperative to resist, since it is always tending toward a terrible,
racist limit or its flipside, a hoary, unearned self-congratulation. Remembering
a road trip through Washington State with her first partner, Heather, she writes,
'we were coming from Spokane / a place so white it felt satanic. she was not' (*P*,
33). Elsewhere she wrestles with what it means for Clive – an actor outside his
day job – to take on a role as a white supremacist whose change of heart makes
him the hero in a liberal, anti-racist play:

> you are frustrated that the script
> depicts the white man as having moved
> beyond his racism, that his speech
>
> after years of silence instigates the hunger strike
> > *P*, 43

At the level of biography or memoir, 'Pet Sounds' moves from Young's relation-
ship with Heather to hers with Clive, and though the politics of the book make
it reasonable to expect that Young would fret over the transition as part of a
capitulation to larger cultural norms – from a cross-racial same-sex partner-

ship to a monoracial, heterosexual pairing – she pivots unexpectedly to the question of culture through the medium of music. The volume keeps returning in particular to the many versions Van Morrison recorded of his epic ballad 'Madame George', whose possibly trans subject, and whose conditions of production, allow Young to think about how race and gender mediate the unstable boundary between love and possession. Referring to the version of 'Madame George' on Van Morrison's 1973 album *T. B. Sheets*, she writes,

> Heather gave me that album or
> I took it when we broke up. I did that to you
> with *Pet Sounds* – the lost objects
> of breaking up so often music
> > *P*, 32

This wry attention to how beloved music ends up shuttling between gift and theft opens out onto a larger question of cultural theft. Across a cluster of poems in the middle of the sequence, Young reflects on how the version she loves best, which featured backup vocals by the all-Black female band The Sweet Inspirations, keeps getting erased in various ways. So she laboriously reconstructs the performance history of the group, who are dismissed by (white, male) rock critic Greil Marcus in his writing on the song. '[B]ecause something is wrong with my brain', she writes,

> because I believe I'm a dumb girl
> and men of a certain class know more than me
> about music, history, Greil Marcus
>
> must know more than me
> I spend a lot of time attempting to figure out
> if The Sweet Inspirations ever went
> by The Sweet Emotions instead.
>
> they did not. Greil Marcus is wrong.
> he is also wrong when he writes
>
> *If one's response to that culture – the culture*
> *as set down by a small number of people*
> *in Mississippi and elsewhere in the American South*
> *from the late 1920s to the early '40s –*
> *is as strong as Van Morrison's plainly was,*

> *how can that culture not be*
> *in the deepest sense one's own?*
> P, 34

Marcus's dismissal of the black women's contribution to the song feels to Young like the gateway to a dubious argument about how sheer love of Black music can make it 'one's own', if you're white. This becomes especially dubious when, as Young notes in another poem in the sequence, the liner notes for *T. B. Sheets* deliberately miscredit the backup vocals to three white men.

Young does not equate her love of the song with a sense of possessing it. Indeed she loves it despite the conditions that produced it. This includes Van Morrison's own gender politics:

> if Madam George is, like [Lester] Bangs said
> and Morrison denied, a lovelorn drag queen
>
> why should that be the saddest thing
> to write a sad song about? And if she is
>
> the wife of Yeats, his medium and muse?
> more or less sad? Morrison said it's whatever
> you want it to be. a swiss cheese sandwich.
>
> that sounds a lot like a woman
> or something a woman would make for him
> P, 37

But the song is part of her. 'Everything I love is born of brutal contact', she writes, just a line above these lines. This is a political problem, one that would seem to call for imagining an utterly different world, probably a world undone by actual revolution. But Young suspects that it cannot be grasped entirely inside the category 'politics', perhaps especially not inside the category 'revolution', at least as it's discussed in old-school Marxist circles:

> I heard some friends, men, speak beautifully
> of all the things they'd miss most
> after the, uh, rev
>
> the pop the jazz the blues
> all the shapes made possible by slavery
> unmake that problem so too its music

couldn't exist. not me, not you and me together
and that's my jam. both things
have to go. those sounds, those guys

I didn't get them. I still don't. I'd miss each other
more than music, myself – can you actually abolish her?
  P, 31

That humorous hesitation at the start of the poem – 'the, uh, rev' – previews the space Young holds open between her scepticism about a model of revolution that addresses earlier forms of dispossession by 'abolishing' them in the sense of erasing them, and her willingness to imagine that perhaps, indeed, she, herself, needs to be 'abolished'. But if she has to go, so do her relationships – 'you and me together' – and that's where she can only imagine abolition in this narrow sense if she becomes an object, 'her'. The baseline three-line stanza of the book breaks apart here – 'can you actually abolish her?' – fracturing the tercet into an off-rhymed couplet and a small, stray third line, adrift on the other side of a carriage return: 'you can try'.

Taken as a whole, 'Pet Sounds' argues that what is lost in this model of revolutionary abolition as erasure is the obverse of what has been lost in the long histories of dispossession that make a revolution necessary in the first place: the radical 'dependency' of 'highly social animals' announced on the poem's first page. That dependent sociability is acted out imperfectly in a language that Young takes care to show is strung between something like the undead ascriptive power of categories, on the one hand, and a vital, inventive, and vulnerable animality in speech that is also a kind of category-breaking conceptualisation. It is actualised throughout the book in humour, imperfect form-making, tenderness, grief and self-awareness. And it keeps looping through the forms of intimacy that categories can't track, a fluidity itself imperfectly captured by the concept of queer. She celebrates the 'basic shittiness of private language', sitting atop her kitchen table, 'talking, honestly, nonsense' but enjoying the feeling of disorientation, 'in the house who were we even' (*P*, 54). One poem lists the names she and Clive have given their kitten ('the old man / pumpkin spice / captain crunch'), and senses the groping behind the humor:

nonreproductive nonsense for a nonhuman companion
I would never call that queer, still
nothing fits
  P, 27

After the mass murder of 49 people at the Pulse queer bar in Orlando, Florida – the climax of the book's narrative – she lists the names of the people killed, and marks the difference between the slurs to which she and Clive have been subjected and the obliterating violence that night:

> faggot, dyke
>
> what didn't kill us
> didn't kill us
>   P, 73

She hopes against hope for a universal queerness, asking like a child, 'if everyone is queer would nobody get hurt?' (P, 72). But she recognises that this desire may itself be hamstrung by its voicing through 'straight mostly white women' who are 'coming out this week on the internet' (P, 72). She tries on 'wife' and 'husband' for herself and Clive, retreats from that – 'I call you my person mostly' – but knows there isn't any queerness without categories to upend:

> if I disinvest us from the categories
> what's left? two cat ladies
> two men and a baby who is a cat
>   P, 74

What subtends the categories that chafe, in 'Pet Sounds', is property – private property, that is, which gives the binaries and the slurs a rigidity that perhaps categories themselves needn't have. I have backgrounded all the economic language in the book, but it is everywhere, and perpetually appears in how relationships are constructed. In the opening poem of the book she calls it 'the shape togetherness was taken by // dispossession and constraint' (P, 3). At the far end of the book's arc, in the final poem, Young describes cobbling together a household and a garden by happenstance,

> a green plastic table
> I haggled down to fourteen dollars
>
> what was in your wallet
> what we found on the street,

and senses in the loose assemblage a life in which the dispossession of having to live by 'purchased wages' opens on to understanding the lie embedded in possession:

we don't own the house
or the yard or the shed
we covered in a tarp

I'm learning to tell the difference
   P, 78

If you only read the final poem, you wouldn't know what 'the difference' is between: ownership and ...? But taken as part of a dynamic whole, the difference is shimmering, and clear. It's between possession and life – life as given shape in a collective language, harried and enabled by animal vulnerabilities that 'the, uh, rev', if it ever were to happen, would need to build with.

Another way to put the book's closing distinction would be to say it's between possession and value – not least linguistic value, shaped by capitalist value and perpetually outmanoeuvring it. The book ends with the beginning of an education we've actually seen in action, disarmingly humble (self-negating as Young is) but resolute in its own way, and clear-eyed about the strong forms of analysis that deepen its modesty. It can feel academic indeed – deadening, even – to say about so unprepossessing a collection of poetry, one so full of open-hearted humour, that it is a 'Marxist-Feminist' book, or that it is 'dialectical'. It feels more legible in terms of the poetic pet sounds made by 'highly social animals'. All that purring and mewling might seem a long way from the dialectic – and perhaps pleasantly so! – but for Hegel, the purposiveness of earth's creatures, their motility, their growth – these were a fundamental ingredient in his sense of dialectical motion, which he felt our minds could only engage inasmuch as we are creatures too. As McCumber puts it, 'Hegel genuinely believes that animals are idealists'.[37]

∴

There is a long debate in studies of Marx that centres on whether and how Marx managed to succeed in connecting his theory of value to an account of how it becomes economically legible in the prices of commodities, that is, over whether Marx was able to reproduce the transformation of value into price. It is an intricate debate. But from a distance, it becomes interesting for how it links anti-Marxist economists eager to demonstrate that Marx didn't prove that the source of value under capitalism is the exploitation of labour, on the one hand,

---

37   McCumber 2014, p. 80.

with Marxists determined to correct what they see as Marx's failure to prove this (or to be explicit enough about having proved it), on the other. The premise on both sides is that if you can make the numbers work out – that is, if you can show that it is at least theoretically possible to calculate a total difference (for a given period) in the net output of capitalist production between what accrues to capitalists as profit and what is paid to workers as wages, then … well, then you'd have proved something, proved that the labour theory of value is correct, that capitalism works not by paying workers but by underpaying them. You'd have proved, in short, that capitalism, as a form of perennial underpayment to workers, *exists*.

But Marx wasn't trying to prove that capitalism exists. As Fred Moseley has argued, one of the problems for Marx's defenders in the debate over the 'transformation problem' is their unwillingness to acknowledge that Marx presupposed fully developed capitalism at the beginning of his analysis, so that the inputs his quantitatively-minded defenders want to prove add up are already value-derived themselves, that is, they are already capitalist money, and can't be used to prove from outside the circuit of capital that there *is* a circuit of capital to begin with.[38] In his landmark 1993 study *Time, Labor and Social Domination*, Moishe Postone puts it this way:

> [Marx's] explicit arguments deriving the existence of value in the first chapter of [*Capital*] are not intended – and should not be seen – as 'proof' of the concept of value … The critique only fully emerges in the course of the presentation itself which, in unfolding the basic structuring social forms of its object of investigation, shows the historicity of that object.[39]

Another way of putting this might be to say that *Capital* is meant to be persuasive, not legitimate. The Marxism that is focused on the legitimation of his theory of value walls off Marx from the very holism that enabled the concept in the first place. It is still the dominant Marxism in and around the academy. A Marxism that accepted its origins in a 'social intuition', however, would be more clear-eyed about its character as rhetoric – 'rhetoric' not in the sceptical sense of ornamented, or hectoring, but in Hans Blumenberg's sense of rhetoric as the kind of thought that grapples with its own situatedness.[40] It may or may not be philosophical. The importance of rethinking Marx's debt to Hegel, in this

---

38   See Moseley 2016.
39   Postone 1993, pp. 141–2.
40   See, for instance, Blumenberg 1987.

light, is not to boost the intellectual prestige or leftist credibility of the philosopher, but to recognise that inasmuch as we need to think philosophically when we think holistically, it is liberating to tap into a philosophy whose attention to the social activity of language as a form of collective concept-making itself implicitly acknowledges philosophy's intellectual non-autonomy. It can enable a theory of value less likely to fork into Marx bros and people who have come to believe they're 'dumb girls'; one that sees its need for poetry.

Poetry benefits, too. As an English professor, I have to say that one of the joys of the flowering of Marxist poetry in English over the last twenty years is the way it has made the task of disentangling the living currents of poetry from the need to defend its philosophical legitimacy so much easier. In his *Theory of The Lyric*, Jonathan Culler gently but insistently turns our attention away from the hostile Platonism that can only ever find in poetry a failure native to representation, and enables us to begin thinking about poems as 'articulating values' rather than subsisting lamely as a 'species of fiction'.[41] This project is nourished by a poetry in which 'values' are so up front. Marxist poetry is not a metonym for all poetry, but it shines a light on all of it.

It is impossible not to feel that time is running out for the institutions and practices of literary criticism we have known since the great expansion of university education after the GI Bill. But we have our opportunities. A return to Marx that sees in his theory of value not a Hegelian subsumption of particulars but an honouring of holism might help us rethink political difference, rather than erase it. A theory of value that sees in abstraction an irreducible element of intuition might allow us to see the helplessly situated character *of* abstraction. And focusing on that heteronomy might assist in re-narrating what it means to think, in the first place: something more collective and less categorical. Abstraction, intuition, poetry: maybe made into a little constellation, they could be a metaphor for 'what we're going to need'.

41   Culler 2015, p. 7.

References

Adorno, Theodor W. 1983 [1966], *Negative Dialectics*, translated by E.B. Ashton, New York: Continuum.

Adorno, Theodor W. 1970, *Aesthetic Theory*, translated by Robert Hullot-Kentor, Minneapolis: University of Minnesota Press.

Adorno, Theodor W. 1996 [1951], *Minima Moralia: Reflections from Damaged Life*, translated by E.F.N. Jephcott, New York: Verso.

Adorno, Theodor W. 1991 [1974], 'Lyric Poetry and Society'. *Notes to Literature, vol. 1*, translated by Shierry Weber Nicholsen, edited by Rolf Tiedemann. New York: Columbia University Press: 37–54.

Adorno, Theodor W. and Horkheimer, Max. 2002 [1944], *The Dialectic of Enlightenment*, translated by Edmund Jephcott, Stanford: Stanford University Press.

Agamben, Giorgio 1993 [1977], *Stanzas: Word and Phantasm in Western Culture*, translated by Ronald L. Martinez, Minneapolis: University of Minnesota Press.

Agamben, Giorgio 1995, 'We Refugees', translated by Michael Rocke, in *Symposium*, 49: 114–19.

Agamben, Giorgio 1998 [1995], *Homo Sacer: Sovereign Power and Bare Life*, translated by Daniel Heller-Roazen, Stanford: Stanford University Press.

Agamben, Giorgio 1999 [1996], *The End of the Poem: Studies in Poetics*, translated by Daniel Heller-Roazen, Stanford: Stanford University Press.

Agamben, Giorgio 2005 [2000], *The Time that Remains: A Commentary on The Letter to The Romans*, translated by Patricia Dailey, Stanford: Stanford University Press.

Alexander, Amir 2004 *Infinitesimal: How a Dangerous Mathematical Theory Shaped the Modern World*, New York: Farrar, Straus and Giroux.

Alexander, Charles P. 1983, 'The New Economy', *Time*, 121, 22: 50–8.

Altieri, Charles 1983, 'An Idea and Ideal of a Literary Canon', *Critical Inquiry*, 10, 1: 37–60.

Altieri, Charles 1998, 'Some Problems about Agency in the Theories of Radical Poetics', in *Postmodernisms Now: Essays on Contemporaneity in the Arts*, edited by Altieri, University Park: Penn State University Press.

Andrews, Bruce 2004, 'The Poetics of L=A=N=G=U=A=G=E', available at www.ubu.com/papers/andrews.html.

Arrighi, Giovanni 1994, *The Long Twentieth Century: Money, Power, and The Origins of Our Times*, London: Verso.

Badiou, Alain 2005 [1998], *Metapolitics*, translated by Jason Barker, London: Verso.

Badiou, Alain 2005 [1998], *Handbook of Inaesthetics*, translated Alberto Toscano, Stanford: Stanford University Press.

Badiou, Alain 2005, *Infinite Thought*, translated by Oliver Feltham and Justin Clemens, London: Continuum.

Balakrishnan, Gopal 2000, 'Hardt and Negri's Empire', *New Left Review*, 5: 142–8.

Barker, Jason 2002, *Alain Badiou: A Critical Introduction*, London: Pluto Press.

Baucom, Ian 2000, 'Globalit, Inc.; Or, the Cultural Logic of Global Literary Studies', *PMLA*, 116, 1: 158–72.

Beech, Dave 2015, *Art and Value: Art's Exceptionalism in Classical, Neoclassical and Marxist Economics*, Boston: Brill.

Beiser, Frederick 2014, *After Hegel: German Philosophy, 1840–1900*, Princeton: Princeton University Press.

Bell, Vance 1997, 'Falling into Time: The Historicity of the Symbol', *Other Voices*, 1, 1: available at http://www.othervoices.org/1.1/vbell/symbol.php.

Benanav, Aaron 2020, *Automation and the Future of Work*, London: Verso.

Benjamin, Walter 1969 [1942], 'Theses on the Philosophy of History', in *Illuminations: Essays and Reflections*, edited by Arendt, Hannah, translated by Zohn, Harry, New York: Schocken Books.

Benjamin, Walter 2009 [1928], *The Origin of German Tragic Drama*, translated by John Osborne, New York: Verso.

Bennett, Jane 2010, *Vibrant Matter*, Durham: Duke University Press.

Berardi, Franco 2012, *The Uprising: On Poetry and Finance*, Cambridge, MA: MIT Press.

Berlin, Isaiah 2000, *Three Critics of the Enlightenment: Vico, Hamann, Herder*, edited by Henry Hardy, Princeton: Princeton University Press.

Bernes, Jasper 2012, *We Are Nothing and So Can You*, Oakland: Tenured Ninja.

Bernes, Jasper 2017, *The Work of Art in the Age of Deindustrialization*, Stanford: Stanford University Press.

Bersani, Leo 1986, *The Freudian Body: Psychoanalysis and Art*, New York: Columbia University Press.

Bersani, Leo 1995, *Homos*, Cambridge: Harvard University Press.

Bhandar, Brenna 2018, *Colonial Lives of Property: Law, Land, and Racial Regimes of Ownership*, Durham: Duke University Press.

Blumenberg, Hans, 1983 [1966], *The Legitimacy of The Modern Age*, translated by Robert Wallace, Cambridge: MIT Press.

Blumenberg, Hans 1987, 'An Anthropological Approach to the Contemporary Significance of Rhetoric', in *After Philosophy: End or Transformation?*, edited by Kenneth Baynes, James Bohman, and Thomas McCarthy, Cambridge: MIT Press.

Boethius 1990, *The Consolation of Philosophy*, translated by S.J. Tester, Cambridge, MA: Harvard University Press.

Bogost, Ian 2012, *Alien Phenomenology, or, What It's Like to Be a Thing*, Minneapolis: University of Minnesota Press.

Boone, Bruce 1983, 'For Jack Spicer: And a Truth Element', *Social Text*, 7: 120.

Brassier, Ray 2007, *Nihil Unbound: Enlightenment and Extinction*, by Basingstoke: Palgrave.

Bredekamp, Horst 1999, 'From Walter Benjamin to Carl Schmitt, via Thomas Hobbes', translated by Melissa Thorson Hause and Jackson Bond, *Critical Inquiry*, 25, 2: 247–66.

Brennan, Timothy 2014, *Borrowed Light: Vico, Hegel and The Colonies*, Stanford: Stanford University Press.

Brenner, Robert 1998, 'Uneven Development and the Long Downturn: The Advanced Capitalist Economies from Boom to Stagnation, 1950–1998', *New Left Review*, 229: 1–264.

Brenner, Robert 2006, *The Economics of Global Turbulence: The Advanced Capitalist Economies from Long Boom to Long Downturn, 1945–2005*, London: Verso.

Breslin, James E.B. 1983, *From Modern to Contemporary: American Poetry, 1945–1965*, Chicago: University of Chicago Press.

Buell, Lawrence 1996, *Environmental Imagination: Thoreau, Nature Writing, and the Formation of American Culture*, Cambridge: Harvard University.

Butler, Judith 1990, *Gender Trouble: Feminism and The Subversion of Identity*, New York: Routledge.

Butler, Judith 1997, *Excitable Speech: A Politics of the Performative*, New York and London: Routledge.

Butler, Judith 2004, 'Doing Justice to Someone: Sex Reassignment and Allegories of Transsexuality', in *Undoing Gender*, New York and London: Routledge.

Chakrabarty, Dipesh 2009, 'The Climate of History: Four Theses', *Critical Inquiry*, 35: 197–222.

Chen, Chris 2013, 'The Limit Point of Capitalist Equality', in *Endnotes*, 3.

Cleaver, Harry 1992, 'The Inversion of Class Perspective in Marxian Theory: from Valorization to Self-Valorization', in *Essays on Open Marxism*, edited by W. Bonefeld, R. Gunn and K. Psychopedis, London: Pluto Press.

Clegg, John J. 2015, 'Capitalism and Slavery', in *Critical Historical Studies*, 2, 2: 281–304.

Clover, Joshua 2006, *The Totality for Kids*, Berkeley: University of California Press.

Joshua Clover and Christopher Nealon, 'Literary and Economic Value', in *The Oxford Research Encyclopedia of Literature* (27 July 2017), https://oxfordre.com/literature/view/10.1093/acrefore/9780190201098.001.0001/acrefore-9780190201098-e-123.

Culler, Jonathan 2015, *Theory of The Lyric*, Cambridge: Harvard University Press.

Curtius, Ernst Robert 1973 [1953], *European Literature and the Latin Middle Ages*, translated by Willard R. Trask, Princeton: Princeton University Press.

Cusset, Francois 2008 [2003], *French Theory: How Foucault, Derrida, Deleuze, & Co. Transformed the Intellectual Life of the United States*, translated by Jeff Fort, Minneapolis: University of Minnesota Press.

Dauben, Joseph W. 1977, 'Georg Cantor and Pope Leo XIII: Mathematics, Theology, and The Infinite', *Journal of The History of Ideas*, 38, 1: 85–108.

de Man, Paul 1983, *Blindness and Insight: Essays in the Rhetoric of Contemporary Criticism*, Minneapolis: University of Minnesota Press.

de Man, Paul 1996a "Phenomenality and Materiality in Kant", in *Aesthetic Ideology*, edited by Andrej Warminski, Minneapolis: University of Minnesota Press.

de Man, Paul 1996b, "Kant and Schiller", in *Aesthetic Ideology*, edited by Andrej Warminski, Minneapolis: University of Minnesota Press.

Davies, Kevin 2000, *Comp.*, Washington, D.C.: Edge Books.

Debord, Guy 2004 [1967], *The Society of the Spectacle*, translated by Ken Knabb, London: Rebel Press.

Debord, Guy 2008 [2004], 'The Rise and Fall of the 'Spectacular' Commodity-Economy', in *A Sick Planet*, translated by Donald Nicholson-Smith, New York: Seagull Books.

Derrida, Jacques 1980 [1967], 'From Restricted to General Economy: A Hegelianism without Reserve', in *Writing and Difference*, translated by Alan Bass, Chicago: University of Chicago Press.

Derrida, Jacques 1986 'Mnemosyne', in *Memoires for Paul de Man*, New York: Columbia University Press.

Dimock, Wai-Chee 2006, *Through Other Continents: American Literature Across Deep Time*, Princeton: Princeton University Press.

Dronke, Peter 1994, *Verse with Prose from Petronius to Dante: The Art and Scope of the Mixed Form*, Cambridge: Harvard University Press.

Dupuy, Jean-Pierre 2000 [1994], *The Mechanization of the Mind: On The Origins of Cognitive Science*, translated by M.B. DeBevoise, Princeton, NJ: Princeton University Press.

During, Simon 2010, *Exit Capitalism: Literary Culture, Theory, and Post-Secular Modernity*, New York: Routledge.

Eagleton, Terry 1990, *The Ideology of The Aesthetic*, Malden, MA: Blackwell.

Edelman, Lee 1994, *Homographesis: Essays in Gay Literary and Cultural Theory*, New York: Routledge.

Edelman, Lee 2004, *No Future: Queer Theory and the Death Drive*, Durham: Duke University Press.

Eliot, T.S. 2005 [1923], 'Ulysses, Order, and Myth', in *Modernism: An Anthology*, edited by Lawrence Rainey, Malden, MA: Blackwell.

Ellis, Cristin 2012, *Political Ecologies: The Contingency of Nature in American Romantic Thought*, Dissertation, Johns Hopkins University.

Elson, Diane 1979, 'The Value Theory of Labour', in *Value: The Representation of Labour in Capitalism*, edited by Diane Elson, Atlantic Heights, N.J.: Humanities Press.

Epstein, Steven 1998, *Impure Science: AIDS, Activism, and the Politics of Knowledge*, Berkeley, University of California Press.

Ellingham, Lewis and Killian, Kevin 1998, *Poet Be Like God: Jack Spicer and the San Francisco Renaissance*, Middletown, CT: Wesleyan University Press.

Federici, Silvia 2004. *Caliban and The Witch*, Brooklyn: Autonomedia,

Felski, Rita 2015, *The Limits of Critique*, Chicago: University of Chicago Press.

Florida, Richard 2002, *The Rise of The Creative Class: And How It's Transforming Work, Leisure, Community and Everyday Life*, New York: Basic Books.

Ford, Simon 2005, *The Situationist International: A User's Guide*, London: Black Dog Publishing.

Fromm, Erich 2011 [1961], *Marx's Concept of Man*, translated by T.B. Bottomore, Eastford, CT: Martino Publishing.

Frye, Northrop 1957, *Anatomy of Criticism*, Princeton: Princeton University Press.

Gilbert, Alan 2000, 're: Reading the Active Reader Theory', *Tripwire*, 6: 118–24.

Gilmore, Ruth Wilson 2002, 'Fatal Couplings of Power and Difference: Notes on Racism and Geography', *The Professional Geographer*, 54, 1: 15–24.

Gonzalez, Maya and Jeanne Neton, 'The Logic of Gender: On The Separation of Spheres and The Process of Abjection', in *Endnotes 3*.

Goux, Jean-Joseph 1990 [1973], *Symbolic Economies: After Marx and Freud*, translated by Jennifer Curtiss Gage, Ithaca, NY: Cornell University Press.

Graeber, David. *Debt: The First Five Thousand Years*. Brooklyn, NY: Melville House, 2012.

Guyatt, Nicholas 2001, *Another American Century? The United States and the World after 2000*, New York: St. Martin's.

Guillory, John 1983, 'The Ideology of Canon Formation: T.S. Eliot and Cleanth Brooks', *Critical Inquiry*, 10, 1: 173–98.

Habermas, Jürgen 1996 [1981], 'Modernity: An Unfinished Project?' In *Habermas and The Unfinished Project of Modernity: Critical Essays on The Philosophical Discourse of Modernity*, edited by Maurizio Passerin d'Entrèves and Seyla Benhabib, Cambridge: Polity Press.

Halpern, Rob 2009 [2006], *Disaster Suites*, Long Beach, California: Palm Press.

Hardt, Michael and Negri, Antonio 2000, *Empire*, Cambridge, MA: Harvard University Press.

Hardt, Michael and Negri, Antonio 2004, *Multitude*, Cambridge, MA: Harvard University Press.

Harman, Graham 2005, *Guerilla Metaphysics: Phenomenology and the Carpentry of Things*, Chicago: Open Court.

Harman, Graham 2011, 'Realism without Materialism', *SubStance*, 40, 2: 52–72.

Harman, Graham 2012, *Weird Realism: Lovecraft and Philosophy*, Alresford: Zero.

Harootunian, Harry 2015, *Marx After Marx: History and Time in The Expansion of Capitalism*, New York: Columbia University Press.

Harris, Cheryl I. 1993, 'Whiteness as Property', *Harvard Law Review*, 106, 8: 1707–1791.

Heilbroner, Robert and Milberg, William S. 1995, *The Crisis of Vision in Modern Economic Thought*, Cambridge: Cambridge University Press.

Heise, Ursula K. 2008, *Sense of Place and Sense of Planet: The Environmental Imagination of the Global*, Oxford: Oxford University Press.

Hejinian, Lyn 1987, *My Life*, Los Angeles: Sun and Moon Press.

Hejinian, Lyn 1994, *The Cold of Poetry*, Los Angeles: Sun and Moon Press.

Hejinian, Lyn 2000, 'The Rejection of Closure', in *The Language of Inquiry*, Berkeley and Los Angeles: University of California Press.

Herndon, Jim 1974, 'Thus Jack Spicer Refuted Child Psychology', *Manroot*, 10: 56.

Herrnstein-Smith, Barbara 1983, 'Contingencies of Value', *Critical Inquiry*, 10, 1: 1–35.

Holsinger, Bruce 2005, *The Premodern Condition: Medievalism and The Making of Theory*, Chicago: University of Chicago Press.

Houlgate, Stephen 1999, 'Schelling's Critique of Hegel's *Science of Logic*', *The Review of Metaphysics*, 53, 1: 99–128.

Hulme, T.E. 2003 [1908], 'A Lecture on Modern Poetry', in *Selected Writings*, edited by Patrick McGuinness, New York: Routledge.

Hulme, T.E. 1936, 'Humanism and the Religious Attitude', in *Speculations: Essays on Humanism and The Philosophy of Art*, London: Kegan Paul, Trench, Trubner & Co.

Huttner, Tobias 2019, ''Not the Abstract Question of Democracy': The Social Ground of Whitman's 'Lilacs'', *ESQ: A Journal of Nineteenth-Century American Literature and Culture*, 65, 4: 642–90.

Huyssen, Andreas 1986, *After The Great Divide: Modernism, Mass Culture, Postmodernism*, Bloomington, IN: Indiana University Press.

Jameson, Fredric 1974, *Marxism and Form: Twentieth-Century Dialectical Theories of Literature*, Princeton: Princeton University Press.

Jameson, Fredric 1981, *The Political Unconscious: Narrative as a Socially Symbolic Act*, Ithaca, NY: Cornell University Press.

Jameson, Fredric 1984, 'Postmodernism, or The Cultural Logic of Late Capitalism', *New Left Review*, 148: 53–92.

Jameson, Fredric 1990, *Late Marxism: Adorno, or, The Persistence of the Dialectic*, New York: Verso.

Jameson, Fredric 1991, *Postmodernism, or the Cultural Logic of Late Capitalism*, Durham, N.C.: Duke University Press.

Jarvis, Simon. 'Soteriology and reciprocity'. *Parataxis: Modernism and Modern Writing* 5 (1993): 30–9.

Jarvis, Simon 2003, 'The Incommunicable Silhouette', *Jacket*, 24, available at jacketmagazine.com/24/jarvis-tis.html

Jay, Martin 1986, *Marxism and Totality: The Adventures of a Concept from Lukács to Habermas*, Berkeley: University of California Press.

Jordan, Z.A. 1967, *Evolution of Dialectical Materialism: A Philosophical and Sociological Analysis*, New York: St. Martin's.

Jost, Walter, and Michael J. Hyde (eds.) 1997, *Rhetoric and Hermeneutics in Our Time*, New Haven, CT: Yale University Press.

Kant, Immanuel 2000 [1790] *Critique of the Power of Judgment*, translated by Paul Guyer and Eric Matthews, edited by Guyer, Cambridge: Cambridge University Press.

Kant, Immanuel 1993 [1796], 'On a Newly Arisen Superior Tone in Philosophy', in *Raising the Tone of Philosophy: Late Essays by Immanuel Kant, Transformative Critique by Jacques Derrida*, edited by Peter Fenves, Baltimore: Johns Hopkins University Press.

Katko, Justin. 'Relativistic Phytosophy: Towards a Commentary on *The* Plant Time Manifold *Transcripts*'. *Glossator* 2 (2010): 245–93.

Kaufman, Robert 1996, 'Legislators of the Post-Everything World: Shelley's Defence of Adorno', *English Literary History*, 63: 707–33.

Kaufman, Robert 2001a, 'Negatively Capable Dialectics: Keats, Vendler, Adorno, and the Theory of the Avant-Garde', *Critical Inquiry*, 27: 354–84.

Kaufman, Robert 2001b, 'Intervention & Commitment Forever! Shelley in 1819, Shelley in Brecht, Shelley in Adorno, Shelley in Benjamin', *Romantic Circles*, available at https://romantic-circles.org/praxis/interventionist/kaufman/kaufman.html.

Kim, Eleana 2001, 'Language Poetry: Dissident Practices and the Makings of a Movement', in Gary Sullivan's online journal readme, available at https://www.academia.edu/456515/.

Klein, Naomi 2007, *The Shock Doctrine: The Rise of Disaster Capitalism*, New York: Metropolitan Books.

Korten, David C. 1995, *When Corporations Rule the World*, Bloomfield, Conn.: Kumarian Press.

Kracauer, Siegfried 1995 [1927], 'Those Who Wait', in *The Mass Ornament: Weimar Essays*, translated by Thomas Levin, Cambridge: Harvard University Press.

Kreiner, Tim 2013, 'The Long Downturn and Its Discontents: Language Writing and the New Left', Dissertation, University of California, Davis.

La Berge, Leigh Clare 2019, 'Abstraction', in *The Bloomsbury Companion to Marx*, edited by Jeff Diamanti, Andrew Pendakis, and Imre Szeman, New York: Bloomsbury Academic.

Lacoue-Labarthe, Philippe 1999 [1986], *Poetry as Experience*, translated by Andrea Tarnowski, Stanford: Stanford University Press.

Laruelle, François 2010 [2002], *Future Christ: A Lesson in Heresy*, translated by Anthony Paul Smith, London: Continuum.

Levi-Strauss, Claude 1966 [1962], *The Savage Mind*, trans George Weidenfeld, Letchworth, Hertfordshire: The Garden City Press Limited.

Lewontin, Richard 2000, *The Triple Helix: Gene, Organism, and Environment*, Cambridge, MA: Harvard University Press.

Lilla, Mark 2001, *The Reckless Mind: Intellectuals in Politics*, New York: New York Review of Books.

Löwith, Karl 1957, *Meaning in History: The Theological Implications of the Philosophy of History*, Chicago: University of Chicago Press.

Lucas, Edward Verrall 1917, 'The Debt', in *A Treasury of War Poetry: British and American Poems of the World War, 1914–1917*, edited by George Herbert Clarke, Boston: Houghton Mifflin Company.

Lukács, Georg 1971 [1923], *History and Class Consciousness: Studies in Marxist Dialectics*, translated by Rodney Livingstone, Cambridge: MIT Press.

Lyotard, Jean-François 1984 [1979], *The Postmodern Condition: A Report on Knowledge*, translated by Geoffrey Bennington and Brian Massumi, Minneapolis: University of Minnesota Press.

Lyotard, Jean-François 1993 [1974], *Libidinal Economy*, translated by Iain Hamilton Grant, Bloomington: Indiana University Press.

Mao, Douglas 1998, *Solid Objects: Modernism and The Test of Production*, Princeton: Princeton University Press.

Mellor, Leo. 'The Amazing Mr. Prynne' (review of *Poems*). *Buzzwords*. http://www.buzzwords.ndo.co.uk/mellor/poems.html.

Mellors, Anthony. *Late Modernist Poetics: From Pound to Prynne*. Manchester: Manchester UP, 2005.

Marcuse, Herbert 1969, *An Essay on Liberation*, Boston: Beacon Press.

Martin, Randy 2002, *The Financialization of Daily Life*, Philadelphia: Temple University Press.

Marx, Karl 1970 [1843], *Critique of Hegel's Philosophy of Right*, edited by Joseph O'Malley, translated by Annette Jolin and Joseph O'Malley, Cambridge: Cambridge University Press.

Marx, Karl 1990 [1867], *Capital Volume 1*, translated by Ben Fowkes, London: Penguin.

Marx, Karl 1993 [1939], *Grundrisse: Foundations of the Critique of Political Economy*, translated by Martin Nicolaus, New York: Penguin.

Marx-Scouras, Danielle 1996, *The Cultural Politics of Tel Quel: Literature and the Left in the Wake of Engagement*, University Park, PA: Penn State University Press.

Matz, Robert 2000, *Defending Literature in Early Modern England: Renaissance Literary Theory in Social Context*, Cambridge: Cambridge University Press.

McCumber, John 2014, *Understanding Hegel's Mature Critique of Kant*, Stanford: Stanford University Press.

McMahon, Robert 2006, *Understanding the Medieval Meditative Ascent: Augustine, Anselm, Boethius, and Dante*, Washington, DC: Catholic University of America Press.

Meillassoux, Quentin 2009 [2006], *After Finitude: An Essay on The Necessity of Contingency*, translated by Ray Brassier, New York: Continuum.

Meillassoux, Quentin 2012 [2011], *The Number and The Siren: A Decipherment of Mal-*

larmé's Coup De Des, translated by Robin Mackay, Falmouth, UK: Urbanomic/Sequence Press.

Miller, Douglas B. 2002, *Symbol and Rhetoric in Ecclesiastes: The Place of* Hebel *in Qohelet's Work*, Atlanta: Society of Biblical Literature.

Moretti, Franco (ed.) 2006–7, *The Novel: History, Geography and Culture*, 2 vols, Princeton: Princeton University Press.

Morrison, Toni 1992, *Playing in the Dark: Whiteness and the Literary Imagination*, Cambridge: Harvard University Press.

Morton, Timothy 2010, *The Ecological Thought*, Cambridge: Harvard University Press.

Moseley, Fred 2016, *Money and Totality: A Macro-Monetary Interpretation of Marx's Logic in* Capital *and the End of the 'Transformation Problem'*, Leiden: Brill.

Moten, Fred 2015, 'Blackness and Poetry', *Arcade*, available at http://arcade.stanford .edu/content/blackness-and-poetry-0

Moxley, Jennifer 2002, *The Sense Record*, Washington, D.C.: Edge Books.

Mullen, Harryette. 2002, *Sleeping with the Dictionary*, Berkeley: University of California Press.

Nancy, Jean-Luc 1991 [1986], 'Literary Communism', in *The Inoperative Community*, translated by Christopher Fynsk, Minneapolis: Minnesota University Press.

Nealon, Chris 2009, 'Reading on The Left'. *Representations*, 108: 22–50.

Nealon, Chris 2010, *The Matter of Capital: Poetry and Crisis in the American Century*, Cambridge: Harvard University Press.

Nealon, Chris 2015, 'Infinity for Marxists', *Mediations: Journal of the Marxist Literary Group*, 28, 2: 47–64.

Negarestani, Reza 2011, "Drafting the Inhuman: Conjectures on Capitalism and Organic Necrocracy," in *The Speculative Turn*, eds. Levi Bryant, Nick Srnicek, and Graham Harman (Melbourne: re.press), 182.

Ngai, Sianne 2005, *Ugly Feelings*, Cambridge, MA: Harvard University Press.

Ngai, Sianne 2015, 'Visceral Abstractions', *GLQ: A Journal of Lesbian and Gay Studies*, 21, 1: 33–63.

Nietzsche, Friedrich 2015 [1874], *The Use and Abuse of History*, translated by Adrian Collins, Eastford, CT: Martino Publishing.

Nietzsche, Friedrich 1999 [1873], 'On Truth and Lying in a Non-Moral Sense' in *The Birth of Tragedy and Other Writings*, translated by Raymond Geuss, Cambridge: Cambridge University Press.

Noys, Benjamin 2014, 'The discreet charm of Bruno Latour', in *(Mis)readings of Marx in Continental Philosophy*, edited by Jernej Habjan and Jessica Whyte, New York: Palgrave Macmillan.

Nussbaum, Martha C. 1992, *Love's Knowledge: Essays on Philosophy and Literature*, Oxford: Oxford University Press.

Oliver, Douglas. 1979, 'J.H. Prynne's 'Of Movement Toward a Natural Place'', *Grosseteste Review*, vol. 12, 1979, 93–6.

Olson, Charles 1997 [1950], 'Projective Verse' in *Collected Prose*, edited by Donald Allen and Benjamin Friedlander, Berkeley: University of California Press.

Olson, Charles 1987 [1953], 'The Kingfishers', in *The Collected Poems of Charles Olson*, edited by George F. Butterick, Berkeley: University of California Press.

Palmer, Michael 2001 [1988], 'Sun', in *Codes Appearing: Poems 1979–1988*, New York: New Directions.

Pavesich, Vida 2008, 'Hans Blumenberg's Philosophical Anthropology: After Heidegger and Cassirer', *Journal of the History of Philosophy*, 46, 3: 421–48.

Peacock, Thomas Love 1923 [1820], 'The Four Ages of Poetry', in *Peacock's Four Ages of Poetry, Shelley's Defence of Poetry, Browning's Essay on Shelley*, edited by H.F.B. Brett-Smith, Oxford: Basil Blackwell.

Perril, Simon. 'Hanging on Your Every Word: J.H. Prynne's *Bands Around The Throat* and a Dialectics of Planned Impurity' http://jacketmagazine.com/24/perril.html

Plato 1994, *Republic*, translated by Robin Waterfield, Oxford: Oxford University Press.

Poovey, Mary 1998, *A History of the Modern Fact: Problems of Knowledge in the Sciences of Wealth and Society*, Chicago, IL: University of Chicago Press.

Poster, Mark 1992, 'Postmodernity and the Politics of Multiculturalism: The Lyotard-Habermas Debate over Social Theory', *Modern Fiction Studies*, 38, 3: 567–80.

Postone, Moishe 1993, *Time, Labor and Social Domination: A Reinterpretation of Marx's Critical Theory*, Cambridge: Cambridge University Press.

Price, Leah 2010, *How to Do Things with Books in Victorian England*, Princeton: Princeton University Press.

Prynne, J.H. 1999 [1971], 'Jeremy Prynne lectures on Maximus IV, V, VI' [1971], in *Minutes of the Charles Olson Society*, 28, available at www.charlesolson.org/Files/Prynnelectu re1.htm.

Prynne, J.H. 2010, 'Mental Ears and Poetic Work', *Chicago Review*, 55, 1: 126–57.

Prynne, J.H. 2015, *Poems*, Northumberland: Bloodaxe Books.

Prynne, J.H. 1999, *Poems*. Newcastle upon Tyne: Bloodaxe Books.

Prynne, J.H. 2010, *Sub Songs*. London: Barque Press.

Prynne, J.H. 1993, 'Stars, Tigers, and the Shapes of Words'. *The William Matthew Lectures 1992*. London: Birckbeck College.

Prynne, J.H. 'Difficulties in the Translation of 'Difficult' Poems'. *Cambridge Literary Review*, I/3 (2010): 151–66.

Rancière, Jacques 2004 [2000], *The Politics of Aesthetics: The Distribution of the Sensible*, translated by Gabriel Rockhill, New York: Bloomsbury.

Reeve, N.H., and Richard Kerridge 1996. *Nearly Too Much: The Poetry of J.H. Prynne*. Liverpool: Liverpool UP.

Reeve, N.H., and Richard Kerridge 2002, 'Deaf to Meaning: On J.H. Prynne's *The Oval Window*'. *Jacket* 20 (2002). Web.

Robbe-Grillet, Alain 1965 [1963], 'Nature, Humanism and Tragedy', translated by Barbara Wright, *New Left Review*, 31: 65–80.

Roberts, Michael 2016, *The Long Depression*, Chicago: Haymarket Books.

Robertson, Lisa 1997, *Debbie: An Epic*, London: Reality Street Editions.

Robertson, Lisa 2001, *The Weather*, Vancouver: New Star Books.

Robinson, Cedric J. 2000 [1983], *Black Marxism: The Making of The Black Radical Tradition*, Chapel Hill: The University of North Carolina Press.

Rorty, Richard 1984, 'Habermas and Lyotard on Post-Modernity'. *Praxis International*, 4, 1: 33–44.

Rose, Gillian 1984, *Dialectic of Nihilism: Poststructuralism and Law*, Oxford: Blackwell.

Ross, Andrew 1999 [1988], 'Uses of Camp', in *Camp: Queer Aesthetics and the Performing Subject*, edited by Fabio Cleto, Ann Arbor: University of Michigan Press.

Roy, Arundhati 2003, 'Mesopotamia. Babylon. The Tigris and Euphrates', *The Guardian*, available at https://www.theguardian.com/world/2003/apr/02/iraq.writersoniraq.

Saint-Amour, Paul K. 2018. 'Weak Theory, Weak Modernism', *Modernism/modernity*, 25, 3: 437–59.

Sartre, Jean-Paul 2004 [1960], *Critique of Dialectical Reason, Volume 1: Theory of Practical Ensembles*, translated by Alan Sheridan Smith, edited by Jonathan Rée, London: Verso.

Schelling, Friedrich Wilhelm Joseph von 2000 [2015], *The Ages of The World*, translated by Jason M. Wirth, Binghamton: State University of New York Press.

Schiller, Friedrich 1967 [1794], *On the Aesthetic Education of Man: In a Series of Letters*, translated by Elizabeth M. Wilkinson and L.A. Willoughby, Oxford: Oxford University Press.

Schmitt, Carl 1985 [1922], *Political Theology: Four Chapters on the Concept of Sovereignty*, translated by George Schwab, Cambridge: MIT Press.

Sedgwick, Eve 1993 [1991], 'How to Bring Your Kids Up Gay: The War on Effeminate Boys', *Tendencies*, Durham, NC: Duke University Press.

Sedgwick, Eve (ed.) 1995, *Shame and Its Sisters: A Silvan Tompkins Reader*, Durham, NC: Duke University Press.

Sedgwick, Eve (ed.) 1997, *Novel Gazing: Queer Readings in Fiction*, NC: Duke University Press.

Sedgwick, Eve and Frank, Adam 1995, 'Shame in the Cybernetic Fold: Reading Silvan Tomkins', *Critical Inquiry*, 21, 2: 496–522.

Sidney, Philip 2002 [1595], *The Defence of Poesy*, in *Sir Philip Sidney: The Major Works*, edited by Katherine Duncan-Jones, Oxford: Oxford University Press.

Shell, Marc 1978, *The Economy of Literature*, Baltimore: Johns Hopkins University Press.

Shelley, Percy Bysshe 2003 [1840], 'The Defence of Poetry', *The Major Works*, edited by Zachary Leader and Michael O'Neill, Oxford: Oxford University Press.

Shelley, Percy Bysshe 2009 [1840], 'A Defence of Poetry', available at https://www.poetryfoundation.org/articles/69388/a-defence-of-poetry.

Shutt, Harry 1998, *The Trouble with Capitalism: An Enquiry into the Causes of Global Economic Failure*, London: Zed Books.

Silliman, Ron 1995 [1977], *The New Sentence*, New York: Roof Books.

Simonds, Sandra 2015, *Steal It Back*, Ardmore, PA: Saturnalia Books.

Smith, Rod 2001, *The Good House*, New York: Spectacular Books.

Spicer, Jack (2008), *My Vocabulary Did This To Me: The Collected Poetry of Jack Spicer*, edited by Peter Gizzi and Kevin Killian, Berkeley, CA: University of California Press.

Spivak, Gayatri Chakravorty 1988, 'Scattered Speculations on the Question of Value', in *In Other Worlds: Essays in Cultural Politics*, New York, Routledge.

Srnicek, Nick 2011, "Capitalism and the Non-Philosophical Subject," in *The Speculative Turn*, eds. Levi Bryant, Nick Srnicek, and Graham Harman (Melbourne: re.press), 164–81.

Sutherland, Keston. Interview with Geoffrey G. O'Brien. *The Claudius App* 3 (2011). Web.

Stewart, Susan 2001, *Poetry and the Fate of the Senses*, Chicago: University of Chicago Press.

Stewart, Susan 2001, *The Poet's Freedom*. Chicago: University of Chicago Press.

Taleb, Nassim Nicholas, 2007, *The Black Swan: The Impact of The Highly Improbable*. New York: Random House.

Thacker, Eugene 2011, *In the Dust of This Planet: Horror of Philosophy, Volume 1*, Alresford: Zero.

Tomba, Massimiliano 2014, 'Adorno's Account of The Anthropological Crisis and the New Type of Human', in *(Mis)readings of Marx in Continental Philosophy*, edited by Jernej Habjan and Jessica Whyte, New York: Palgrave Macmillan.

Unger, Roberto Mangabeira 1987, *Social Theory: Its Situation and Its Task*, Cambridge: Cambridge University Press.

Vico, Giambattista 1984 [1725], *The New Science of Giambattista Vico*, translated by Thomas Goddard Bergin and Max Harold Fisch, Ithaca: Cornell University Press.

Virno, Paolo 2004 [2001], *A Grammar of The Multitude*, translated by Isabella Bertoletti, James Cascaito and Andrea Casson Cambridge, MA: MIT Press, 2004.

Ward, Dana 2013, *The Crisis of Infinite Worlds*, New York: Futurepoem.

Warsh, David 2006, *Knowledge and The Wealth of Nations: A Story of Economic Discovery*, New York: W.W. Norton.

Watney, Simon 1994, *Practices of Freedom: Selected Writing on HIV/AIDS*, Durham: Duke University Press.

Watten, Barrett 2000, 'The Turn to Language and the 1960s', *Critical Inquiry*, 29, 1: 139–84.

Wolin, Richard 2010, *The Wind from The East: French Intellectuals, the Cultural Revolution, and the Legacy of the 1960s*, Princeton: Princeton University Press.

Wood, Ellen Meiksins 2012, *Liberty and Property: A Social History of Western Political Thought from the Renaissance to Enlightenment*, New York: Verso.

Young, Stephanie 2019, *Pet Sounds*, New York: Nightboat.

Zieman, Katherine 2008, *Singing the New Song: Literacy and Liturgy in Late Medieval England*, Philadelphia: University of Pennsylvania Press.

Žižek, Slavoj 2001 [1992], *Enjoy Your Symptom! Jacques Lacan in Hollywood and Out*, New York: Routledge.

Index

www.ingramcontent.com/pod-product-compliance
Lightning Source LLC
Chambersburg PA
CBHW071146130626
46553CB00004B/1546